ALSO BY WYLIE SYPHER

Rococo to Cubism in Art and Literature
Four Stages of Renaissance Style
Loss of the Self in Modern Literature
Guinea's Captive Kings

Editor

Enlightened England
Art History, An Anthology of Modern Criticism
Comedy

LITERATURE *and* TECHNOLOGY

WYLIE SYPHER

LITERATURE

and

TECHNOLOGY

The Alien Vision

RANDOM HOUSE   NEW YORK

700
£994

FIRST PRINTING

Copyright © 1968 by Wylie Sypher

All rights reserved under International and Pan-American Copyright Conventions. Published in the United States by Random House, Inc., New York, and simultaneously in Canada by Random House of Canada Limited, Toronto.

Acknowledgment is hereby made to Alfred A. Knopf, Inc. for permission to reprint from "Esthétique du Mal" from THE COLLECTED POEMS OF WALLACE STEVENS, by Wallace Stevens, and to Hill and Wang, Inc. for permission to reprint from BRECHT ON THEATRE, translated by John Willett.

Library of Congress Catalog Card Number: 68-14516

Manufactured in the United States of America by The Haddon Craftsmen, Inc., Scranton, Pa.

ACKNOWLEDGMENTS

For permission to quote from copyrighted material I am indebted as follows: to Alfred A. Knopf for the lines from Wallace Stevens's "Esthétique du Mal"; to Grove Press for passages from Alain Robbe-Grillet's *For a New Novel,* translated by Richard Howard; to Hill and Wang for passages from John Willett's *Brecht on Theatre;* to *The American Scholar* for certain passages that were printed in slightly different form in an essay in that periodical.

I am also most grateful to Jason Epstein, Alice E. Mayhew, and all those at Random House who have given frequent, careful, and patient help.

W. S.

For L. J. S., again

"Between foolish art and foolish science, there may indeed be all manner of reciprocal mischievous influence; but between wise art and wise science there is essential relation, for each other's help and dignity."

John Ruskin: *The Eagle's Nest*, Lecture III

"This tie between Science and Art has never ceased to exist throughout the history of human culture."

Naum Gabo: *The Constructive Idea in Art*

"Il n'y a pas d'opposition naturelle entre l'art et la technique. . . . Tout au contraire, l'art et la technique ont, jusqu'ici, toujours été liés l'un à l'autre."

Pierre Francastel: "Technique et
Esthétique" in *La Réalité Figurative*

Contents

∽

IV. Alien Worlds

V. Participation

VI. Proximity

Introduction

TO EVERYONE'S RELIEF the squabble about the two cultures has subsided. It began with unaccountable blunders on both sides: overlooking, for example, that during the later nineteenth century and even thereafter the poet, the novelist, and the painter often staked as much on method as did the scientist. So obsessed was the aesthetic movement with method that some of Walter Pater's artful pages are a kind of literary technism, calculated to the last phrase and cadence, manipulated to the finest detail. Illogically enough, the most literary literature reacted against an increasingly technological culture by resorting to a refinement of technique. Meanwhile science itself was identified with the use of a certain method precisely and restrictively employed. In speaking of the nineteenth century, Whitehead said, "What is peculiar and new to the century, differentiating it from all its predecessors, is its technology." Its great invention was "the invention of the method of invention." The arts of the time were inventive in this sense, that each sought to exploit a method.

Reliance on method, especially in painting, was characteristic of the renaissance, a period in which mediaeval craft was being changed to a new order of experience called Art. As the academies took over, art became Fine Art and there were erected whole systems of rules and genres with institutional cachet. Then, when the nineteenth century rebelled against such academism, many of its experiments in realism, impressionism, symbolism, and decadence were as programmatic as the so-called scientific method. At times Seurat spoke as if he wished to engineer painting, and Zola as if he wanted to engineer the novel. Such anxiety about exploiting a medium induced an overesteem of technique, converting the arts to various projects in method. Methodologies were constantly supported by systems of criticism, leading at last to a "new" criticism elaborated in the wake of Hulme, Pound, Eliot, Richards, and Empson, and innumerable techniques for understanding poetry.

The heavy investment in method suggests that the artist was subject to the same imperatives as the scientist and that the fissure between science and art was not so wide as is alleged, or the kind of fissure one might think, since both were highly specialized executions or procedures. Obvious as this dependence on method is, the more notable circumstance is the affiliation of these methodologies in art and science with certain attitudes tracing back to renaissance notions of exactitude, precision, detached observation, and accurate imitation. Behind all such notions is an impulse toward efficiency, frugality, a restraint or rejection of pleasure that is nearly puritan in rigor. In a general sense one might call it a psychology of thrift, a control that is a mode of precaution, privation, or repression, a mentality expressing itself in its sparest and most impersonal form in engineering, the choice of methods that most economically yield the designed results. A law of parsimony worked in aestheticism as it did in science.

Such privative or puritan discipline is associated with the notion of distance, the detachment that makes the artist or scientist a neutral spectator, isolating him from the realm of Nature or Beauty by exclusion or disengagement. The distancing of Art from Life was greatest during the aesthetic era, precisely at the time when the scientist was distancing himself by the so-called scientific method of controlled observation, a method enabling him to erect a system of abstract laws that find their analogue in the remote Beauty envisioned by Mallarmé. Asceticism in method made artist and scientist negative, or absent, agents, each alien in his own way from the domain he erected. The most effective artistic control of his medium required of the symbolist poet an act of exclusion, refusal, or nonparticipation. In the novel, also, the methodological approach indicates that the man of letters, consciously or unconsciously, was affected by the technical estrangement from which the scientist suffered. Therefore we are concerned with the attitudes behind the methods rather than with the methods themselves.

During the nineteenth century there developed a distinction between pure and applied science. The latter has become so dominant that we now speak of our technological society. If it is allowable to make a distinction between science and technology, one may say that the thrifty, puritan, predictive use of method is more active in technology than in "pure" science, which is exploratory and relatively agnostic. To the extent, then, that the aesthete was bound by his method he resembles the technologist. There is a difference between the aesthetes and their romantic predecessors: the romantics were less bemused by their methods than by their feelings and thus produced few critical systems; but the aesthetes were technicians in the sense that they were devoted to methods even at the expense of their feelings, which they were prone to regulate. Thus the aesthetes exhibit, sometimes in accentuated form, the privative disciplines, the puritan detachment and estrangement, that had inhered in science since the renaissance. Accordingly I have tried to indicate how the attitudes and motives implicit in aestheticism are related to attitudes and motives that appear in an earlier phase, and especially in some of Shakespeare's plays, which are astonishingly sensitive to the psychology of thrift. And this theme of thrift is inextricably involved with the distancing that is a refusal and an alienation. Since alienation takes economic and psychological guises, I have been led to comments upon the Marxist and Freudian meanings of distancing.

If alienation is a mark of technological society, it is also a symptom of the distancing that aesthetes presumed to be necessary to Art. When the notion of aesthetic distance appeared during the renaissance, the craftsman became the artist, and the idea of imitation ("mimesis") was often equated with holding a mirror up to nature. One of the glaring fallacies of criticism from the renaissance to the romantics was the neglect of the notion that the Greeks usually associated with imitation—the notion of participating ("methexis"). Plato used the term "methexis" to refer to the way in which things participate in Forms; but implicit in Aristotle's discussion of mimesis is a recognition that art is not only imitation but likewise a mode of participating. This reciprocity between imitation and participation appears in Aristotle's belief that art is a craft, or "techne," a physiological activity, and I have tried to suggest that the resolution of the technological difficulty may be a return to craft—which is not methodological. Craft is muscular skill; it is not ideological; it is not puritanical; it requires no distanced world of Art; it enables the artist to improvise and to participate. The romantics, who had no coherent methodology, did seek to participate. But the later nineteenth century, intoxicated by its methodologies, distanced art in many ways. Style became a technological artifice.

With the twentieth century has come a reaction against this distancing; the traditional theories of imitation, which often meant alienation, have collapsed before our need to participate, as is apparent in action painting and the obscure intimacy of the new-wave novel. And while technologists themselves have been reintroducing the craft ideal into engineering, a number of "new" French critics have been insisting that Style is a fraud: they wish to draw literature back to the everyday idiom of the spoken word and are far more modest about Art than were the aesthetes—as well as more agnostic and more tolerant of the usual.

In saying all this I am assuming that engineering is hostile to art. In many ways it has been. Nevertheless these chapters are not intended to disparage technology or science. The distinction between the two is blurring, for advanced technologies are among the most adventurous of scientific activities. Besides, it has been pointed out that the admiration for "pure" science (whatever that may be) in contrast to "applied" science is a snobbism. For one thing, there are likewise a "pure" and an "applied" art, and the advantage is not always with the "pure." Architecture, the matrix of all the plastic arts, has always been an "applied" design, as portraiture is "applied" painting. Drama is "applied" literature, as is laureate verse, elegy, or any occasional writing. Furthermore, technology itself is now very responsive to what is happening in the arts. The concordat between technism and the arts, formalized by the Bauhaus, has been ratified as form has followed function and function, form. Above all, those who have read Aristotle comprehendingly must grant that the artist has always been a kind of technician, art being an ability to execute in a medium. So my purpose is neither to condescend to technology nor to deny the artist's need to control his métier. I am convinced that technology and the arts will continue to stimulate each other, particularly in their vanguard phases.

Notwithstanding, it happens that during the last century technology, limited in its aims and methods, contaminated both science and art, interdicting each by its law of parsimony, its principle of minimal expenditure, its fallacies of specification and exactitude, its manipulation of techniques. Not science but technology has roused our apprehension of being controlled. I do not share this alarm simply because the arts seem to be a continuing revolt against the tyranny of techniques. Although the results of technological imperatives have not always been rewarding in literature, there is convincing evidence that literature and other arts can, at least on occasions, adapt the technological method and divert it to non-technological purposes: the purposes of concrete poetry or music, for instance.

If it is foolish to generalize about technology or science, it is still vainer to generalize about art. One uses the terms technology, science, and art only under duress, for in fact there are only technicians, scientists, and artists, each with his problem, method, and solution. Since I am emphasizing the commitment of the arts to methods and the ideologies based on methods, I have arbitrarily stressed the work of certain writers and painters. It is clear, for example, that Zola's realism, which serves my purpose, is unlike George Eliot's realism, though both are "realists." It is equally clear that a writer such as D. H. Lawrence might have benefited from a more disciplined method. By the same token I have slighted Courbet, whose realism is immethodical; also, I have only glanced at Stendhal, whose inconclusive empiricism is almost a rebuttal of *the* scientific method and whose finesse in execution is anything but systematic. Or again, symbolist methodology gave us some of our most poetic poetry, and impressionist methods opened up the entire range of modern painting. Whatever their limitations, these methods richly justified themselves as stimulants, if as nothing else.

In discussing the implications of technism I have plundered what others have written. My debt is open, I trust, to the critics Lewis Mumford, E. H. Gombrich,

Anton Ehrenzweig, Jacob Bronowski, Georg Lukacs, Claude Lévi-Strauss, Roland Barthes, Lucien Goldmann, Gyorgy Kepes, and many others. It may appear that I am endorsing Norman O. Brown's formulas for a Dionysiac self; but a Dionysiac self is neither so desirable nor accessible as Brown implies, and I prefer to revert to Nietzsche and his romantic forbear, Blake. I am less taken with a Dionysiac view of selfhood than with a Dionysiac view of art—a view that is implicit in Freud, though Freud would hardly have granted as much.

The further I went, the more I was aware that nearly everything here is to be found in a writer whose moralizing and confusion cannot diminish his relevance: John Ruskin. And what Ruskin failed to say, William Morris— or his scion, Herbert Read—did. These critics are more helpful than the overstimulated Marshall McLuhan, whom I have also invoked. Constantly in the background is that other nineteenth-century colossus, Karl Marx, whose aesthetic is being recovered now that we can no longer take his economics seriously. Among critics of such diversity I have sought some coherence.

LITERATURE *and* TECHNOLOGY

I

Conquest
by Method

❦

Technical Anesthesia

WHILE SPEAKING of the "crisis in literature" during the 1880's, Mallarmé accused "official prosody" of
relying upon "cut and dried rules," an orthodox ever-
ready keyboard. But the new poet, the symbolist, could for
the first time in history build his own instrument "with an
individual technique," transposing verse into a "rhythmic
totality" that is absolutely pure. "If the poem is to be pure,
the poet's voice must be stilled and the initiative be taken
by the words themselves," which will "thus replace the
audible breathing in lyric poetry of old—replace the
poet's own personal and passionate control of verse." The
pure poem is born of its own medium; it is an anonymous
fabric from which the poet is "absent," for the erratic
breathing of the romantic writer, so audible in earlier
years, was a concession to the Chance, or *Hasard*, that
must be excluded from the absolute work of art. Thus
"the pure work implies the elocutionary disappearance of

(3)

the poet, who yields to words" that "take light from mutual reflection, like an actual trail of fire over precious stones, replacing the old lyric afflatus or the enthusiastic direction of the phrase."

In effect Mallarmé is seeking to replace one kind of impersonality with another. The impersonality of official verse with its mechanical rules is to be replaced by the impersonality of language itself, a structure "of perfect fulness and clarity, the totality of universal relationships" —the Book. Properly employed, the medium creates the Poem, which is a construct of words erected by manipulating a technique.

Echoes of this impersonal theory of poetry have carried down to our own day. T. E. Hulme called for "a new technique, a new convention" that could reach a "formalism" like Pope's. But it was T. S. Eliot who most effectively phrased our impersonal theory of poetry, reaffirming that the poet does not have a personality to exploit but only a medium. His early "programme for the *métier* of poetry" depends almost as heavily as Mallarmé's upon a method, a technique that almost of itself achieves the poem. The poet is a catalyst whose activity is to a degree neutral; he is an agent who is present, yet whose presence is a mode of absence. Reacting, nearly like Mallarmé, against a romantic involvement, Eliot suggests that a poem can occur without the intervention of personality, for it should arise, instead, from the poet's sensitivity to (that is, his "feeling" for) his medium. The poet seems auxiliary to what gets written, being responsible in a somewhat secondary sense for the accomplishment of his verse. He speaks thus impersonally to escape from his temperament; the poem phrases itself at some distance from his own existence. Paul Valéry subscribes to this view of the poet: "I see taking shape in him an agent, a living system for producing verses."

During the nineteenth century there was, continuingly, a crisis in the arts, a crisis manifest not only in theories of impersonal poetry but more generally in Parnassian and other kinds of realism, in decadence or aestheticism, in various commitments to art for art's sake, and in developments in painting from impressionism and Art Nouveau to Seurat and the cubists. However different these manifestations are, they share a diligent consciousness of method, and if we seek a parallel to this attention to method, we find it in the prevailing attitude toward science, which was supposed to be a certain method, used impersonally, to reveal the abstract laws of nature. In this era science was nearly identical with the scientific method, as it was naïvely called, and Huxley spoke for his age in proclaiming "an unhesitating faith that the free employment of reason in accordance with scientific method is the sole method of reaching truth."

Such addiction to method throws doubt on the supposition that there were two cultures, as we have been terming them. The nineteenth-century aesthete may have been at odds with the scientist on many counts; yet aestheticism and science were, in a sense, only two aspects of a culture that produced both. As Pierre Francastel has noted, any society molds the specialists it needs, whether they be mechanics or artists: technologies foster a certain community of consciousness. Especially during its latter decades the nineteenth century was a culture dominated by methodologies, and methodology attracts a kind of man Nietzsche called theoretic.

The wearisome debate about our two cultures misconceived the relations between science and literature, obscuring the fact that the opposition, so far as it exists, is not between science and literature (or other arts) but between technology and both science and the arts. The curious circumstance is that, although the aesthetes repudiated science, a good deal of the "arty" art of the nineteenth century was receptive to certain technological premises or motives.

Admittedly the distinction between science and technology is treacherous and often denied. We are told that there is no clear line between pure and applied science, for all science, as Bacon said, has the purpose of using nature in the interest of man. Undeniably technology has had beneficial effects that it would be bigoted to depreciate. However, there is a difference between some motives in pure science and the motives in technology, a difference that sometimes reduces itself to a concern for truth versus a concern for efficiency or immediate results. "The body of technical science," says Bronowski, "burdens and threatens us because we are trying to employ the body without the spirit." Human nature being what it is, science can be diverted from its interest in truth, its attempt to benefit man, into a quest for power, for manipulating people and imposing programs. Insofar as technology is employed to carry out programs, there is a practical difference between science and technology. Since programs are devised or managed by officials, or bureaucrats, the distinction between science and technology (or "applied science") is psychological and procedural. Our doubt about technology is due to our fear of being engineered. The question is not one of pure versus applied science but of how science is applied. Government-sponsored science is hardly pure, and perhaps not science.

To make a firmer distinction between motives in pure science and motives in technology, we may invoke Daniel Bell's phrase: the "technological imperative," which is a dread of waste, a concern for efficiency that arises from a psychology of parsimony, or, to use the term we shall need later on, thrift. It is a principle of minimal effort, usually directed toward the solution of immediate problems instead of toward investigating the nature of the problems themselves. To this extent "pure" science is a wasteful activity, often inspired by what Karl Popper calls a wish to corroborate by experiment or otherwise. To this extent, too, "pure" science is a speculative activity

like philosophy, where questions are often more consequential than any possible answers. The technologist is
usually seeking a solution that applies locally in a given
condition. An example would be the sacrifice of the city
for the sake of a highway to relieve congestion in a certain area.

Percy Bridgman mentions that an experiment can be
performed for quite different purposes: either to find an
answer to a special need or to gratify a curiosity that has
no immediate result. From a technological point of view
the latter kind of experiment may be extravagant, having
something in common with that other extravagance we
call art. Yet even this distinction is unreliable, for works
of art have been created to meet a local need or to satisfy
a local interest. Athenian drama was written under certain political controls, and Shakespeare's plays were
"good theatre." Lewis Mumford has described the sym-
phony orchestra as a triumph of technics.

Howbeit, the contrast between the scientific and the
technological holds good at extremes, and Daniel Bell illustrates the technological or bureaucratic extreme by
Frederick W. Taylor's "scientific management." As a master of "social physics" Taylor applied a utilitarian calculus
to make work more efficient, carrying the principle of
division of labor to its last absurdity by analyzing how
pig iron could be handled more cheaply. He proved that
a workman could be trained to shovel 47 tons a day instead of 12: after reckoning the weight of the shovel, its
size, its bite, the arc of the swing, the number of steps and
other motions, Taylor eliminated all useless (i.e., non-
profitable) effort and insured the employer "maximum
prosperity." This industrial economy is based—like Mallarmé's poetic economy—upon an elimination of the accidental, or what the symbolists called Chance, *Hasard,
Prose.* Existentialists call it the contingent, in contrast to
the necessary, agreeing with Whitehead and other modern scientists that the most convincing evidence of reality

is its uncertainty, the individual irregularity, leap, or willfulness that should not surprise us even if we cannot predict it. The engineer (the applied scientist at his extreme) must master the contingent. The technologist dreads surprises; indeed, he must not be surprised. He predicts everything—and, in a sense, discovers nothing. Technism might be defined as a conquest without surprise—or perhaps a conclusion without risk.

More than a century ago Dickens presented the technological hero in grotesque form in the person of Thomas Gradgrind, "A man of realities. A man of facts and calculations. A man who proceeds upon the principle that two and two are four, and nothing over, and who is not to be talked into allowing anything over. . . . With a rule and a pair of scales, and the multiplication table always in his pocket, Sir, ready to weigh and measure any parcel of human nature, and tell you exactly what it comes to. It is a mere question of figures, a case of simple arithmetic." Gradgrind embodies the notion of technological efficiency or parsimony that Dickens rejected in favor of a principle of surplus or extravagance. Immethodical and impulsive as he was, Dickens never engineered anything, even if he wrote for the market.

Social critics like Jacques Ellul and Herbert Marcuse have warned that the danger of the Gradgrind mentality is not in technique but in the loss of control over these techniques. Earlier societies freely used techniques at their disposal; but their techniques were confined to limited domains, applied as they were within larger social, moral, or religious contexts. Our case is different, Ellul claims, since technology has become our metaphysic, even our magic. The computer is our oracle; the statistician is our *deus ex machina.* Our techniques are more than mere machines, for a canon of efficiency controls all our activity.

Once techniques have been applied to experiences originally foreign to the machine, their intervention is self-augmenting. Ellul goes so far as to say that the difference between democracies and totalitarian states is the latter's awareness of how to exploit techniques to subject men to an idea of order, to the planning contrived by specialists whose decisions are necessarily a form of human engineering. "Inside the technical circle, the choice among methods, mechanism, organizations, and formulas is carried out automatically. Man is stripped of his choice, and he is satisfied. He accepts the situation when he sides with technique." In advanced societies decision can be remanded to the computer.

Ellul calls this situation technological anesthesia, since the technician can delude us into believing we are free when we are not. Techniques can absorb our very hostility to techniques, because the technician can calculate our resentment in advance and provide for it in his program. To leave us ignorant of being manipulated is the technician's supreme feat. There is an alarming cynicism in Ellul's comment that "true technique will know how to maintain the illusion of liberty, choice, and individuality; but these will have been carefully calculated so that they will be integrated into the mathematical reality merely as appearances." If technique is adequate, it deals with contingencies and renders invisible the controls that are the ultimate human engineering. The technological Elysium is established by inducing us to believe we are free in order that we may be more efficiently managed by forgetting the formulas that govern us. Whereas earlier cultures used techniques in war, marketing, or scientific inquiry, we have allowed technology to expand out of context and accepted it as a way of politics and life. As Ellul sees it, the only escape is dream or madness, hallucination being a response least accessible to techniques. But here again, as Giorgio de Chirico noted, mechanism has penetrated the subconscious. However, the ugliness of our arts seems to be a way of exhibiting our distress about this fatality, which, in Herbert Marcuse's phrase, "repulses all alternatives."

This view may be too pessimistic, since the very consciousness of technological peril is a means of resisting. More important, the artist has never been successfully engineered; as will be suggested later, art may be the most effectual resistance to technological autocracy. Nor is the technologist always so malign as Ellul implies. Besides, to reject technology because it is abused is as unwarranted as rejecting the machine because it has been misused. For us the significant point is that the technological is not always synonymous with the scientific. Techniques precede and often support science, but during the nineteenth century science became identified with the use of a certain method that was adaptable to the technological imperative, associated as it was with a naïve ideal of "objectivity," a naïve materialism, a naïve logic of induction, a naïve reliance upon observation, a compulsion to discipline the mind by making it "accurate." All this made it possible to corrupt the official scientific method into a technological means to administer, to control, to secure certain results. The scientific method was put to limited uses, and the scientist himself became a methodologist— like the poet or the painter. The nineteenth century was a century of methodologies, in science, in history, in philosophy, in the arts. Here is a point of contact between the so-called two cultures.

Two Cultures

This debate is a stale business, but since it involves what Arnold termed "instrument knowledge" (technology), we must spend a moment on it. The droll fact is that Lord Snow is closer to Arnold's position than is Leavis. The closing passages of the Rede Lecture show that Snow's concern is a social one, like Arnold's, for he wants to see a new world where the gap closes between rich and poor countries. Snow's motive accords with Arnold's in his essay on "Equality," dealing with the gap between rich and poor as a crippling condition that must be removed if England is to attain anything that might be called culture. If Arnold's culture is a study of perfection, it is also a "moral and social passion for doing good," a general perfection, an aspiration to diminish misery, "to leave the world better and happier than we found it." Snow is justified in claiming that the scientist looks toward this social betterment more earnestly than our novelists and poets, who have been occupied mainly with our unhappiness and sickness.

Snow also admits a difference between "pure" scientists and technologists, remarking upon the leftism of many scientists and the inherent conservatism of engineers. He notes an incompatibility between the technological and the scientific attitudes, and he distinguishes between the scientific and the industrial revolutions, the latter depending upon machines. Although scientists have often failed to see that technological problems can be "pure," satisfying, or "beautiful," technology itself remains a "branch of human experience that people can learn with predictable results."

The echoes of Arnold are clear enough, for in his language "instrument knowledge" is a special discipline not directly related to "the sense for beauty, the sense for conduct." Arnold includes among "instrument knowledges" the conventional study of classical languages: "When I speak of knowing Greek and Roman antiquity, therefore, as a help to knowing ourselves and the world, I mean more than a knowledge of so much vocabulary, so much grammar, so many portions of authors in the Greek and Latin languages." Arnold agreed with Huxley that to know ourselves and our world we must know scientific theory: "There is, therefore, really no question between Professor Huxley and me as to whether knowing the great results of the modern scientific study of nature is not required as a part of our culture, as well as knowing the products of literature and art." The main question was simply how much of the curriculum should be devoted to science. Arnold complains that as things stand "the student of the natural sciences only, will know nothing of humane letters," and thus be overspecialized.

Snow has his own variation on this theme but incorrectly presumes that science has not directly influenced literature and art. This is a blunder easy to make if one regards English education, where there has indeed been a sad incomprehension between men of letters and scientists facing each other with frozen smiles across a gulf wider than it was in the days of Arnold and Huxley. The brusqueness of Leavis's response ironically justifies Snow's complaint. Nevertheless Snow heightens the difficulty when he supposes one is scientifically illiterate if he is unable to state the second law of thermodynamics—which is like supposing one is linguistically illiterate if he cannot repeat Verner's law of consonantal shifts. Both are specialists' knowledge.

Snow and Leavis alike ignore how our theatre, our novels, our verse (as in computer poetry) show the effects of technology as well as science. Theories of relativity have been invoked to explain the new vision in painting from cubism onward. Techniques used in the psychology of vision have contributed to op art; topology, electronics, and field dynamics have affected abstract expressionism, concrete music, lettrist verse. The interaction between technology, science, and the arts has never been more pervasive. Technologists, in their turn, have been responsive to the methods of abstract expressionism. Snow betrays himself when he alleges that "There seems to be no place where the cultures meet."

Across the gulf Edgar Wind, professor of art at Oxford, laments that the disjunction between scientist and artist leads painters to adapt the most advanced—that is, the most fashionable—aspects of science, which are the least profitable to them as artists. Perhaps. But the most advanced science is usually the most stimulating, the least official, the very area where the two cultures find them-

selves in an open situation congenial to experiment, accommodating the contingencies and uncertainties that
can bring surprise, at least, if not discovery. The fully
validated scientific theory becomes official, and when the
artist seeks the official, he becomes academic. Inter-
changes between the two cultures have constantly occurred along the frontiers of advanced scientific thought.
The renaissance painters were excited by the new science: witness Leonardo. So, also, Milton used the cosmology of his day—arbitrarily, to be sure; and Alexander
Pope eagerly adapted Newtonian law to his poetry, much
as James Thomson adapted optics. During the nineteenth
century technology brought increasing pressure to bear
upon the arts: if Baudelaire rejected photography as the
enemy, Degas adapted it to his own uses, while the impressionists were adapting the prismatic analysis.

Lord Snow evidently based his opinions upon Eric
Ashby's book *Technology and the Academics* (1958), a
discussion of the reluctance of English universities to
admit science into the curriculum. Properly enough
Ashby judges that the scientific revolution in England
occurred outside the walls of the academy and generally
against opposition from the humanities. Doubtless, class
structure, on which Oxbridge relied, had a good deal to
do with this antagonism toward science. To this degree
Snow is justified in accusing the humanists of "not listen-
ing at all." They tried not to listen, though Arnold and
others did. Ashby points out that while Germany and
France offered technological training, England had only
its dismal institutes for mechanics. By way of bridging
the two cultures, Ashby asks that universities re-focus
education upon a core of technical studies around which
are grouped a fringe of humanities auxiliary to specializa-
tions, which must be the axis of a new humanism. This
rather desperate view has been restated by Martin
Green in *Science and the Shabby Curate of Poetry*
(1964), urging mutual tolerance by scientists and hu-

manists and proposing that science fiction be used to initiate technicians to literature. This will hardly do. The social passion for a better world requires technicians, and unless the humanities can prove themselves essential to a better world, there is small reason to tolerate them as a fringe of "culture," especially as mere science fiction.

The educational dilemma occupying all these critics was hotly debated during the nineteenth century in different language: the fine versus the applied arts. The fissure between the two appeared during the renaissance and is an aspect of the history of academies and the whole Aristotelian theory of imitation. England met the dilemma in the 1830's when Parliamentary committees tried to decide how far and in what manner the "grand style" of painting should be taught in schools of design founded under the Board of Trade for the express purpose of adapting the arts to the needs of industry, these schools being an early version of the Bauhaus.[1] The academies with their study of the human figure, were supposed to have proprietary rights to the "grand style"; but early in the century William Hazlitt had already called the academicians "a society of hucksters in the Fine Arts," and their Royal Academy a "mercantile body, like any other mercantile body, consisting chiefly of manufacturers of portraits, who have got a regular monopoly of this branch of trade." In brief, fine art was seen as a fraud that roused the contempt of everyone outside the establishment: Blake, Benjamin Robert Haydon, the pre-Raphaelites, and George Moore. The upper floors of the Victoria and Albert Museum are a mausoleum for the official British painting that passed for High Art. In France the antiacademic revolt led to the Salon des Refusées. In England a Select Committee on Arts and Manufacture planned a curriculum for industrial designing in which the human figure, the warrant of High Art, was not taught. The School of Design opened in 1837 with a syllabus including elementary outline drawing, the study of fabrics, and decorative patterns for commercial products. But the students felt deprived of culture and continually agitated for study of the human figure.

The long and contentious history of fine versus applied art leads to William Morris's efforts to re-establish the so-called minor or decorative arts, to the arts-and-crafts movements, to Art Nouveau, and eventually to the Bauhaus. The torrential outpouring of Ruskin's criticism should have suggested to the Victorians that there is no necessary opposition between high and decorative art, science and art, or art and industry. But Ruskin's approach to art and art criticism by way of geology, botany, crystallography, mineralogy, topography, meteorology, chemistry, and other sciences went largely for naught. So he laments in *Deucalion,* "And still, with increasingly evil results to all of us, the separation is every day widening between the man of science and the artist—in that, whether painter, sculptor, or musician, the latter is pre-eminently a person who sees with his Eyes, hears with his Ears, and labours with his Body." Ruskin sought in science itself the fidelity to experience he found lacking in art; thus "of all writers on art, I suppose there is no one who appeals so often as I do to physical science." Yet it was left to Gropius and the Bauhaus Manifesto of 1919 to reconcile science with art and art with industry: "Architects, sculptors, painters, we must all go back to handicraft. . . . There is no essential difference between artist and craftsman." Speaking of his basic Bauhaus course, Johannes Itten says, "First, imagination and creative ability must be freed and strengthened. When this is accomplished, technical-practical requirements can be brought in and finally also economic considerations of the market."

For the Bauhaus, for Ruskin and Arnold, there are not two cultures but two aspects of a culture that has been unalterably affected by science. Conversely, science has been affected by the arts, for as Gerald Holton remarks, scientist and artist are today concerned with an allegorical representation of reality; and one eminent technologist grants that the artist is often in advance of the scientists because "the practice of art permits creative application of its principles while learning about them."

So the case is hardly as grim as Snow fears, and instead of making his ill-tempered reply, Leavis might better have rested in a position he took in *New Bearings in English Poetry* (1932), where he pleaded for intelligence in literature. The poet, he claimed, is more conscious than others of what his age is experiencing, and "if the poetry and the intelligence of the age lose touch with each other, poetry will cease to matter much, and the age will be lacking in finer awareness." Leavis accused Tennyson of not being intelligent and of withdrawing into an alien world; isolating his mind from his verse, he retired to a palace of art where his allusions to science did not enlarge his comprehension of life. Strangely enough, Leavis is here in some agreement with Snow: however uncongenial the age may be to poetry, Leavis disapproves of the inadequacy, or bad faith, which sanctions the notion that only certain topics are poetical—"flowers, dawn, dew, birds, love, archaisms and country place-names." Leavis calls upon the poet to be tough-minded, to acknowledge that a Rolls-Royce is as eligible for poetry as a rose. He notes, too, that tough-mindedness is not identical with intelligence, for if Browning had been a little more intelligent, he might not have been so robust.

The history of literature suggests that the unintelligence of the nineteenth-century artist is exceptional rather than normal. Euripides was a highly intelligent writer, as was Lucretius. Dante easily accommodated his art to scholastic thought. The new art forms of the renaissance were based upon complex notions of harmony and proportion and were steeped in a neo-scholasticism. An early version of the idea of relativity is inherent in *Gulliver's Travels*. Optics and botany inspired some rather sensitive poems during the eighteenth century, and the associationist psychology furnished Wordsworth with a theory about his poetic experience. Obviously the poet or painter has often dealt imaginatively with contemporary science insofar as science, as Arnold said, has forced general conceptions upon the culture that nourished it.

However this may be, there does exist—and did during the nineteenth century—a certain maladjustment between our two cultures, especially in the resistance by the artist to the practical or technological effects of science. Wordsworth dreaded railways, Dickens hated Coketown, Ruskin was infuriated by cast-iron gothic. We are even more conscious than Ruskin of the distinction between the effects of science and the effects of technology and deal with it more subtly.

There is, for instance, our awareness that improved methods of reproducing art objects enable us to live in a museum without walls. Giving a new turn to the notion that photography is the enemy, Edgar Wind is convinced that a knowledge of, or a taste for, art is more widespread than in any era in western history; yet he is doubtful whether this expansion of our aesthetic horizon is not a diffusion rather than an extension. We are more knowing than ever about painting, but our familiarity, owing to the easy accessibility of art objects, causes immunity to art. Our appreciation is facile, but it is secondary to our deeper interests, which center in science and economics. Now that we all have a taste for the arts, the arts have become merely fashionable. This, of course, is Harold Rosenberg's anxiety about the tradition of the new, which means that a knowledge of art is most useful at cocktail parties. Or as Wind says, if our response to art is authentic, it should be a shock—and we are shocked by nothing. The deluge of art objects has benumbed us. Our knowingness is a safety zone protecting us against disturbance or even bafflement.

Wind asks, also, how far our taste is formed by the kind of painting that can be most readily and accurately reproduced; and, in turn, whether the most successful modern painting is not that best suited for reproduction. Such conditions lead toward a mechanization of taste and judgment. Accessibility means vulgarization, the supremacy of an art most marketable. Likewise there is evidence that we appreciate stereophonic brilliance more than the score or its rendering. The ordinary recording is a kind of falsification, a composite of passages heard not as they are played in any actual performance, but as they are synthetized into a "perfect" reproduction. Technology has invaded the domain of culture in ways Ruskin and earlier critics could not have predicted. The museum without walls has liabilities Malraux did not suspect.

Wind believes that the artist himself, not the scientist, is partly to blame for ejecting art into a marginal position. Quite apart from the technological dilutions just mentioned, there has been the artist's own failure in imagination or intelligence (which is essentially Leavis's complaint). Wind suspects that the artist began to capitulate to science during the renaissance: in the sixteenth century Ariosto refused to face the fact that firearms had done away with chivalry and thus withdrew into the fantastic world of the *Orlando Furioso,* in which neither he nor the reader could have any faith. "If chivalry died, it did not die by firearms alone; it died in and through the imagination."

In effect Wind is restating Thomas Love Peacock's indictment that the poet refuses the present, seeking to live nostalgically in a bygone realm, trying to salvage "exploded superstitions" by appealing to "factitious sentiment." In *The Four Ages of Poetry* Peacock submits that the poet now speaks only to a public

> whose minds are not awakened to the desire of valuable knowledge, and who are indifferent to anything beyond being charmed, moved, excited, affected, and exalted; charmed by harmony, moved by sentiment, excited by passion, affected by pathos, and exalted by sublimity:

harmony, which is language on the rack of Procrustes; sentiment, which is canting egoism in the mask of refined feeling; passion, which is the commotion of a weak and selfish mind; pathos, which is the whining of an unmanly spirit; and sublimity, which is the inflation of an empty head: when we consider that the great and permanent interests of human society become more and more the main spring of intellectual pursuit . . . the poetical audience will not only continually diminish in proportion of its number to that of the rest of the reading public, but will also sink lower and lower in the comparison of intellectual acquirement . . . because intellectual power and intellectual acquisition have turned themselves into other and better channels.

Peacock was not only dealing with two cultures; he mustered against the poet Plato's objections—and Wind's. The accusation of unintelligence cannot be met by appealing to Coleridge's axiom that poetry requires a willing suspension of disbelief. If poetry is to be defended, it must be defended on better grounds than any willing suspension of disbelief, which is tantamount to erecting a tariff wall about the poem, protecting it within a safety zone.

A recent attempt to protect poetry from the rigors of science and reason rests on a belief that it must be mythical, and one may conjecture that our obsessive quest for myth, in spite of all the aid offered by Jung, amounts to not much more than a willing suspension of disbelief. The poetic myth as we now find it is a fabrication, since the poet is aware of what is mythical; and as one critic has put it, when we really think mythically, we are not aware of being mythical. The quest for myth has been one way of decerebrating poetry. The nineteenth century decerebrated art by guarding it within another kind of safety zone, the world of Beauty. Leavis and Wind agree that the nineteenth-century artist, averse to the world about him, often withdrew toward a marginal vision where art could "reign as its own master," losing touch "with other forces that shape our experience." This centrifugal impulse sent the arts toward a peripheral aesthetic realm of "fastidious exile." Tennyson did not retire alone to his Palace of Art.

The Palace of Art was a refuge from the industrial dominion established by science or by technology. Nevertheless the most literary of all nineteenth-century movements, symbolism, did not after all succeed in evading technology, for it was a kind of technology developed within the arts themselves. In a sense the two cultures were only two faces of the same technological compulsion. The crux of the matter is Wind's remark that the most agile artistic imagination "is not at its best when it apes a science from which it is in fact cut off." Art aping science: the aping was most apish whenever painter, poet, or novelist attempted to use the methods of the scientist. The prevailing theories of science embody the intelligence of an era and are thus available to the artistic imagination, as the Newtonian cosmology was available to Pope and others inspired by the spacious firmament or as Chevreul's theory of color was available to the impressionists. But to ape *the* scientific method as it was conceived in the nineteenth century is to rely upon a kind of technology.

Limited Initiative

Consciousness of method is, of course, precisely what identifies the renaissance as an era distinct from the middle ages, as the work of Uccello, Leonardo, and Alberti indicates. And renaissance methodologies in the arts were heavily indebted to the new science. Yet the artist's fascination with method during the renaissance is inherently different from the nineteenth-century reliance on method, because renaissance science, as Copernicus and Bacon show, was an uncertain and incoherent performance tinged with ancient and mediaeval myth. By the nineteenth century, however, science was nearly synonymous with a rigorous notion of method that was orthodox to the degree of being official. In fact the nineteenth-century view of science was narrow and inadequate because it depended so heavily upon an unquestioned and unquestioning ritual of observation, experiment, and induction leading to "laws."

We have long since recognized the naïveté of this view of science, for as Whitehead says, science is a mode of thought rather than a method of observation or experiment. The very conception of *the* scientific method has yielded to our awareness that each science has its own method, that sciences intersect, that even the notion of method is undependable, that operationalism is a basis for science, that science frequently amounts to what the scientist does. With his limited view of scientific method Huxley minimized the effect of chance, hunch, imagination, purpose, reason, without which science could not have gained its larger interpretations.

A generation ago Whitehead remarked that since the renaissance, science has never bothered to justify its premises and borrowed what rationality it needed from preceding systems. The irrational element in science has been emphasized by Arthur Koestler, who describes the scientist as a kind of sleep-walker blundering into theories that could not have been conceived by sequential logic or any accumulation of evidence, let alone experiment. An experiment is sometimes a post facto means of verifying what has already been imaginatively established. One is reminded of Wallace Stevens's axiom that "we live in concepts of the imagination before the reason has established them. If this is true, then reason is simply the methodizer of the imagination." Koestler describes the origin of a scientific theory as an act of creation resulting from "bisociation" or perceiving a situation as existing within two incompatible contexts—the incompatible contexts being like the ambiguity inherent in a tragic view of man, his strengths and failings. The great scientific discovery is a leap to a new synthesis, a leap resembling play or artistic creation. Karl Popper has also rejected the notion that science is an induction leading to demonstrable knowledge. Instead, the scientist is one whose theories are liable to a certain kind of verification: they must be validated by a criterion of fallibility, a process of applying rival or alternative theories to test them by degrees of falsifiability. Huxley was unsophisticated enough to presume that *a* method leads to truth.

As for method in the arts, the Greeks were hardly the first to know that poetry or painting is mastery of a craft, techne, or métier. Aristotle termed art an intellectual virtue that exercises certain methods, or techniques: "art is a state concerned with making involving a true course of reasoning, and lack of art on the contrary is a state concerned with making, involving a false course of reasoning." (He adds that in a sense art and chance are concerned with the same objects, for they alike deal with the variable.) For the Greeks art and technique were synonymous, as they usually were for mediaeval and renaissance craftsmen. Then, thanks to neo-Platonism, or romanticism, there came a distinction between *techné* and *ars:* for art (not technique) belonged to the realm of the absolute—Beauty, the Infinite, the One, the "pure" Conception, Idea, or Form.

It is ironic that the symbolists as heirs of the most transcendental romantics should have staked so much on method ("techne"). No group of poets was more afflicted by the "malady of precision," and Valéry, the last and most intelligent symbolist, wrote his friend Pierre Louÿs in 1890 about *vers sagement calculée* by an "algebra" that would prevent a poem from being a mere sequence of happy phrasings. Though the calculations are not evident in the finished poem, the method of composing it demands severe patience, diligence, and exactitude. Valéry was enchanted by method—not only Leonardo's method, but the method of mathematics, dance, and architecture as well as verse.

It is curious that Valéry should have endorsed method as a creative force in poetry and yet have been so doubtful about its social consequences when it appears in the guise of technology. In his essay "Conquest by Method" he anticipates what Ellul says about the domination of techniques. The basis of our culture, Valéry states, is the "anonymous and urgent science" called method, which is capable of being used by mediocre men who are carried to success, or at least efficiency, by techniques in which they are disciplined. Valéry guesses that this urgent science appeared first in England when Bacon advocated a command of nature by method. Implicit in Valéry's remarks is a distinction between Leonardo's method, fusing *ars* with *techné,* and Bacon's method addressed toward technological ends. It is almost the distinction between the use of method in pure and applied science and is reflected in Valéry's contrast between dancing and walking, which, "like prose, has a definite aim."

There is likewise the method of Descartes, who hoped to attain "a knowledge of all things of which my mind was capable." The Cartesian method was not Bacon's method of experiment; yet it afforded Descartes "certain and simple rules, such that, if a man observe them accurately, he shall never assume what is false as true, and will never spend his mental efforts to no purpose, but will always gradually increase his knowledge and so arrive at a true understanding of all that does not surpass his powers." Much like Bacon, Descartes had an innocent confidence that an attentive method is the Theseus-thread to guide man through the labyrinth of uncertain questions. "Method consists entirely in the order and disposition of the objects toward which our mental vision must be directed if we would find out any truth. . . . If we wish our science to be complete, those matters which promote the end we have in view must one and all be scrutinized by a movement of thought which is continuous and nowhere interrupted; they must also be included in an enumeration which is both adequate and methodical."

Valéry is more cordial to Descartes' method than to Bacon's, for he evidently distrusts Bacon's leaning toward practicality and technism: he observes that the Germans, not the British or French, have made a conquest of the world by method, by the efficiency and economy of the Prussian military system, which was "elevated to the plane of general policy." Valéry might have quoted Treitschke, but he goes on to say, "Germany owes all to something that is most antipathetic to certain temperaments—particularly to the English and the French. That thing is *discipline*." The German superiority in the practical world is due, he thinks, to strict method: the German manufacturer leaves nothing to chance—"instead of *inventing* the form of the object, he makes inquiries," thereby reducing the risk in his enterprise to a minimum. In war and on the market German methodology diminishes the role of chance. Valéry attributes German success to the accuracy he calls an "intensive cultivation of limited initiative." A carefully used method "provides a simple, sure solution to every individual case. . . . All it asks is obedience and *never anything extraordinary*." Method is what can be duplicated, and its very repeatability adds immeasurably to the resources of mediocre successors who continue, without great ingenuity, to use or modify it. An efficient method reduces the hazards of enterprise: if conditions on the market are studied, a product can be offered that satisfies every consumer.

In 1897, when Valéry wrote his essay, Europe was moving into an era when method would become the effectual force in politics and business; Whitehead says that during the nineteenth century "a new method entered into life," breaking up the old culture; Ortega calls it the age of technism. Valéry's thesis, then, is hardly original. It is odd, however, that he should seem to have quite different attitudes toward method in technology and method in poetry. He predicts that Germanic methods will be the reigning discipline of the coming century precisely because "Method calls for true mediocrity in the individual, or rather for greatness only in the most elementary talents, such as patience and the ability to give attention to everything, without preference or feeling. Finally, the will to work." An effective method "greatly reduces the need to invent" and makes research cumulative. "Surprises can be foreseen," since methodical planning can deal with all possible cases. The ventures of the German General Staff have aims that are "clear, simple, and vast" and are based on the premise that "the true enemy is the accidental."

In writing thus did Valéry consider that the poet fabricating his *vers sagement calculée* exercises puritanical virtues having something in common with the methodological virtues of the mediocre men he distrusts in technology? Did he recognize that the attempt to exclude chance in military and economic ventures finds its poetic cognate in Mallarmé's dread of *Hasard*? Of course Valéry has much else to say about poetry—yet to ask such questions is not entirely perverse, since the symbolists were so earnestly given to their method. *Un Coup de Dés* is a desperate venture in writing a pure poem by calculating everything, by ruling out the surprises of Chance—the throw of the dice, which is the aesthetic threat. The symbolists surrendered prose to the realm of Chance; but the Poem (the Book) should be so duly controlled that the casual, the contingent, the irrelevant should be eliminated. The symbolist poem was devoted to a conquest by method, a program of artistic discipline that banished the accidental as utterly as a laboratory experiment (which was also firmly controlled). The poem, manifesting its pure Beauty, would appear in all its clarity as the supreme artifact uncontaminated by the hazard of photography or

(25

prose, the disorder of life, the accidents in actuality. To his torment Mallarmé found it impossible to evade the uncertainties of *Hasard;* therefore his pure Poem is inaccessible. This is to grant that the poem cannot be created by method. Yet symbolist verse is the most daring venture in literary methodology, a strategy of conquest by the Word, a system for creating an art capable of excluding *l'imprevu.* We are not concerned here with symbolist failures but with the obsessive methods that marked so many nineteenth-century artistic ventures. There is a community of consciousness between Flaubert's effort to give attention to everything which could make his novel "scientific" and Huxley's insistence that the scientist should expose his thinking to "every possible kind of verification, and to take care, moreover, that this is done intentionally, and not left to a mere accident."

If the method is adequate, aesthetic law is as absolute as natural law. The irony lies in Valéry's remark about the limited initiative of methodologists, who subject themselves to the technological imperative. The nineteenth century invented methodologies for everything in business, in science, in art: the scientific method, the historical method, the realistic or naturalistic method, the Parnassian or symbolist method in poetry, in painting, in music—Wagnerism, impressionism, pointillism, pre-Raphaelitism, Nabism. To every one attached a program or a theory. Valéry mentions the theoretical approach to experience behind all these methodologies; he points out that one of the uninvestigated areas of the history of ideas is the formulation of a theory of theories. The methodologies of the nineteenth century belong in such a theory, and they were fostered in a society almost instinctively technological in its approach. The nineteenth century was deeply committed to experimentation in many directions, though behind many of its experiments was a limited initiative. The methodologist often explained too much by his method, which led him to invariable laws.

By returning to the unpredictable, to the actuality of the *imprevu* and the contingent, existentialism is a way of reacting against these methodologies. Karl Jaspers mentions the tendency in recent philosophy and science to distrust closed systems based upon rigorous method. Through recognizing exceptions, he says, we remain open to possible truths: "An indispensable approach to the truth would be lost without the exceptions." One might almost say that artistically the exception has become, for us, more significant than the rule. The contingent is a hazard that can no longer be ignored in art or science. Meanwhile the technologist continues to deal with the contingent by laws of probability, a calculus that rationalizes the exception.

Having a method, Valéry explains, is conforming to logic, and the exploitation of method by writers and painters of the last century led to a logic of purity. In the domain of pure and absolute art the poet seemed to exist at the pole opposite to science. Actually, however, the aesthete closed the circuit of his revolt from science at the very instant he attained his highest artistic purity by exploiting his medium at its limits. Edgar Wind notes that "pure patterns are the easiest to mechanize," and the symbolist who made his conquest by method was an aesthetic technologist in the sense that he aped the scientist. Thus we come upon Valéry's own definition of a poem as "a kind of machine for producing the poetic state of mind by means of words." When the poet or painter aped a "scientific" method, he was often unhappily successful, since he subjected art to technology. This happened more obviously to the naturalists than to the symbolists; it happened obviously to Zola, but it also happened to many pre-Raphaelites, to some impressionists, and to most aesthetes like Pater. It is still happening in so-called functional architecture, which is too often engineering, not architecture. But it never happened to John Ruskin or William Morris. The significance of Ruskin as critic of the arts and society is that however moralizing he may be, he never confused science with technology, or artistic techne (craft) with technological method. Indeed one might add that Ruskin's moral and social convictions led him to treat technological problems within the larger contexts which they now lack.

The Logic of Purity

Essentially the question is how far the arts can, or should, be purified by method. On this count the scientist has been more intelligent than the artist or critic, for he has come to recognize that his science cannot be pure. In Michael Polanyi's phrase, science is now admittedly a form of personal knowledge, since any method is the scientist's own method, not an absolute instrument. Meantime a faith in the value of method by and perhaps for itself persists among novelists and painters more strongly than among scientists. Ever since Gide made his seductive attempt to write "pure" fiction by stripping it of character, event, dialogue, and other elements that do "not specifically belong to the novel," there have been efforts to formalize methods. Witness *Finnegans Wake* and fold-in novels, which are as methodological as Mallarmé's *Coup de Dés*. Our drama since Pirandello has sometimes been an exercise in method; even the actor devised his Method. The film has purified the technique of the camera, as in *Last Year at Marienbad*. The cleansing of painting has occasionally amounted to white on white or monochrome blue.

Robert Penn Warren has asked whether poems should be pure, and decides that although all poetry wants to be pure, poems themselves are seldom pure. If we delete from a poem impurities like the beliefs I. A. Richards once called illicit, we are likely to sterilize the poem or to make it so artificial a fabric that it becomes a museum item or a document. Warren thinks of Poe, Shelley, the symbolists and imagists as pure—poets who mastered their intended techniques. If they are not so pure as Warren thinks, yet it is true that a poem most heavily indebted to its method is a poem easiest to fabricate. This is one telling count against computer poetry: it is hard to contaminate it with impurities. *Lycidas,* by contrast, is a poem deeply contaminated with impurities, filled with incompatibles in attitude and even technique. It is a poem that maintains itself almost by its perversions of method.

Of all the areas of literary activity, our modern criticism has been the one where methodology has been supreme. While scientists have been liberating themselves from the tyranny of method, literary critics have been erecting systems that stake nearly everything on method, ignoring Matthew Arnold's warning that the only safeguard is not to be abstract. Without denying the need for, or the vigor of, the "new" criticism, one may judge that from the 1920's onward there has been a more total conquest by critical method than at any period since the renaissance. Our age of criticism has achieved a terminology so exact that the academic critic has at his disposal a vocabulary almost technological in precision. We can discriminate levels of meaning, ambiguities, tones, intentions, signs, and symbols. The growth of linguistic studies has supported the ambition to use critical definitions as refined as they are formal. One critic has "by definition" constructed a *lexicon rhetoricae* enabling us to "analyze the five aspects of form" in literature; another furnishes an anatomy of criticism synoptic enough to embrace and order all genres. Critical methods have become autonomous, so professional that in judging a novel or poem there are specialized approaches through psychology (Jungian or Freudian), anthropology, sociology, history, and aesthetics.

More academic still, some neo-Aristotelians have been proving that criticism is a department of philosophy. It is proposed that "the number of possible critical positions is relative to the number of possible philosophic positions; and that the latter is determined by two principal considerations: (1) the number of aspects of a subject which can be brought into discussion, as constituting its *subject-matter;* (2) the kinds of basic dialectic which may be exerted upon the subject-matter." A criticism "integral in its dialectic" can resolve questions "by referring poetry, for example, to some analogue of poetry, finding characteristics of poetry which are shared by the analogue." There is likewise a differential dialectic for finding the characteristics of poetry by separating poetry from its analogues. Such critical technique "can make available to the poet a calculus of the frame of mind of the audience, of the nature of emotions, etc."

This critical scholasticism is as severe and as "scientific" as the philological scholasticism of an earlier generation of academicians. Cyril Connolly has charged that "Criticism is now an exact science with its own terminology." The analysis of paradox and texture has led to "close readings" of the image and encouraged an approach to poetry that seems nearly technological. Methods of reading a poem have replaced the poem.

One of the influential figures in this technological criticism has been I. A. Richards, who was sensitive to the methods and demands of science. In 1926 in *Science and Poetry* he attempted to salvage literature in an age dominated by mathematics and the theory of relativity. He hoped to treat poetry as pseudostatement, "a form of words whose scientific truth or falsity is irrelevant to the purpose in hand." The purpose in hand is gaining an advantageous or economical organization of "our impulses and attitudes" by lowering or releasing conflicts within the self. Pseudostatement is, however, rather limited, for it is not subject to verification objectively, like scientific statement. The value of a pseudostatement is reckoned by its "serviceableness to the whole personality," and since man is a "system of interests," poetry can be justified as a means of psychotherapy.

There is nothing objectionable in this rephrasing of the notion of catharsis; the point, rather, is Richards's effort to purify the poem from beliefs that are "illicit" simply because science has made it impossible any longer to believe them. Thus Richards wrote his curious footnote (since qualified) on *The Waste Land* as a poem where Eliot made "a complete severance between his poetry and *all* beliefs." Having excluded from his consideration of the poem all "irrelevant" impurities, the critic faces poetic statement as a naked linguistic texture to be analyzed. Lately Richards has acknowledged the shortcomings of this kind of criticism, which reduces itself to structural linguistics: "The linguistic structuralist is so often in danger of confining his attention to the relations of words with other words only," that he ignores the poet's involvement with what is uttered. What is being said depends in part on who is saying it, and under what conditions. Also "what is said depends on how it is said, and how it is said on what is said." Richards is not, of course, arguing that a poem is merely a way of verbally packaging a message or "precipitate"; he is simply warning the critic that a poem may not be as pure as it was once thought to be.

Richards's retreat from his early position is typical of the *detente* now occurring in criticism. R. P. Blackmur always held that criticism is "the discourse of an amateur," formal though it may be. He insisted that "the critic can have little authority as pedagogue," and that any rational approach to literature is tolerable if it can fasten "at any point upon the work itself." The reaction against technological criticism is carried further in William Righter's *Logic and Criticism* (1963), which disposes of a great many recent systems by calling them pedagogy. Much renaissance criticism was pedagogy, just as much of the older philological criticism was pedagogy. Righter suspects that the pursuit of logic in criticism is not so salutary as it once seemed, and that our methodologies have led to closed judgments. Although the genteel appreciation that passed for criticism among the Victorians was superficial, self-indulgent, and belletristic, Righter surmises that "in criticism there are no arguments, only observations."

When criticism is thoroughly methodized, the critic becomes a professional, a specialist, or, worse, an official or functionary. In the past, Righter notes, critics have seldom, even in the renaissance, attempted "pure" criticism, for the most academic critics were also moralists; in spite of their concern for genre and rule, they viewed literature from an ethical angle, the beautiful being, for them, a facet of the good. As Righter says, we seldom read great critics of the past to throw light on literature, but rather to perceive how "society saw both itself and the literature that mattered to it." The very blunders of these critics are profitable because of "something they brought to their subject," not what they extracted from it. So by recent standards, their criticism was impure as well as unsystematic. Their contribution extended beyond the limits of their method.

The larger conquests in criticism, then, are unlikely to come by method only, or by formal lexicons. Criticism cannot have the exactitude or efficiency of technology: "The complexity of literature allows us to entertain multiple attitudes towards any serious figure or major work." And criticism must remain open if only for the reason that "the circumstances under which a work is examined are never twice the same." The pluralism required of the critic has its scientific parallel in the principle of indeterminacy or complementarity, allowing the observer to describe the same phenomenon as it appears within different contexts or by different scales of measurement. Whitehead and Bronowski have both assured us that exactness is a fake.

Thus we may judge that overreliance upon method in science, in criticism, and in the arts is in the long run an evidence of what Valéry calls limited initiative. Practically, the difference between science and technology is defined by this criterion of limited initiative, which manifests itself in the programmatic. Valéry associated the modern consciousness of method with changes that occurred during the renaissance, and it is true that within renaissance art there was a fascination with method for the sake of method, that is, a mannerist tendency. Mannerism might be characterized as an art that sacrifices vision to method, and a considerable part of nineteenth-century art is mannerist in this way. Yet the renaissance exploiting of method in painting by Parmigianino or Bronzino, for instance, could achieve surprises because the method was still exploratory, a way of experimenting or reaching conclusions not entirely predictable. Mannerist art was a means of revising or even rejecting the classical theories of composition. Furthermore the renaissance was a period of incoherent thought; the idea of a world order barely concealed an underlying sense of disorder. Mannerist methods could not be fully theorized or systematized; they were an aspect of craft rather than science or philosophy.

The case is a little different as the nineteenth century develops, for it was a period much given to absolutes in both science and art, and to every method attached a theory that seemed to be based upon certain laws. The limited initiatives inherent in nineteenth-century methodologies result from a rather simplistic view of things, which, in general, was encouraged by the naïve science of the day, with its mechanical explanations that were themselves theoretic. The nineteenth-century world view made it possible for methods to be programmatic, and to that extent technological.

John Stuart Mill is doubtless correct in stating that Jeremy Bentham was "the great subversive" who established the supremacy of method. With his "practical mind" Bentham was effective because he was one of those mediocre men whose method was available to successors with the gift for patient attention to everything. Dreading generalities, always mindful of the "facts," Bentham was able to reach his gigantic and theoretic synthesis by method alone. "Few great thinkers," Mill says, "have ever been so deficient" as Bentham, whose doctrines are less important than "his mode of arriving at them." Mill characterizes Bentham by Carlyle's phrase, "the completeness of limited men." The revolt of the masses, in brief, begins with Bentham's esteem for technique. Not Bentham's opinions but Bentham's methods "constituted the novelty and the value of what he did":

> Bentham's method may be shortly described as the method of *detail;* of treating wholes by separating them into their parts, abstractions by resolving them into Things—classes and generalities by distinguishing them into the individuals of which they are made up; and breaking every question into pieces before attempting to solve it. (J. S. Mill: *Bentham*)

Bentham's hedonistic calculus is a simplistic and programmatic methodology based on the premise that "Nature has placed mankind under the governance of two sovereign masters, pain and pleasure," values which can be accurately denoted by estimating intensity, duration, certainty or uncertainty, propinquity or remoteness, fecundity, and purity.

How far does Bentham's calculus, a primitive phase of human engineering and a manifestation of the technological imperative, reappear in the aesthetic calculus of certain literary methods, notably in realism or naturalism, in decadence, in symbolism with its intent to master *Hasard*, its *vers sagement calculée,* its interest in the artifice that has been compared to the cult of the machine? However the aesthetes scorned industry, they resorted to their own technological methods. It is often assumed that during the nineteenth century art and science expressed two incompatible attitudes, that science damaged art by driving it toward transcendental realms alien from the realm of actuality. The artist did, in fact, seek transcendental realms and tried to soar like Icarus. But the economy of art often resembled the economy of a technological order. The methods of science and art were equally prescriptive.

II

Romantics
and Aesthetes

❦

Romantic Empiricism

AT THE RISK of oversimplifying one may say
that neither the romantics nor some of their successors
like Ruskin felt the conflict between science and the arts,
though the aesthetes and decadents did. But inconsistently enough, the aesthetes, including Parnassians and
symbolists, resorted to a brand of technology in art, perhaps because their initiative was more limited than the romantic initiative. They were more fully committed to a
conquest by method, and their method sometimes was a
mystique. For present purposes one may take Baudelaire
as the writer who brought into literature an awareness of
method that made poetic technique almost programmatic.
Parnassians and symbolists have been called neoroman-
tics, and in truth they are indelibly romantic in their
subjectivity, their revolt, their egoism, their devotion to
dreams. Yet they are unlike the romantics because they
are also indelibly "literary." That is, they were aware of

artifice as the first generation of romantics was not. In spite of Hugo's egalitarian vocabulary and Wordsworth's attempt to give poetry a new language, the romantics lacked any program or coherent method. They voiced new and rebellious attitudes, but they invented little in the way of technique. That was left for the realists and aesthetes after Gautier and the pre-Raphaelites. The decadents are sometimes labeled Alexandrian, and the term reminds us of Nietzsche's distinction between theoretic and tragic man. The realists and aesthetes were theoretic men; the romantics were not. Nietzsche identified the technician of his day as a mystagogue.

The romantics were, for the most part, receptive to science perhaps because at the opening of the nineteenth century both poetry and science were inherently empirical. Making a direct appeal to experience—to their feelings—the romantics were marked by a kind of realism different from the theoretic realism of the naturalistic novel, which was subservient to a methodology of observation and verification. So there are two different questions: the relation between empiricism and literature and the relation between technology and literature. It is not a question of simple oppositions, since there are always interactions. The romantic situation has something in common with the classic Greek situation, when science was a mode of philosophy. Also, with all its dissimilar temperaments the romantic era was less sophisticated than the later nineteenth century in the sense that the romantic poets spoke by direct address, whereas later poetry became increasingly oblique as the use of various methods intervened between the personality of the poet and his poem. After Poe and Baudelaire all poetry became to an extent a highly conscious artifact.

The cordiality of the romantic imagination to science is due to an empiricism that tests every experience against a personal and immediate response, a response often at odds with reason.[2] The validity of romantic experience is warranted by its being immethodical; the authenticity of the romantic poet comes from his inwardness, his faculty for surrender to a passing mood; he often addresses himself to the contingent. Some romantic poets like Shelley were rationalists, envisioning an Idea; yet their reasoning was unsystematic to the degree of being irresponsible. The Idea revealed to them in ecstasy was an assertion of the supremacy of their consciousness, an experience nearly manic in its intensity. As visionary Shelley speaks as abstractly as a scientist or Symbolist, but his vision is not depersonalized or depersonalizing like the vision of Beauty that requires the disappearance of the poet in Mallarmé's art. Shelley is not an Alexandrian or theoretic man in Nietzsche's sense; he says, "We want the creative faculty to imagine that which we know; we want the generous impulse to act that which we imagine; we want the poetry of life: our calculations have outrun our conception; we have eaten more than we can digest." His rationalism is an ardent affirmation of moral or political belief, an epiphany rather than a demonstration.

Shelley took his skylark flight to unknown modes of being without sensing any antagonism toward the science of his day. His enthusiasm for chemistry, physics, and theories of electricity explains some of the obscure imagery in verses like "The Cloud," for instance, and the Spirit pervading his universe is evidently magnetic force. He is not only a Platonist but also a necessitarian or materialist in the tradition of Holbach and the *philosophes*. The early "Notes" to *Queen Mab* affirm his belief in a "necessity" that amounts nearly to scientific determinism: "He who asserts the doctrine of Necessity means that, contemplating the events which compose the moral and material universe, he beholds only an immense and uninterrupted chain of causes and effects. . . . The idea of Necessity is obtained by our experience of the connection between objects, the uniformity of the operations of Nature. . . . Every human being is irresistibly impelled to act precisely as he does act." The figure of Demogorgon in *Prometheus Unbound* symbolizes a determinism that is natural, political, and ethical. Shelley's opposition to conventional Christianity arises from his vision of an ordered plurality of worlds, "the indefinite immensity of the Universe." To this extent he is a poet of Newtonian physics.

This devotion to science did not prevent Shelley from writing his *Defence of Poetry*, the most fruitful and prophetic document in the history of romantic criticism. The *Defence* contains every notion on which the French critics from Baudelaire to Valéry established their poetic methodology: notions of *correspondance*, music, the word as hieroglyph, ascent to another world, the illumination or ecstasy waking the mind to transitory brightness, the anguish and madness that are pleasure. Yet compared with the Parnassians and symbolists, Shelley has no serious interest in poetic method and defines poetry "in a general sense" as "the expression of the imagination," by which he seems to mean an extraordinary sensitivity: the poet is a man "more delicately organized than other men, and sensible to pain and pleasure, both his own and that of others, in a degree unknown to them."

Shelley's essentially romantic definition of poetry is quite in accord with De Quincey's notion of poetry as an "iris" of passion, desire, and emotion, and also with Hazlitt's similar notion of poetry as a highly wrought enthusiasm of feeling. And that other great document of romantic criticism, Wordsworth's "Preface," takes the poet to be a man of more than usual organic sensibility. Like Shelley, Wordsworth readily accepted the science of his day, notably the associationist psychology popularized by David Hartley. If this psychology did not explain what Wordsworth most strove to explain—the relation between his animal sensations and his visionary trances—he nevertheless used the theory of associated ideas much as later poets used Freudian psychoanalysis. In his "Preface"

Wordsworth explains that his purpose was to study how ordinary things present themselves to the mind in unusual aspects while we are in a state of excitement. He supposed that by being sensitive to these cluster-images the poet could reveal "the primary laws of our nature," tracing how the flow of feeling is modified by past feelings that reappear almost subconsciously. Wordsworth was convinced that there is no barrier between poetry and science insofar as science affects us as "enjoying and suffering beings." He was entirely willing to follow the scientist by "carrying sensations into the midst of the objects of science itself." Like Shelley he speaks of poetry as a finer spirit of knowledge assuming the very countenance of science: the "remotest discoveries of the Chemist, the Botanist, or Mineralogist" are subjects for poetry whenever they affect our daily experience.

Like Shelley, too, Wordsworth is more concerned with poetic emotion and poetic experience than with poetic method. To be sure, he rejected the methods of eighteenth-century poetry, which required a special language, and he intended to substitute another method involving the language of prose; but his theory and his practice are alike immethodical and inconsistent. He retained the old meters, he failed to use the language of prose in much of his best verse, and he revised the subjects of poetry rather than poetic technique. His deeper interest was not method but his sensibility, his animal sensations, his awareness of the "goings on" in his mind and in nature. The revision of poetic method was left to Poe and his French disciples.

Nor can it be claimed that Coleridge, for all his pretentious metaphysical explanations, furnished any satisfactory theory of composition, since his interest, too, was chiefly in the supremacy of the creative imagination. Notwithstanding his scattered remarks about the versification of "Christabel" and the *Lyrical Ballads*, Coleridge devoted himself mainly to discourses on the nature and operation of the imagination and the esemplastic quality of the organic poem. The sign of poetic genius is the ability to modify images by "a predominant passion." Of all the romantics, Blake possibly aside, Byron had the most prodigious technical facility; but one can hardly claim that he made any genuine contribution to the development of poetic method. As Auden has said, Byron was essentially a comic poet who, so far as his method goes, was an opportunist, first experimenting with Spenserian verse, then with ottava rima, until he found the vehicle best suited to his ingenuity. Whatever aesthetic theory he had was derived from his practice. Unless we except Blake, Keats probably had more serious interest in poetic method than any of the romantics; but here again, Keats was untheoretic, and his profound observations on poetry are an expression of his temperament, not an attempt to specify a method.

Compared with the French groups, the Parnassians and symbolists, the English romantics are an anarchic company. It might be hard to name poets more divergent in method than Blake, Wordsworth, Byron, Shelley, and Keats. These are the great romantics, and they are such by reason of their dispositions, their responses and feelings, rather than by reason of any agreement about execution. The English romantics had no accepted theory of their métier, although there was a consistent emphasis upon the sanction of feeling. The romantics validated their poetry by their personality, not by their method, about which they were sadly at odds.

They are poets who practiced one of the most authentic forms of empiricism in their century. As Robert Langbaum puts it, they wrote a poetry of experience. They were not "against science," but, rather, intent upon knowing their world by testing everything against their feelings. For the romantic the life of things is apparent "at the moment when experience is immediate and unanalyzed." In romantic poetry all thought is tinged with feeling. When he does think, the romantic finds, like Keats, that a thought is not valid until it is proved on the pulses. By seeking this authenticity of experience the English romantics, at least, resorted to an elemental empiricism that science itself once had.

In his eagerness to test everything against feeling, the romantic was often willing to leave his experiences unrationalized or even disorganized. This incoherence of what is experienced became intolerable in scientific empiricism, which needed to be more completely rationalized. Langbaum mentions Faust as a romantic hero whose "formulations evolve because he senses at each point that his understanding of the experience is inadequate to his total apprehension of it." The romantic experience often exceeds the ability to conceptualize the experience. Whitehead found this true of Wordsworth, who "expresses the concrete facts of our apprehension" without distorting them by a scientific analysis that proceeds by induction and leads to logical conclusions. One of the most sophisticated of all romantic heroes, Stendhal's Julien, is never able to conceive his experiences satisfactorily but spends his life in "the continuous attention with which he watched his own slightest actions." Julien's most scrupulous observations do not lead him to stable conclusions. The value of romantic experience is inherent in the experience itself rather than in the propositions that might be made on the basis of the evidence.

Thus, Langbaum says, the romantic appeal to experience is "an attempt to salvage on science's own empiric grounds the validity of the individual perception against scientific abstractions." Nor was the romantic particularly concerned with the method of acquiring his experiences. He was more intent upon being susceptible to experience. This is one reason why romantic art tends to make consciousness an absolute. Valéry called upon the poet for "as much consciousness as possible," but he tried to discipline this heightened consciousness by his method. The romantic sought a maximum degree of consciousness, but often presented consciousness in its immediate state, leaving it as primal recognition, in an unsupervised condition.

Something of this formlessness of primal experience is in Keats, who realized the value of leaving his responses in a "negative" or conditional state: ". . . it struck me what quality went to form a Man of Achievement, especially in Literature, and which Shakespeare possessed so enormously—I mean Negative Capability, that is, when a man is capable of being in uncertainties, mysteries, doubts, without any irritable reaching after fact or reason." Therefore the poetical character seems to Keats to have no identity, existing in the world outside the self, enjoying experiences that do not need to be ratified by reason: ". . . it has no self—It is everything and nothing —It has no character—it enjoys light and shade; it lives in gusto, be it foul or fair, high or low." For Keats, truth is beauty because beauty is undeniable immediate experience, the poetic empiricism best described by Keats himself as a possibility of continuing discovery through what is seen, heard, or touched; thus "the Simple imaginative Mind may have its rewards in the repetition of its own silent Working coming continually on the Spirit with a fine Suddenness."

The fine suddenness is a mode of empiricism that James Joyce termed an epiphany, that instant when the soul of an object—perhaps the commonest object—leaps to us from the vestment of its appearance. The young Stephen Dedalus had such an epiphany when he saw the peasant girl wading along the shore at Howth, an Irish Venus in all her fleshliness, who is suddenly and miraculously transformed to a luminous image, a thing of beauty that is a joy forever, whose loveliness will never pass into nothing. This metamorphosis of the object into an aesthetic image, in "silent stasis," is a transcendence stimulated through a total surrender to the poetic empiricism of which Keats speaks. By their perceiving things so in-

tensely he and Joyce could irradiate the object to a revelation that transvalued the material to an essence. They
encounter the object with a primal naïveté that allows
them to preserve in all its surprise the full structure of the
event. When he first looked at the Elgin Marbles, Keats
felt only the overwhelming presence of the stony figures
that spoke to him of his own destined mortality and failure. Then occurred the moment when the statues were
transfigured (the theological phrase is needed) into an
abiding vision of the essence of Greek grandeur, the
claritas and *quidditas* of Athenian culture symbolized by
a "billowy main, a sun, a shadow of a magnitude." So also
Stephen Dedalus has his moment of revelation or ecstasy
when the flesh of the Irish girl becomes the splendor of
truth "beheld by the imagination, which is appeased by
the most satisfying relations of the sensible." And the
marble Grecian urn appeased Keats to the full.

Certain romantics like Blake and Shelley did try to
ratify their experiences by thought, but in such cases
their thought was itself a mode of experience, an
epiphany. The meridian of romantic thought as revelation is not really in Valéry but in Blake, who, however,
avoided the danger of rationalistic coherence or consistency by his dialectic, his belief that opposites must exist,
unreconciled, in human experience: "There is a Negation
& there is a Contrary: the Negation must be destroyed to
redeem the Contraries. The Negation is the Spectre, the
Reasoning Power in Man," the power that sacrifices contraries for the sake of systems. Blake's innocence is a state
of primal empiricism, able to accept the lust of the goat
as the glory of God. Shelley is more given to ideologies;
but in Shelley, again, thought at the meridian is an hys-
teric seizure. The notion that the romantic poet suffered
from a dissociation of sensibility is not entirely sustained
by this kind of rationalism—which might be called a
mode of irrationalism insofar as thought itself is a moment of apocalypse, a height of consciousness synthe-

sizing mind with feeling. Shelley's ideas are often illuminations, comprehensions so intense that they amount to revelations. Certainly there is no dissociation of sensibility in Keats's "Eve of Saint Agnes," where a thought comes to Porphyro like a full-blown rose making purple riot in his heart. It might even be claimed that Wordsworth's thoughts gathered about the setting sun are evidence of a unified sensibility.

As poets of experience, many romantics threw themselves into the world in order to know the world, for their empiricism was more primitive than the laboratory empiricism of the scientist, who was required to occupy, according to his method, a position of the detached observer, organizing and controlling his experiment and drawing conclusions. The difference between scientific and romantic appeal to experience is mostly a difference in regulation, scope, and immediacy. The romantic testing is less directed, less stable, less confined, and less distanced. It is liable to the injuries of time, the transitoriness of feelings that pass into nothingness, bringing a sense of irony or cynicism, and leaving the poet in "a dim vast vale of tears, vacant and desolate." If the scientist organizes his disillusions under the guise of knowledge,[3] the romantic disillusions are left in a state of opposition; thus occurs the Byronic reversal from tears to laughter: "And if I laugh at any mortal thing, 'Tis that I may not weep." Romantic empiricism is betrayed by its very authenticity.

As observer, the scientist plays a role, but a more limiting and specified role than the many roles available to the romantic who wishes to prove everything on his pulses. Each romantic role is an experiment. "I take at random," says Stendhal, "whatever fate throws in my path." Julien Sorel commits himself to every sort of experiment indiscriminately and speaks of his life as "a succession of hazards." He complains that civilization and the police have left "no room for the unexpected." As empiricist, therefore, the scientist is eligible only for type-casting, the ex-

perimenter who plays a single role. More exactly, perhaps, the "pure" scientist is less restricted by his role than
is the technologist, the applied scientist or specialist in a
certain procedure. The romantic is an unspecialized role-
player, and his changing roles lead him to contradictory
experiences. Byron played the sentimentalist and the roué;
Shelley played the rationalist and the mystic; Faust's
experiences are comic, tragic, dandiacal, and sentimental;
Fabrizio del Dongo at last finds the role of dreamer most
congenial. Romantic role-playing has an existential immediacy even though romantic sensibility is incoherent.

Such heroes are victimized by their feelings, which
fluctuate so often that their personalities dissolve into a
succession of momentary responses, each having its own
validity. Julien Sorel suffers from Hamlet's personality
diffusion, his negative identity. Stendhal confides, "I do
not really know myself after all, and it is this that sometimes saddens me in the middle of the night when I brood
over it." The diffusion and perplexity of romantic experience is recorded in Wordsworth's *Prelude:*

> ... the soul,
> Remembering *how* she felt, but *what* she felt
> Remembering not ... (II)

The texture of romantic experience is how one feels, not
what one feels. One may not clearly know what one feels,
though one knows what one thinks. The "meaning," or
content, of felt experience may be obscure, confused, or
contradictory, though there is no doubt about how one
felt. Thus, feeling is incommunicable in that it has no
subject but is, rather, an attitude toward, or an angle on,
reality. The romantic experience of nature, for instance, is
not a "what" but a "how": how Wordsworth feels uplifted
to unknown modes of being though he cannot say what
these modes of being are.

In sum, the romantic empiricism was not regulated by
any method, whereas the scientific empiricism was grad-

ually controlled by the so-called scientific method. The gulf opened between the romantics and their successors, whether Parnassian, symbolist, realist, or decadent, when these latter became increasingly attracted to their various methodologies, which brought into their work a more specialized consciousness. Each group in poetry and painting and fiction evolved its critical theory, its expertise. Meanwhile science was also being identified with certain procedures that ultimately had the effect of transforming science into a technological activity. Oddly enough, the scientists emancipated themselves from the tyranny of their method before the poets, novelists, and literary critics freed themselves from their fascination with their own brand of technology, their theoretic approach to art. The group of new French critics including Roland Barthes has at last proclaimed the "death of style" in behalf of a zero degree of writing (*écriture*), undoing the tourniquet that confined so much nineteenth-century literature to an exercise in method. At a considerably earlier date, however, a generation of scientists including Heisenberg, Whitehead, Bridgman, and Polanyi, among many others, made a Goedelian leap outside the confines of *the* scientific method, all of them insisting that the activity known as science is a certain kind of instrumentalism leading to alternative explanations of the same phenomenon. Karl Friedrich Gauss supposedly remarked, "I have the solution, but don't yet know how I am to arrive at it."

Craft as Bricolage

The romantic quest for experience is significant because it is close to the early empiricism of the "concrete" science in savage societies, the science that phrases itself in totemism and myth. The primitive mind seems to have felt the same need as the romantics (and today's scientist): to test things by immediate experience without trying to conceptualize a world order or to structure this experience systematically. Claude Lévi-Strauss calls this primitive empiricism a "first" science. He describes it by the term *bricolage,* which was originally used to denote the "know how" certain persons have in playing games, then to describe the amateur skill of someone who can build things by a do-it-yourself kind of pottering, a non-professional and instinctive craftsmanship. *Bricolage* is a way of knowing reality by what one does with one's hands. It is nontheoretic. Fellows who rebuild their jalopies are *bricoleurs.* A great deal of Leonardo da Vinci's work in both art and science was *bricolage;* the charge has been made again and again that Leonardo was a failed scientist because he never sustained his inventiveness by theories, which is only one way of saying he was not academic. Painters who used junk for *Merzbilden* were *bricoleurs,* and Tinguely's ready-mades are sardonic versions of *bricolage.* A great deal of "informal" modern painting is a sophisticated variant of primitive *bricolage,* as is apparent in Dubuffet's *assemblages* and texturologies. A talent for *bricolage* was sanctioned in cubist collage and dadaist jokes, an extension of the play instinct, which has been continued in pop art and all the ingenuities suggesting connections between objects immediately at hand but not ordinarily associated.

The *bricoleur* uses a logic of the hand and eye, not of the head; he sabotages theory, and his principle of composition is a naked craft impulse, an operationalism in art. If science is what scientists do, then this kind of art is what the painter does with his hand—nothing more. It resembles the zero degree of language that is spoken, not written with a "style" in mind. Its empiricism is crude, deprived of any logic of form; it is what a Happening was supposed to be—before Happenings became a convention. The *bricolage* in modern art is, in fact, cruder than the *bricolage*-science of primitive societies, which has a quite formal scheme of totemism. Claude Lévi-

Strauss interprets the totemic organization of early society as a form of *bricolage* enabling man to live in his tribal world. Totemism is a science sufficient for the occasion, providing a way of life for family and caste, a "logic of the concrete." The classifications that apply to one situation do not apply to another, since there is no world-embracing theoretical ordering of nature but only a kind of social instrumentalism.

The logic of primitive groups is magic, a mode of causality that does not extend into the universe as a natural law, but works pragmatically in given local circumstances. Even if there is no consistent *mise en structure* for this "first" science, each situation has its own immanent and inherent causality, a *bricolage* of magic enabling primitive man to establish whatever relations he needs between events. It is a logic that does not need to distinguish between the contingent and the universal. The logic of a given occasion arises within the occasion itself.

This empirical or magical causality-for-the-occasion is at the root of Wordsworth's primitive organic sensibility, which is as immediate as anything in romantic experience. As a boy Wordsworth sensed in nature:

> . . . a dark
> Inscrutable workmanship that reconciles
> Discordant elements, makes them cling together
> In one society. (*Prelude*, I)

At moments the "hallowed and pure motions of the sense" had "an intellectual charm" which did not come from thought but from a feeling that he was "an inmate of this active universe":

> Along his infant veins are interfused
> The gravitation and the filial bond
> Of nature that connect him with the world. (*Prelude*, II)

For Wordsworth and for the totemic "first" science the world is like an

> ... interminable building reared
> By observation of affinities
> In objects where no brotherhood exists
> To passive minds. (*Prelude*, II)

This elemental and thoroughgoing empiricism is a "sensuous cognition of reality," and Wordsworth feels more strongly than any other poet that "there is no object standing between the Poet and the image of things." He exists in a world Piaget has called diffuse animism, contemplating his own passions "as manifested in the goings-on of the Universe." According to the researches of Henri Wallon the child at first experiences space only as a sensory-motor construction which is a reflex of his own body; then he discovers the world of objects existing solidly and stably outside himself; and at last he posits a rational space in which these objects are arranged.[4] A great deal of primitive art belongs in an ambiguous area where there is no clear boundary between the self and the outside world, where space has topological or half-projective form rather than Euclidean or theoretic structure. That is, for the primitive mind, space is not homogeneous but created around the objects that present themselves to consciousness. There is no space; there are only spaces, and these spaces are molded by the sensation of the object that exists only as it presents itself. In this primitive spatial recognition the object is an aspect of consciousness, or, as Wordsworth has it, nothing stands between him and his image of things. There is something radically primitive about Wordsworth's note to the "Intimations" ode stating, "I was often unable to think of external things as having external existence. . . . Many times . . . I grasped at a wall or tree to recall myself from this abyss of idealism."

It is not idealism, but the diffuse animism that Cassirer associates with the radical empiricism of primitive consciousness, which is unable to establish a margin between the self and the world. In this primitive phase of consciousness the *presence* of the object reveals itself with "irresistible force" because there is no barrier between it and the self. The perception of things is like a revelation, and the object fills consciousness without its being fitted into any conceptual scheme of time or space. The primitive perception endows things with "sacred" values that are qualitative rather than quantitative, a realism that is "discontinuous," or often "polysensorial" because there is a tactile as well as a visual consciousness of the object. Since there is no sense that the self is different from reality, no margin between the seer and what is seen, there are no degrees of reality, and the image is the thing. When Wordsworth grasps a tree or wall in an effort to think of things as having their own external existence, he is struggling to break the spell of a primitive animistic consciousness.

Under this spell of organic sensibility there is no "tragic isolation of the self" from the domain of nature. Shades of the prison house close in as this elemental empiricism yields, under the influence of reason, to an awareness that things have their own *mise en structure,* that the self is alienated from the world outside. At this point thought takes over, and the mind fits things into its constructs of space, time, causality, and the notions establishing the difference between perception and conception, image and thing, subjective and objective. The fissure opens between a mythical, or artistic, consciousness of the world and a philosophic, scientific, theoretic consciousness of the world. Heidegger has said that art must recover the "thingly" recognition of things-standing-in-themselves "unconcealed" in their *Dasein,* their "undisguised presence." In thinking about things we disguise their presence. If we are to avoid this encroachment of thought, "Everything that might interpose itself between the thing and us in apprehending and talking about the thing must first be set aside. Only then do we yield ourselves to the undisguised presence of the thing. But we do not first need to call or arrange for this situation in which we let things encounter us without mediation." Robbe-Grillet has made an effort to recover the primitive sense of the presence of things without the disguise of thinking them into being: "Let it be first of all by their *presence* that objects and gestures establish themselves, and let this presence continue to prevail over whatever explanatory theory that may try to enclose them in a system of references, whether emotional, sociological, Freudian or metaphysical."

Wordsworth's mythical sensibility, in contrast to rational consciousness, operates in an area of experience between image and concept, the area of the "sign" where image "cohabits" with idea. This is the area of "savage thought," an elemental logic integrating man with his world. It is the area of Wordsworth's poetic empiricism, when all his thoughts "were steeped in feeling":

> To every natural form, rocks, fruits, or flower,
> Even the loose stones that cover the highway,
> I gave a moral life: I saw them feel,
> Or linked them to some feeling: the great mass
> Lay bedded in the quickening soul, and all
> That I beheld respired with inward meaning.
> (*Prelude*, III)

If science works on a scale of a world that is only conceived (rather than felt), Wordsworth's art reduces his world to an image homologous to its model, as Lévi-Strauss says, where every object carries its own value as metaphor. As poetic *bricoleur* Wordsworth treats a flower, a field, or a tree as an *objet de connaissance*, illustrating Whitehead's aphorism that "art is the habit of enjoying vivid values." In treating the object as sign or *objet de connaissance*, Wordsworth lays the basis for symbolism, but unlike the symbolists, he is entirely unable to theorize, or even to explain, his method. Indeed, his greatest verse is a direct result of his perplexity about the operation of his imagination.

At the close of his book, *La Pensée Sauvage*, Lévi-Strauss describes the analogical cast of this logic of the concrete-fastening-upon-the-world by many contacts—presenting things as if they were mirrored back and forth on the walls of a chamber without being arranged in a consistent scheme. Paleolithic man was already using this magical logic when he painted the Lascaux Caves, which are like this chamber. The prehistoric artist used a logic of the concrete or an empiricism different from our rational science but no less given to what is "real," to things standing-in-themselves.

The Rigors of Method

If romantic empiricism is closer to primitive magical logic than to the empiricism of the so-called realists, the cause is apparent enough: much of this sophisticated realism was governed by theories and methods that were programmatic and thus an aspect of technology, as we use the term. The romantics were receptive to science, and realists often operated under the auspices of science —but realists often confused science with a certain methodology. The immediacy of romantic experience is not the same as the immediacy sought by realists, who, as Lévi-Strauss would say, tried to work on the scale of the world outside, which to them is forever alien as it was not to Wordsworth. The realist has been defined in Gautier's phrase as one "for whom the world exists." The world existed for the romantic, too, but he did not try to know it by a scientific method; he authenticated experience by his sensibility.

Insofar as post-romantic writing was increasingly subjected to certain methods, the critical activity took priority over the creative. In discussing the function of criticism, Matthew Arnold mentions that creative activity depends upon an atmosphere that only criticism can furnish. He judges that the romantics were premature because they did not "know enough," a strange view, since the romantics were for the most part not only intelligent but well informed. But they did lack any critical theory of their métier as such, Coleridge and the German aestheticians notwithstanding. And it is true that the movements and countermovements after romanticism—realism, *Parnasse,* symobolism, naturalism, decadence—were creative activities that sprang from the very anxiety about method, since they were all in one way or another attempts to exploit a medium and experiments that had to be performed. Yet the heightened consciousness of method had the effect of inducing certain repressions and alienations characteristic of technology; in the long run subservience to method injured the empiricism of art and science alike.

To define the realist as one for whom the world exists is neither discriminating nor accurate, for realism is a far more complex attitude than the so-called realists themselves supposed. Harry Levin has said that "we can define realism by its context." Exactly. Since the context has continually changed, there have been all sorts of realism, mostly influenced by science—whether Ptolemaic, astrological, Newtonian, or Darwinian—and always influenced by the social order. Generations of Marxist critics have linked the realism of the modern novel with the bourgeois society created by industry. Amiel spoke of realism as an "intrusion of technology into literature," a helpful remark, since each of the plural realisms had its own method. If realism thrives under the auspices of science, one of the most effectual aspects of science brought to bear upon nineteenth-century realism is its methodology. Balzac supposed he could deal with his society by applying to it the classification of species arranged according to Cuvier, Buffon, and other biologists or botanists. Zola invoked the method of Claude Bernard in medicine. Flaubert hoped to give his fiction "the precision of science," and de Maupassant assumed that the novelist must always find the exact word. The realists were determined to discard romantic "scrap iron" (the mythologies of the past), but what they most had in common was a consciousness of method as it was employed in science. So far as realism is concerned, the theories of science seem less relevant than the method. This concern with method makes some realistic novels like monographs.

The compulsion to use certain methods is as obvious among Parnassians and symbolists as it is among naturalists. Often it was a method that enforced a fiction of authorial silence—the cancellation of the writer from his own text in the interest of Art, a cancellation as impossible to attain in art as it was in science, where the experimenter pretended to be a mere observer, devoted to objectivity. In accepting this fiction, realists, naturalists, and symbolists made literature a technical feat. This explains in part why so-called realism leads directly toward aestheticism and decadence. Art for the sake of art echoes many of the romantic refinements of feeling, but always with the consciousness of aesthetic effect, always with an anxiety about a method that insures the "purity" of the work. Only a proper method can guarantee this purity, this artifact which must be erected in the world of Forms. The romantics tried to live life as art, but they were not worried about aesthetic effects, as were the decadents and even the realists such as Flaubert, Gautier, and Huysmans.

However the romantics may have dedicated themselves to the Ideal, they did not make a fetish of Style. But the post-romantics tried to transcend by a discipline calculated to exploit their medium. There seems, consequently, to be a difference between the romantic transcendentalism and the transcendentalism of the symbolists, the first being positive and affirmative, the second negative, privative, and finally empty—the disappearance or Nothingness of the blank white page and the vacant mirror. The final symbolist negation is Style turning back upon

itself by the achievement of a total method. It is perhaps
characteristic of German methodology that within the
heart of the romantic period Schelling and Hegel should
have laid the foundation for this total methodology in
literature. Hegel speaks of technical skill as essential to
art: "The fact is that an important aspect of the creating
process is merely facility in the use of a medium; that is
to say, a work of art possesses a purely technical side,
which extends to the borders of mere handicraft." Schelling in discussing the relation between art and nature
argues that art must, like science, strive to represent nature as it "actually is," seeking a "particularity" of form:
the artist must not fear "hardness and severity," since
"determinateness of form in Nature is never a negation,
but ever an affirmation." The life of the plant is embodied
in its "exact and severe outline," and the artist "must deny
himself and descend into the Particular, without shun-
ning isolation, nor the pain, the anguish of Form." Precision, exactitude, control of medium: through Form the
artist reaches Essence.

From this privative and disciplinary notion derive the
sundry principles on which the Parnassians worked, and
all those poets who strove for purity of form by excluding
the excessive, the hazards of Chance. Parnassian beauty
as it appears in Gautier's *Emaux et Camées* is chiseled,
hard, glittering, nearly an imagism in its exactitude and
definition:

> Oui, l'oeuvre sort plus belle
> D'une forme au travail
> Rebelle
> Vers, marbre, onyx, émail.

This *assouplissement de la technique* attracted Baudelaire to Poe. Impossible as it is to take "The Philosophy of
Composition" seriously, Poe's essay is testimony to the
obsession with method which becomes a tradition in
French poetry from Baudelaire to Valéry, the verse which
can in general be called symbolist. Charles Maurice, writ-

ing in 1893, spoke of this new verse as "the inevitable union of the critical with the poetic spirit." Rejecting the belief that poetry is "a species of fine frenzy, an ecstatic intuition," Poe is willing to place in full view the "wheels and pinions" of poetic operation, the first determination of what effect is desired, the "calculation" of tone, atmosphere, event. With nearly technological finesse Poe works on the principle that "objects should be attained through means best adapted for their attainment." The elevation of soul wrought by the poem comes through an economy of means, circumscriptions, cautious selections and rejections, all directed toward a design that is clearly preconceived. As much consciousness as possible, said Valéry, and Poe is conscious of a method controlled by an almost puritan notion of parsimony. The poem "which is a poem and nothing more," the poem *per se,* written solely for the poem's sake" as a "rhythmical creation of Beauty," has a precision that seemed to Valéry like an algebra. It is an isolation of consciousness.

Poe's law of parsimony is operative in symbolist and decadent art, and however Baudelaire may be devoted to *volupté,* he is post-romantic in his awareness of method. A similar kind of Occam's razor was used in the so-called scientific method: not to waste motions, not to make unnecessary hypotheses, not to squander effort. Poe's diligence in giving attention to everything is, artistically, an "intensive cultivation of limited initiative" corresponding to the commonplace desire of the technologist to economize, calculate, and guarantee precision.

Symbolist poets were conscious of their inspiration as Shelley was not. The induced hallucination begins with Baudelaire's "elevation," lifting the poet toward *les champs lumineux et sereins.* This flight is prearranged, and Baudelaire admires Poe's ability to leave nothing to chance, every word being designed to perfect the composition. (Baudelaire is ravished by Gautier's style, a miracle of precision like *une profonde science mathématique.*) The induced hallucination was the basis for De

Quincey's *Confessions of an English Opium-Eater*, which with Coleridge's "Kubla Khan" brings into English romanticism a method of reaching an artificial paradise. It might be claimed that De Quincey and Coleridge were the only English romantics who were aware of this method, a technique to create illusion by opiates, and one not lost upon Baudelaire, whose elevation was attained by hashish. Under the influence of drugs Baudelaire inhabits an artificial domain where, like De Quincey, he loses a sense of his own identity, becoming an impersonal observer, seeing things "objectively" and vividly as does the scientist in his laboratory—that other artificial paradise of nineteenth-century culture. "It sometimes happens," says Baudelaire, "that one's personality vanishes, and the objectivity attributed to pantheistic poets, occurs in you so remarkably that the regard of things outside makes you forget your own existence so that you identify yourself with them." This objectivity is not pantheistic but the hallucinatory impression that haunted De Quincey in his psychedelic moments. In any case it is ironic that under the spell of drugs the poet achieved a negation of the self more radical than the scientist achieved in his laboratory.

The poetic method of obliterating the self is no more, and no less, contrived than the scientific method. At least the poet was not deluded about the artifice of his method, whether by drugs, words, rhythm, or other effort to "find a language." After Baudelaire, the medium becomes entirely pure: *vers en lui même*. The technique of *correspondance* and analogy is refined until Mallarmé makes the world disappear into *une Conception Pure*, at last leaving the poet as Valéry sees him *un sagace algébriste, un calculateur infaillible de l'effet à produire*.[5] Pierre Reverdy alleged that art begins where chance ends, and Valéry spoke of his own verses as exercises in *le calcul logique, le dessin, la versification régulière*, a music that authenticates silence.

Art for art is an ideal that penetrates realism itself from

Flaubert onward, enchanting even the novelist with the possibilities of Style within the realm of prose and evidence and factuality. Realism itself is a paradox, since it is admittedly one of the most artificial of all styles. George Moore stated, "No more literary school than the realists has ever existed," and Roland Barthes now repeats that the entire naturalistic convention is one of the most spectacular fabrications in the history of literature. Realists believed that literature should refuse the literary ("And all the rest is literature"—"take eloquence and wring its neck"). Yet refusing the literary in the interests of precision, style, and observation eventually led to a literature that was nothing except literary. Barthes summarizes the case: realism had to end in preciosity.

The absurdity of realism with its malaise about method is clear enough in Flaubert, who sacrificed himself to his technique. He urges Mlle. de Chantpie, "When you read the great masters, try to grasp their method, to draw near to the heart of them, and you will rise from your studies dazzled with joy." Flaubert seeks in perfection of literary technique a refuge from the bitterness of life: "And one does avoid it by living in Art." His most revealing confession is a letter to Louise Colet mentioning his hope to write a book about nothing, to "be held together by the strength of its style. I believe that the future of art lies in this direction," where the subject becomes nearly invisible and only the language is the fiction. This would be the "pure" novel. (Flaubert was prophetic: Gide would exploit the technique for writing the pure novel as an art form in *The Counterfeiters*.) Flaubert predicts that "the more Art develops, the more scientific it will be." He is not an experimental novelist in Zola's sense, but he agrees with Zola that a proper method is everything. Although he objects to Zola's belief that environment accounts for what happens, he is as committed to method as Zola.

The most extreme instance of aping the methods of science is Zola's "experimental novel," adopting the techniques used in medicine. Zola believed he could gain "a foothold in the realm of truth" by treating fiction as a "provoked observation" able to "verify" its art. The novelist should become "the photographer of phenomena, his observation should be an exact representation of nature. The moment that the result of the experiment manifests itself, the experimentalist finds himself face to face with a true observation which he has called forth, and which he must ascertain, as all observation, without any preconceived idea. The experimentalist should then disappear, or rather transform himself instantly into the observer." In adopting Claude Bernard's method, Zola is convinced that "the mechanism is all there." What can be carried from chemistry or physics into medicine can also be carried from medicine into the novel. Although he admits that "the method is but the tool," Zola concludes with a wholly unguarded assurance, "We have a method; we should go forward" as experimental moralists.

"Everything is reduced," says Zola, "to a question of method." In view of Valéry's remarks on the ease of duplicating method and the mediocrity of methodological man, it is significant that Zola defines the experimental novelist as one who does not "interpose his personal interests," but submits to the evidence of facts before him: "Therefore in naturalism there could be neither innovators nor leaders; there are simply workmen, some more skillful than others," each taking part in "a vast movement, a march forward," "each one in his own specialty" advancing a program. Ortega y Gasset speaks of these new men as a type unparalleled in history, the functionary who is not a scientist but a technician devoted to efficiency.

Zola could not abide by his own limited program. His effort to document his fiction, to write novels that excluded the fictional, led to melodrama and even symbolism; and it is observed that at the heart of Zola's experimental novels are symbolic figures of the Human Beast, the Animated Machine, the grotesque characters who belong in Dickens. *Germinal,* his greatest novel, is documentary in its early pages; then follows the nightmare underworld of the mine, and the lyrical close that is a metaphor of revolution coming like grass in spring. This experiment is an act of rebellion, and Zola is a romantic who betrays his own neutral method (about which he may not have been serious).

While discussing the symbolists Arthur Symons detected some agreement, however tenuous, between Zola's realism and the idealism of decadent poets. Symons speaks of Zola's method as a "distorted idealism" and revises Zola's definition of the novel: it is not nature seen through a temperament but rather through a formula. The symbolist formula is more sophisticated, but nevertheless a formula: for a poetry different from the impassioned, reckless personal vision of Blake or Shelley. The formula is supposed to obliterate the poet, and the Goncourts saw the implications of this impersonal philosophy of composition when they wrote in their journals, "After reading Edgar Allan Poe. Something the critics have not noticed: a new literary world, pointing to the literature of the twentieth century. Scientific miracles, fables on the pattern A plus B; a clear-sighted sickly literature. No more poetry but analytic fantasy. Something monomaniacal." There was something monomaniacal running through the formulas for style by which Valéry at last succeeded in "resolving consciously" all the problems of writing poetry:

> Je cherche un mot (dit le poète), un mot qui soit:
>   féminin,
>   de deux syllabes,
>   contenant P ou F,
>   terminé par une muette,
>   et synonyme de brisure, désagrégation;
>   et pas savant, pas rare.
>   Six conditions—au moins!
>   ("Autres Rhumbs")

This reliance upon formulas brings "the savour of the artificial" into various styles in all the arts: the pastiche of historical styles in architecture, the strained observation of pre-Raphaelite painting, the precisions of naturalists, symbolists, and decadents. Baudelaire specified the faculty of the modern poet as *le sentiment de l'artificiel*, a fascination with *maquillage* (make-up), which is the technology of Beauty. Théodore Hannon wrote verses on *maquillage:*

> Mon âme, tu le sais, ma mie,
> N'aime que l'artificiel.

Gautier recognized the paradox that the decadents detested the machine but cultivated artifice, and in his "Notice" of 1868 linked this literary technism with a culture that had become overripe:

> . . . style ingénieux, compliqué, savant, plein de nuances et de recherches, reculant toujours les bornes de la langue, empruntant à tous les vocabulaires techniques, prenant des couleurs à toutes les palettes, des notes à tous les claviers; . . . mais tel est bien l'idiom nécessaire et fatal des peuples et des civilisations où la vie factice a remplacé la vie naturelle . . .

Henry James said that Gautier's novels are "written in what is called a studio light." The most realistic passages in *Mlle. de Maupin* are compositions arranged in the atelier, requiring the controlled methods of the laboratory, for the studio and the laboratory were devices for observing nature. Gautier's care for "enumerations, lists, catalogues" produces an art that James compares to goldsmith's work; like the Parnassian he traces with delicate hand the marble vein until he defines the contour of Apollo's profile. Gautier's "faculty for visual discrimination was extraordinary," his stories reminding James of "those small cabinet paintings of the contemporary French school, replete with archaeological details as to costume and furniture, which hang under glass in immense gilt frames and form the delight of connoisseurs." (A propos of James's remark: Edgar Wind has said that after Giovanni Morelli, art criticism became a mode of connoisseurship, a technique of attending only to insignificant details, establishing the authenticity of a painting by dissociating it into fragments of evidence scientific in exactitude.) Attentive as he was to the pictorial, Gautier "cared for nothing and knew nothing in men and women but the epidermis." And the observer in his laboratory sometimes cared for nothing but the epidermis. Gautier's "irresistible need" for what is "describable and phraseable" causes him to write works that belong in the salon. James speaks of Gautier's fiction as "tinged with intellectual passion," the passion for reading the dictionary.

In an essay on the failure of nineteenth-century painting George Moore makes the same complaint that James made about Gautier's novels, namely, that the realistic subjects of the time made the painter literary, a manager of stage-effects, or a librettist. Take, for instance, a work by Alma Tadema, "where, in a circular recess of white marble, Sappho reads to a Greek poet. . . . The interest of the picture is purely archaeological." The ornament in Sappho's hair is represented scrupulously according to the information supplied by the latest researches; and if further researches discover that this kind of ornament was not worn until a century later, the painting becomes old-fashioned. Speaking of the fallacy of the documented painting, Moore remarks, "Once the painter accepts truth for aim and end, it becomes impossible to set a limit upon his investigations." His art becomes a form of inventory, and the inventory undergoes continual revision, so that his work is dated.

The Privations of Art

The attraction to studio artifice makes the vices of decadence outrageously literary—calculated corruptions like those of Des Esseintes, as alien from human experience as experiments in the laboratory. This art-view of life substitutes for existence a method of existing and ends in Axël's deciding that his servants can live for him. Such alienation has something in common with the situation of the scientist who let the rest of us live while he demonstrated in the laboratory that life is a certain combination of carbonic acid, water, and nitrogenous compounds. This kind of science and art is highly theoretic, a studio effect that results from dealing scrupulously with instruments and observing from a distance. It has been called a "spiritual paraplegia," a form of *impuissance*. It is also a mode of absence associated with the *conception pure* of symbolist verse, a Thought being thought. "J'entrerais dans la Disparition suprême," Mallarmé wrote to Cazalis. Such absence is achieved by a technique of exclusion: exclusion of chance, of matter, of everything but the word, which itself becomes an ellipsis, a "typographical equation." The extreme of this poetic method is a form of Destruction, which was Mallarmé's Beatrice.

But artifice took other forms than Destruction, notably in the verbal contrivances of literary archaeology: the Lang, Leaf, and Myers translation of the *Iliad* into the "grand style" of Biblical language—simple or severe, as Arnold had it. Arnold's own attempt to identify the "Celtic" element in language is symptomatic of this verbal archaeology. An oddity of nineteenth-century criticism is that Pater the stylist should have mentioned Tennyson's *ascesis* in language, since it would be hard to name a poet whose vocabulary has more liturgical inflation:

> And o'er his head the Holy Vessel hung
> Clothed in white samite or a luminous cloud.
> And with exceeding swiftness ran the boat . . .
> ("Holy Grail")

This is the artificial language of Rossetti's "Blessed Damozel," and Robert Buchanan asked what to expect from a Victorian poet who refers to damozels, citherns, and citoles. Rossetti's language is no more contrived than Parnassian idiom. Gautier recommended using terms not only from the dictionary but from the sciences: *bitumes, déliquescences, burgau, blancs de chlorose, gris plombé.*[6] A little glossary for decadents printed in 1888 listed such words as *errance, flavescent, torpide, attirance.* There is also the famous Mallarméan *Ptyx.* The attempt to reach an art that was autonomous and absolute led to a style Barthes calls "intemporal," that is, artifactual, a rhetorical pastiche, the pluralistic *écriture* of a middle class that has rejected its own language. Moore calls it an "episcopal style."

Most of these stylizations were pedantries as *recherché* as the ecclesiological architecture prescribed by the Camden Society, which endorsed only the "middle-pointed" of the fourteenth century. The ecclesiological anxiety about the form of rood screens, vestments, floral motifs, pews, sash windows, corbels, rounded apses, and liturgy was a symptom of the studio culture that passed for art. The historical studies of the Camden Society and the Tractarian anxiety to be orthodox in rite and dogma are signs of a monomania about method that is also illustrated by the Early English Text Society, which inspired a poet as talented as Hopkins to write a language that makes Milton seem conversational by comparison. At least Milton's style was in the main stream of epic and Biblical tradition.

The archaizing vocabulary of Tennyson, Rossetti, and Hopkins is a glossary of inkhorn terms that are not gothic but pseudobardic.[7] While he was at Manresa House, Hopkins urged, "We must enlarge our stock by the revival of obsolete words and inflections from native sources." This advice expresses the philological interests of Trench and Furnival with their distaste for Latinisms. Trench wanted to replace "impenetrability" by "unthoroughfaresomeness" and "redemption" by "again-buying."

William Barnes proposed to discard "photograph" for "flameprint," "commiserate" for "overyearn," "music" for "gleecraft," "dormitory" for "sleepstow," and "subjective" and "objective" for "inwoning" and "outwoning."

There was some point in Pound's suggesting to young Tom Eliot that poetry should be as well written as prose. But Pound must have for the moment forgotten the prose in George Moore's *Brook Kerith* and Charles Doughty's *Arabia Deserta,* a text given wholly to rhetorical formulas:

> What mean these lofty walls; is not the site too small for a city? neither is the soil very fit hereabout for husbandry. . . . We are about to go down into the sandstones—whereof are the most sands of Arabia. . . . When this sun was nigh setting, I remembered their unlucky prayer-hour! . . . He who brought me the bowl (not one of them) was a manly young man, of no common behaviour; and he showed in his words an excellent understanding. I bade him sup with me.—"I have supped."—"Yet eat a morsel . . ."

The passage indicates how vocabulary itself became a machine, a contrivance as artificial as any apparatus invented for manufacture and one to be exploited in the interests of a dubious creed of productivity. This "gregorian codification" of language persists as a tradition from Gautier and Tennyson through Rimbaud, Meredith, Swinburne, Valéry, Pound himself, and Joyce, who is one of the great technologists of the word. Proust wrote, "Perhaps it is rather by the quality of the language than by the particular aesthetic that we can judge the level which intellectual and moral work has reached." Or, more crudely put: language is a kind of instrument to turn out an *art*-product.

It is surprising to what extent Walter Pater's canon of style anticipates what T. S. Eliot said or implied about the impersonal use of the medium of language. This notion of style amounts to a strategy of fabrication, imposing a law of parsimony, a discipline that is frugal and exacting. For Pater style is a methodology where aesthetic and scientific ideals of precision intersect. When the use of the medium itself becomes art, then the writer must deal scrupulously with his vehicle, and Pater's overestimation of his technique is not unlike Huxley's overestimation of the scientific method. Instead of Zola's experimental formula Pater uses a formula of language, "the right vocabulary": the writer "has winnowed and searched through his vocabulary, is conscious of the words he would select in systematic reading of a dictionary, and still more of the words he would reject." Pater assumes that finesse in method—in this case frugality and accuracy of language—is the means by which prose becomes art. He invites comparison between the scientist's observation of fact and the transcription of feelings into "the finer accommodation of speech."

The writer must obey the recondite laws of language "for the material in which he works is no more a creation of his own than the sculptor's marble" or the data from nature recorded by the scientist. The poet needs the self-denial Zola demanded of the experimental novelist. For both, method is everything. Pater's man of letters has a scholarly conscience: "his punctilious observance of the proprieties of his medium" is "the science of the instrument he plays on." The poet is an agent who, in Eliot's sense of the term, is an impersonal catalyst in whose sensibility occurs a structure of language: "The house he has built is rather a body he has informed." Certain writers, Pater thinks, have a way of absorbing language with a result that resembles inspiration. Pater gives new meaning to Buffon's axiom "le style est l'homme même," for "if the style be the man, in all the colour and intensity of a veritable apprehension, it will be in a real sense 'impersonal.'"

The work of art is a fabric consciously erected by a "process of execution" that is comparable to the "provoked observation" of scientific experiment as Zola understood it. In fact, Zola's notion that the novel gets written inevitably if the novelist uses the experimental method is very close to Pater's notion that literature gets written almost involuntarily if the writer obeys the laws of his medium ("the purity of this medium, its laws or tricks of refraction"). This notion reappears in Eliot's suggestion that the poem is a receptacle for "feelings, phrases, images" combined in new forms, and also in Valéry's opinion that poetry "is an art of language; certain combinations of words produce an emotion that others do not produce, and which we shall call *poetic*."

It seems callous to call this aesthetic technism, yet both scientists and aesthetes valued a method affording "a skillful economy of means." The "fine fastidious scholarship" of the stylist demands a "frugal closeness" in phrasing: "surplusage! he will dread that, as the runner on his muscles. For in truth all art does but consist in the removal of surplusage." Pater's renunciations are not so severe as the symbolist elimination, but his "literary architecture" governs all contingencies by the "design of a single, almost visual image, vigorously informing an entire, perhaps very intricate, composition, which shall be austere, ornate, argumentative, fanciful, yet true from first to last to that vision within." Loose accretions will not suffice, but only the "tight hold" that enables one "to give the phrase, the sentence, the structural member, the entire composition, song, or essay, a similar unity with its subject and with itself: style is in the right way when it tends towards that." Like Valéry, Pater speaks of "the necessity of *mind* in style," and like Eliot, he takes "the special function of mind in style" to be the writer's way "of absorbing language."

Pater admires Flaubert as "the martyr of literary style" and quotes Maupassant's passage describing Flaubert's quest for the unique word; it is a passage that recalls Huxley's warning that a fallacy in scientific method, no matter how trivial, leads to mischievous, if not fatal, results: "Possessed of an absolute belief that there exists but one way of expressing one thing, one word to call it by, one adjective to qualify, one verb to animate it, he gave himself to superhuman labour for the discovery, in every phrase, of that word, that verb, that epithet. A thousand preoccupations would beset him at the same moment, always with this desperate certitude fixed in his spirit: Among all the expressions in the world, all forms and turns of expression, there is but *one*—one form, one mode —to express what I want to say." This commitment to exactitude is symptomatic of a technological malaise in science as well as the fine arts.

Commenting upon nineteenth-century science as a version of puritanism relentless in its concern for accuracy to the last decimal point, Bronowski has said, "Exact measurement became an end in itself, until it seemed to carry an almost moral sense of undeviating righteousness."[8] It was an era when "empirical method became a fetish, an addiction to observation in itself and for its own sake." Pater's empiricism, his way of isolating the "single sharp impression," was a limiting artistic initiative that caused a certain paralysis or *impuissance*. His refined and over-anxious method excluded a great deal of human experience, the oceanic impulses to which the romantics could yield. Pater speaks of the need to accommodate language to the vision within, but the notion of purity of medium or style intervenes and becomes an absolute in the "fine" arts. Thus he is forced to renunciations the romantics did not need: Coleridge writes that when he looked at the moon he seemed "rather to be seeking, as it were *asking* for, a symbolic language for something within me that always and for ever exists, than observing anything new. Even when that latter is the case, yet still I have always an obscure feeling as if that new phenomenon were the dim awaking of a forgotten or hidden truth of my inner nature." Pater's law of style is a form of repression or thrift in art that corresponds to the thrift of laboratory experiments carefully controlled to exclude the disturbing or contingent factors of personality.

When art is the exploitation of a medium, the writer perverts the Greek notion of techne and falls victim to what the Marxists call skill fetishism, as is clear from Pater's remarks on the prose artist:

> His punctilious observance of the proprieties of his medium will diffuse through all he writes a general air of sensibility, of refined usage. *Exclusiones debitae naturae*— the exclusions, or rejections, which nature demands—we know how large a part these play, according to Bacon, in the science of nature. In a somewhat changed sense, we might say that the art of the scholar is summed up in the observance of those rejections demanded by the nature of his medium, the material he must use.

Devoted to Beauty as he is, the aesthete commands an art that is precautionary, essentially a tactic of refusal quite in contrast to the egotistic excesses of the romantics, whose empiricism had a more generous and undisciplined range. Pater exists at the other artistic pole of the century, where artists and scientists submit to a technological canon of parsimony, dreading waste, the exuberance that Blake called beauty. All the flagrant vices in Huysmans are as invented as the exquisite impressions of Pater's Florian Deleal. The most exotic experiences are the most carefully regulated, and the precautions behind technology appear in the aesthetic program to convert life to art. The aesthete pays lip service to *luxe,* but his Beauty is not Dionysiac.

The purest economy of phrase is a mode of conception. Pater quotes Flaubert approvingly: "For the idea only exists by virtue of the form." This is aesthetic scholasticism, and the scientist's precisions were a kindred scholasticism. Pater's style is a technological feat, a version of engineering in art, a manifestation of Taylorism in aesthetics; his fastidiousness is a mark of the minimal initiative of men whose instrument works for them. Pater suspects that the future of art may lie "in the naturalisation of the vocabulary of science" because science seeks "truth to bare fact," a studied economy that enables the scientists to attain a "true literary ideal." "Say what you have to say in the simplest, the most direct and exact manner possible. . . . Here is the office of ornament: here also the purpose of restraint in ornament." In dread of the otiose Pater appeals to Schiller, who said that the artist is known by what he omits. Yet in spite of this care for accuracy the aesthetic language is as artificial as the language of the scientific laboratory, a vocabulary so highly specialized that Pater's addiction to words like "comely" and "diaphanous" leads to mannerism, not to a "direct manner."

John Ruskin continually warned against this monomania about method, causing art to ape science. He traced the difficulty back to the renaissance, when the painter with his new "pride of science" or "pride of system," his "learning and demonstration," committed his art to certain methods: "His life was devoted, not to the objects of art, but to the cunning of it; and the sciences of composition and light and shade were pursued as if there were abstract good in them;—as if, like astronomy or mathematics, they were ends in themselves, irrespective of anything to be effected by them; . . . a fatal change of aim took place throughout the whole world of art. In early times art was employed for the display of religious facts; now, religious facts were employed for the display of art." Using his moral Victorian phrase, Ruskin says that renaissance painting tended to "setting Beauty above Truth, and seeking for it always at the expense of truth."

A more tolerable phrasing might be: craft is not identical with method as the notion of method was accepted by the aesthetes, since craft is an instinctive faculty rather than a theoretic use of the medium. Although Aristotle designated art as one of the intellectual virtues involving a true course of reasoning, he added that art deals with the variable, and that doing and making have something in common since chance is involved with both: "art loves chance, and chance loves art." The effort to methodize art is a specialization of the notion of techne, for by excluding the variable it equates artistic talent with "contriving and considering" only. With his strong pragmatic tendency Aristotle would hardly have understood exploiting the medium for its own sake. The exchange of craft for method explains the mannerism in *fin de siècle* arts. Method is craft rationalized, theorized, converted to an abstraction.

The exploitation of a medium for its own sake might be called the technical alienation of art, since craft, or the command of a métier, is a way of making something; but the methodologist seems more concerned with the expertise of his technique than with what is brought into being —which is a way of estranging art from its end. Such an exhibition of method is techne inverted upon itself, an act of limited initiative.

The monomania about method has a secondary effect of causing another estrangement: the artist's sense that his work has no use in the community, since it justifies itself only as a technical feat or, as might be said, as an exhibitionism that can only be mannered. The mediaeval craftsman must have known that his work was in real demand and that his prescribed skill had a social sanction. But the estrangement of the so-called fine arts, in contrast to the so-called applied arts, cast the artist back upon himself in an isolation that left him to exercise his métier for its own sake. Thus the problem of craft as different from an autotelic use of medium arises in the later nineteenth century.

As Jean Cassou has explained, the only training in craft was given in schools of applied art; those who revolutionized the fine arts had to think through their methods alone, usually being ignorant of skills that formerly had been passed down by the guilds. In the fine arts the only methods that could be studied were those of academic painting, against which every talented painter rebelled. So he was cast back from the official system upon his own experiments, which often martyred him because they were refused by the public. Baudelaire lamented this anarchic condition, and the need for a dependable knowledge of one's craft was constantly voiced during the whole century by Ruskin, by Morris, by Viollet-le-Duc, as it was later by Eliot. In quest of a satisfactory métier some painters have been driven toward such applied arts as ceramics and tapestry-designing—the arts William Morris fostered, frankly admitting them to be "minor," "applied," or "decorative."

The rather desperate resort of Parnassians and symbolists, pre-Raphaelites and impressionists, decadents and imagists to their methodologies was a consequence of the breakdown in craftsmanship, the traditional practice of one's medium. Seeking the satisfaction of their craft instinct, they were often led to rely upon methods that resembled technism, methods as deceptive and fallacious as the so-called scientific method. For by the nineteenth-century science had lost its original talent for *bricolage,* its earlier unsophisticated empiricism that had something in common with craft in the arts.

One of the most deceptive fictions of the scientific method was the existence of the detached, impersonal observer—the experimenter who distanced himself from nature for the sake of examining facts. The facts appeared most clearly under controlled laboratory conditions—and we now suspect they are not facts after all. The myth of the detached observer has been dispelled; but it had some injurious effects in the arts. It was symptomatic of a culture that has been called visual.

III

Mimesis: The Visual

The Mirror of Nature

WHEN PATER MENTIONED that the artistic experience fines itself down to the "single sharp impression" he was acknowledging that the nineteenth century was among the most visual periods of western culture, the most given to ideals of precise observation—a spectator-view shared by novelists, painters, scientists, and, to an extent, by poets, who became "visionary," although poetic vision did not always mean observation. In Shelley, for example, the visionary faculty was a mode of participating rather than observing, and many symbolists sought to transcend to the Unseen. Yet the figure of the poet as seer or as visionary or *voyant* is itself witness to what extent our culture is visual, to what extent we have taken an optical approach to reality, as the usual one, whether in art or science. Lucien Febvre has called sight the intellectual sense enabling us to abstract ideas from experience, and Marshall

McLuhan has argued that ever since the invention of typography we have isolated the visual sense and thus become one-dimensional men insensitive to auditory, tactile, or haptic responses. It is, of course, undeniable that since the renaissance art and science have widely approved the idea of holding the mirror up to nature. Even Wordsworth hoped to keep his eye fixed on the incidents of common life.

The proposal, however, that the arts after the renaissance were entirely dominated by the sense of sight is open to serious doubt. If it is true that renaissance painting was affected by Alberti's system of the visual pyramid, it is equally true that the notion of musical harmony was inherent in the mathematics of composition: the optical, the plastic, and the sonorous were indissoluble, and the music of the spheres could still be heard in renaissance science, as it could be in poetry and architecture. The ideal of harmony persists through Shelley's theory of poetry, through symbolist *correspondances* (colors, odors, tones *se répondent*), through Pater's theory that all arts approach the musical. "The pure line's gracious flow" was resonant, and the last harmonies of the nineteenth century were the abstract colors of Monet's impressionist compositions. A provisional conclusion to the problem of visual art is offered by Robbe-Grillet, who admits that the sight is a privileged sense which endows our world with a kind of structure, which establishes intelligible distances, which leaves things in their place. But, he cautions, there are risks: for the sense of sight isolates details, thus falsifies their situation—so that absurdity is not far away. And absurdity can bring on a feeling of nausea. Nevertheless the artist must work with available means, and "the sense of sight remains, in spite of everything, our best weapon" simply because, however it may falsify experience into a static or artificial structure, it at least defines one's position in his world.

Without, therefore, claiming that the ills of our culture

are caused by typography or isolating the visual sense, we can turn to the problem of the spectator-view of reality which actually did arise with the renaissance ambition to hold the mirror up to nature, the theory that a painting is like a view through a window. It is a theory that leads to difficulties and ambiguities, and it is associated with the scientific impulse to observe. One of the difficulties is that the spectator is distanced—or estranged—from what is viewed: the symbolists wished to leave the seen in order to reach the unseen, yet the problem of symbolist verse is not, perhaps, its antivisual direction but its infinite distance, which is complete alienation. A symbolist vision of the horizon or of absence is not a view through a window, but it is still, in many ways, a spectator- or alienated-view; the dream, the silence, the echoes are a reaction against the precisions of a scientific or geometric reality, but they are *another* world. The ambiguity is always, in poetry and science, the relation between the observer and the observed world.

Art historians are very sensitive to the implications of the spectator-view taken by renaissance painters, the view on which Alberti based his theory. It is a theatrical view, as Pierre Francastel explains: "During four centuries man-as-actor will reside, for the human imagination, in a 'world-theater' which will have a cubical design and fixed planes limited in number like those of the Western stage."[9] The Newtonian conception of space was scenographic or theatrical in this sense. Another art historian, Paul Laporte, illustrates the rigidity of this renaissance space by Duerer's block-printings for the *Art of Measurement,* which can be seen "accurately" only from a fixed point of view. The renaissance was conscious of man's "ability to detach himself from his experience and to look at this experience, as it were, from the outside" —as stranger:

What he calls the objective world is a consequence of his detachment; what he calls the objective is his own creation subsequent to the role of spectator he has chosen for himself. What he calls the objective world is possible only because he has chosen a point outside from which he can look at it. The objectivity and eternal presence of Renaissance art is achieved only by a conscious and intentional elimination of involvement. The world is motionless and timeless just because there is no involvement. (Paul Laporte: "Painting, Dialectics, and Existentialism")

Ever since this detachment there has been a conflict within the artist between his impulse to involve himself with the world and his obligation to view the world objectively, from a distance that prevents involvement. It is an aspect of the conflict Whitehead found basic in our civilization: between a "scientific" fatality and a feeling that man is a self-determining organism; between realism and expressionism, between evidence furnished by the facts and evidence furnished by the feelings.

Ruskin blundered into this dilemma in the course of discussing whether art should give "the truth of impression" (the world distorted by emotion) or the "truth of form" (the most "finished" representation of things as they look to the eye of a patient observer). As usual, he is more discerning than might be expected: "With this romantic love of beauty, forced to seek in history, and in external nature the satisfaction it cannot find in ordinary life, we mingle a more rational passion, the due and just result of newly awakened powers of attention." Ruskin wrote irritated footnotes in an attempt to find a tenable position between "two of the most objectionable words that were ever coined by the troublesomeness of metaphysicians,—namely, 'Objective' and 'Subjective,'" and he only confounds himself by inventing his own desperate categories:

So that, finally, that which is the subject of examination or object of attention, uniting thus in itself the characters of subness and obness . . . and we also, who suppose ourselves the objects of every arrangement, and are certainly the subjects of every sensual impression, thus uniting in ourselves, in an obverse or adverse manner, the characters of obness and subness, must both become metaphysically dejected or rejected, nothing remaining in *us* objective, but subjectivity, and the very objectivity of the object being lost in the abyss of this subjectivity of the Human. (*Modern Painters,* "Of the Pathetic Fallacy")

This is not far astray, for behind this riddle is Ruskin's recognition that the arts of his day were given to visual observation but that the observer, not the object, is actually the center of the experience: "The power, therefore, of thus fully *perceiving* any natural object depends upon our being able to group and fasten all our fancies about it as a center." Ruskin has anticipated the principle of Gestalt psychology that we see what we are structured to see. Recently a psychologist has asked, "How can experience of a constant world arise from the ever-changing flux of sensory impressions? This is the central puzzle."[10] Artist and scientist once solved the puzzle scenographically by constructing a world-stage measurable by an eye fixed at a certain point. The universe was a constant that could be thought because it could be accurately seen. Consciously or otherwise artists and scientists fell back upon the supposition made by Locke and Addison that sight is the most perfect of our senses and that we can conceive the world more reliably by vision than by touch, smell, taste, or even hearing. The world so visually constructed was an abstraction amenable to geometry and to mathematics. Since it was possible to be accurate only by measuring, and since measurement is chiefly an optical scaling, facts seemed to be most factual when they were optically precise. The "pursuit of facts" was nearly synonymous with "the manipulation of exact measurements." Art and science staked almost everything on accurate observation: Millais used a magnifying glass to study the leaves he painted.

The obsession with accurate measurement was partly

due to the static and "eternal" nature of the nineteenth-century reality, so clearly defined. The world of modern science and art is harder to visualize because it is a constant passage or process, discontinuous and contoured into topological relations having no "visible outline." It is a world accessible to other kinds of sensory intelligence than sight alone. Gerald Holton has questioned whether the method of classroom demonstration is any longer useful in teaching science, since it is a merely visual kind of pedagogy.[11] He suggests that the crucial activity in a lecture-demonstration is the teacher's way of touching or handling the apparatus: if the touch is tender, it can be as revealing as a dramatic gesture—like the way a woman brushes her hair. It is exploratory, not demonstrative. So far as it relies upon mere depiction, a demonstration is not scientific. An experiment requires a sensory acquaintance not of the eye alone.

Nineteenth-century realism, like nineteenth-century science, was often a mode of demonstration that gave form to experience by visualizing so exact as to appear "factual." But as Barthes and others have insisted, the fact was an artifact, and the most neutral observation was a convention manufactured from formal signs that led to preciosity. The perception of fact was not a means of immersing the scientist in experience but a way of alienating experience. The precision of realists and decadents was a specification based upon limited evidence that derived meaning only from a preconceived structure called nature. This art was a demonstration of what, in a sense, was already known rather than a means of discovery. Realism, especially, was like a lecture-demonstration in which the technique was not immanent but imposed.

The experimental method seemed to Zola a "solid foundation" for the novelist's art. "The observer relates purely and simply the phenomena which he has under his eyes. He should be the photographer of phenomena, his observations should be an exact representation of nature."

Zola accepts the facts, and the facts verify. Experiment is "but provoked observation"—*pour voir.*

Symbolist poets reacted against this kind of observation, but they, also, were committed to the faculty of *vision,* whether in Rimbaud's hallucinations or vision in its privative form, the empty mirror and blank white page in all its Mallarméan purity. Baudelaire envisioned Beauty as a stony dream, motionless and white like a swan, an austere study

> De purs miroirs qui font toutes choses plus belles:
> Mes yeux, mes larges yeux aux clartés éternelles.
>
> ("La Beauté")

Yet Baudelaire and the symbolists inherited from the romantics a sensitivity to what could be felt in the flesh, to the tactile, the auditory. The romantics were never observers in Zola's sense. Shelley's harmonies were heard as well as seen, and his flaming color was more than an optical impression. By the same token Verlaine heard the music that Hegel attributed to romantic art, and Swinburne scored his verse with the heard melodies of Keats. Browning, too, has his own harsh auditory quality. Notwithstanding, the poet was perhaps first of all a *voyant* of one sort or another, a seer, as Carlyle said; and whether he sought the seen or the unseen, he felt the tyranny of the visual. The Keatsian stained-glass effects were highly visible in the pre-Raphaelites, and it is a question whether Tennyson is pre-Raphaelite or Parnassian:

> . . . The great brand
> Made lightnings in the splendor of the moon,
> And flashing round and round, and whirled in an arch,
> Shot like a streamer of the northern morn,
> Seen where the moving isles of winter shock
> By night, with noises of the northern sea.
> So flashed and fell the brand Excalibur;
> But ere he dipped the surface, rose an arm,
> Clothed in white samite, mystic, wonderful,
> And caught him by the hilt . . . (*Morte d'Arthur*)

Ruskin noted that Tennyson's faculties are centered in *perceiving*.

The emphasis on visual accuracy was nowhere more apparent than in the art criticism of the age. The ability to draw what was seen—or, more precisely speaking, what was known—became almost identical with style as it was understood by the academies. Stendhal has a bitter page on the ability to "paint bodies": "Correct, scholarly drawing imitated from antiquity as the school of David comprehends it is an exact science like arithmetic, geometry, trigonometry, etc. That is to say, with infinite patience . . . one can arrive in two or three years at a knowledge of the conformation and the exact position of a hundred muscles which cover the human body and be able to reproduce them with a brush . . . To acquire the *exact science* of drawing was to be a genius." This insistence on observing details, which was a method of learning rather than seeing, fostered an illustrative art; for academic "history" painting was no less illustrative than the pre-Raphaelitism that returned to "nature." Even Ruskin often argued that the more facts a painter gives, the greater he is. The tyranny of the visual was more oppressive in painting than in the novel.

This commitment to visual accuracy accounts for the prevailing myth about renaissance art. Jacob Burckhardt's *Cicerone* (1853–54) taught the century how to look at renaissance painting, which seemed to be a birth of naturalism. Overlooking almost entirely the schematic, theoretic aspects of renaissance style, Burckhardt takes *quattrocento* painting as evidence of a new spirit entering art: the painter who was still in the service of the Church performed more than the Church required by giving "a copy of the real world." In learning to observe, he redeemed art from mediaeval typology (it is a myth that is still with us):

> . . . the artist is absorbed in the examination and the repre-
> sentation of the outward appearance of things, and by de-

grees learns to express all the various manifestations of the human form as well as of its surroundings (realism). Instead of general types . . . we have individuals; the traditional system of expression, of gestures and draperies, is replaced by the endless variety of real life, which has a special expression for each occasion. Simple beauty . . . now gives place to the distinctness and fulness in detail which is the principal idea of modern art; and wherever it does appear, it is a different and sensuous beauty, which must not be stinted of its share in the real and earthly.

Burckhardt rejoices in the secularizing that led renaissance painting to all that is natural—all that was excluded, he says, from mediaeval art. He looks upon Byzantine art as a shell which had to be broken by painters who were wise enough to put aside "meager" religious images in order to give "free scope to the individual character." Burckhardt had doubts about Dante: was the *Comedy* great "on account of his symbolism or in spite of it"? This view of renaissance art as naturalism became official art history:

Now . . . begins an enthusiastic study of the nude, and, in general, of the human figure and its action; in the flow of the garments also they seek to give the character of the individual and of the given moment; actual materials are represented, in easel pictures especially, with inimitable delicacy: the richest possible variety of colours and the picturesque contrasts of the personages acting become the essential principle. . . . Lastly, quite a new feeling for space grows up . . . so that nearness and distance, motion backwards and forwards, may serve as essential means of illustration; and instead of simply indicating the localities, as far as was necessary to be intelligible, we now find a real landscape, and a real architecture given more or less in perspective.

Burckhardt explains that if Filippo Lippi's "Coronation of the Virgin" at Spoleto lacks the earnestness of Giotto, it compensates by "the lifelike expression of accessory groups." Lippi's easel paintings convey a pleasure in nat-

ural beauty, and his Madonna is "a figure out of Floren-
tine domestic life." Of the "Coronation" at Florence
Burckhardt writes "it gives an impression of over-fulness,
because the subject, a Glory, is represented in a definite
earthly spot."

While Burckhardt was lauding renaissance naturalism,
Ruskin in *Stones of Venice* (1851–53) was admiring
gothic, also, for its naturalism, "that is to say, the love of
natural objects for their own sake, and the effort to represent them frankly, unconstrained by artistical laws." In
fact, Ruskin probably speaks more accurately than Burckhardt when he finds that a sure sign of the best gothic
style is the precision with which foliage is represented,
for gothic was at least as naturalistic as renaissance. In
their nineteenth-century enthusiasm for visual accuracy
the art critics devised a myth about the gothic and a
myth about the renaissance: both gothic and renaissance
were alleged to be naturalistic; yet renaissance was supposed, also, to be a revolt against gothic. Here is a case
where an inconsistency resolves itself into an identity of
opposites, since these conflicting myths about gothic and
renaissance are only two aspects of the same commitment
to naturalistic art. It is a view Browning held in his poem
on Filippo Lippi, which recapitulates Burckhardt's reading of *quattrocento* painting: the world is good, and
Lippo has a store of attentive remarks about the look of
things, faces, arms, legs, the contour of mountains, the
figures of man, woman, child. Lippo asks:

> . . . Have you noticed, now,
> Your cullion's hanging face? A bit of chalk,
> And trust me you should, though!

Lippo calls it the value and significance of flesh, and one
of the conventional defenses of realistic art was its capacity to give a pleasure of recognition, a heightened awareness of reality—if reality is accurately seen (Browning
imagines Andrea del Sarto correcting Raphael's wrongly

drawn arm). Ruskin praised naturalism because it was a reverential admiration of God's work; Browning praised naturalism because it was a pagan relish of a world that means intensely and means good, of itself.

Ruskin understood better than either Browning or Burckhardt what was involved in the change from mediaeval to renaissance composition, which brought about perspective systems and a reinterpretation of space. Mediaeval composition was partly a result of designing on the wall itself: as the craftsman laid out his mural in red outlines (*sinopia*) over the surface to be covered, the painting was born during the very process of its being designed and executed. But with the desire for accurate perspective ("pride of science," Ruskin called it) came a method of preparatory cartoons, preliminary drawings on paper so that the design might tally more accurately with what the painter observed. This practice of making preliminary sketches on paper caused a separation of imagination and observation as "opposing forces," along with a documentary presentation of nature, a care for coherent pictorial reportage answerable to facts studied in detail and verified at leisure. Thus painting became a way of reminding us of what we already know. Observation became a fetish, and the painter began to hold the mirror up to nature.

His painting became mimesis in a rather literal sense. There was born a faith in what Huxley called the method of scientific investigation, the aim of which was "the discovery of a rational order which pervades the universe," this rational order being a system of perspective based upon a vanishing point. The premises of this painting as prescribed by Alberti are visual, and the vision is rationalized. Dante's mediaeval world order was also rationalized and visual, but the renaissance schema rationalizes and envisions from a new and special point of view. Observations fit into a scheme of "nature" conceived by mathematicians. In his essay, "The Method of Scientific Investigation," Huxley repeats the assumptions on which the renaissance painter, as seen by Burckhardt, works: ". . . the subject matter of physical science is furnished by observation, which cannot extend beyond the limits of our faculties. . . . All physical science starts from certain postulates. One of them is the objective existence of a material world. . . . Another postulate is the universality of the law of causation; that nothing happens without a cause . . . and that the state of the physical universe, at any given moment, is the consequence of its state at any preceding moment. Another is that any of the rules, or so-called 'laws of Nature,' by which the relation of phenomena is truly defined, is true for all time." If, then, our observation is accurate, we can determine the "constant relations of the phenomena thus defined, and their expression in rules or laws," the laws of matter and motion which, in turn, are verified by the experiments we perform. This (circular) reasoning is the strongest foundation on which knowledge can rest. Is it any wonder that Whitehead accused the scientists of the past of never examining their premises? Is it any wonder that Robbe-Grillet accuses the old realistic novel of representing a world order "linked to an entire rationalistic and organizing system": "All the technical elements of the narrative—systematic use of the past tense and the third person, unconditional adoption of chronological development, linear plots, regular trajectory of the passions, impulse of each episode toward a conclusion, etc.—everything tended to impose the image of a stable, coherent, continuous, unequivocal, entirely decipherable universe." The stable, intelligible scenography of renaissance perspective does signify a disappearance of God and a reconstruction of a world that is a theatre of the mind.

It is a world created from the standpoint of the observer: not only standing outside but at a fixed locus, an assigned position. The renaissance humanism, so far as it means this assigned point of view, is not humanism at all, but a way of detaching man from the world by making him a spectator: artist and scientist are *voyeurs*. In other words, the question of perspective involves what Nietzsche termed a "pathos of distance," which implies more than the separation of hero from herd. The "pathos of distance" describes the disengagement of artist and scientist after the renaissance. It is a disengagement that gives a monotone to science, a monotone that is heard again in naturalistic novels and the fatigued voice of Flaubert. The pathos is reversible, for if it distances the world from the artist, it likewise excludes the artist from any sympathetic response to what he observes. Rossetti, for instance, in a letter asks John Lucas Tupper, "Are there any opportunities at the Hospital of seeing such a thing as a dying boy? Consequent emotions in bystanders desirable—mother especially so—If you have any youth in such position, and he is accessible, I wish you would let me know before the looks are entirely vacant."

Mimesis and Methexis

The renaissance ambition to hold the mirror up, to give everything its very form, overspecializes the sense of sight and creates a theatre that disallows a mode of artistic action inherent in Greek thought and practice—participation (methexis). Mimesis and methexis: two ideas Aristotle associated in his theory of tragedy, which was a ritual and rhythmic performance. So much was made of mimesis, supported as it was by the scientific imperative to observe, that the artist was finally excluded almost by definition from the theatre in which he had a leading role. Paradoxically enough the new self-awareness of the renaissance man brought about a "tragic isolation of the self" as an observer looking at the world from the outside, objectively. The world so seen was a construct of the spectator; it was coherent, stable, thinkable, and determinate because he was not involved in it. Hamlet's notion of holding up the mirror makes the world a stage where men and women are merely players whose sound and fury signifies nothing if the artist is distanced enough. Hamlet, of course, like the romantics, could not distance himself, and feels like a monster when he sees the player carried away by his own theatrical fiction. He is already in revolt against the renaissance perspective that stakes everything on mimesis; his *cue* for passion turns him from art to life, and he feels that his performance must be an act of participating as well as imitating. In qualifying his notion of holding up the mirror, Hamlet has already reached an existential position resembling Robbe-Grillet's view of the modern novel: "To limit one's self to description is obviously to reject all the other modes of approaching the object: sympathy as unrealistic, tragedy as alienating, comprehension as answerable to the realm of science exclusively." The mirror images a reality that pre-exists; but the form of things begins to blur when the artist participates: Hamlet is certain about the form of things as reflected in the mirror, but he is lost when the player is carried away by his own gestures, when theatre becomes a mode of participation. As Robbe-Grillet says, fiction once made us see things, but now it confuses their outlines or makes them incomprehensible because the writer is engaged with his world.

The consciousness of being a spectator excluded from the great stage of what is "out there" is one reason for the hostility of the Lear world. Gloucester remarks that although we can explain the eclipses of sun and moon, yet we are scourged by them nonetheless. A sense of helplessness before the observed world is an especially modern form of fatalism, undermining the optimism of a scientific method assuming that an inspection of nature makes her handmaiden to man. Huxley himself warned that nature's discipline is often a blow given without notice. Thus Lear asks, "Is man no more than this?" And Kent answers, "It is the stars, the stars above us, govern our conditions; else one self mate could not beget such different issues." This grim neutrality of the observed world, radically inhuman, gives a Learlike tone to Bertrand Russell's tragic judgment: "Brief and powerless is Man's life; on him and all his race the slow, sure doom falls pitiless and dark. Blind to good and evil, reckless of destruction, omnipotent matter rolls on its relentless way."

The distancing in science corresponds to "keeping the ideal plane" in painting, like a proscenium arch behind which there was a world constructed in logical scale. This aesthetic distance was chosen in behalf of accuracy of observation, but every sort of rationalizing was required to sustain this illusion in painting, in theatre, in science. The great painters and playwrights were never taken in by this figment. They employed perspective arbitrarily, and Shakespeare habitually broke the plane between stage and audience.

The theory of aesthetic distance has been taken more seriously by some moderns than by the renaissance artists who devised it. The most notable recent version (1912) is Edward Bullough's "psychical" objectivity, the aesthetic contemplation that removes art from actuality. Bullough notes that the aesthetic distancing which is "a factor in all Art" is "negative" or "inhibitory." Although he insists that distancing in art is not neutral, as it is in scientific observing, he adds that aesthetic detachment places the art object in a perspective endowing it with an "appearance of unreality." The reversal of this perspective is fatal in art, for without any distance between us and the art object, aesthetic response is impossible. Thus Bullough accepts a paradox: art requires both involvement and distancing, "the utmost decrease of Distance without its disappearance." He calls this the distance-limit; it is the perilous margin between mimesis and methexis, a narrowness of distance evident in the greatest periods of the arts. Leaving the contradiction unresolved, Bullough decides that the most important consideration is to have "consistency of Distance." The paradox of aesthetic distancing is clearest, perhaps, in symbolist poetry, which took the Icarus flight toward *les champs lumineux et sereins* as a means of participating in the supernal realm of the Idea: the extremest distance as a mode of utter union or identification. The more one thinks about the notion of distancing, the nearer he may be to deciding that the entire problem is factitious in both art and science, tracing back to the renaissance hypothesis of the fixed eye seeing the world as through a window. It is a problem induced by an artificial perspective. Yet it has major effects in art and science.

One of the most ambiguous uses of the distance-limit is Berenson's theory of "the aesthetic moment" when a life-enhancing feeling arises from a heightened visual impression of things "presented in a way to make us feel that we are perceiving them more quickly, grasping them more deeply than we do ordinarily."[12] At this moment there is a tension between distance and empathy, a realizing of things seen as "ideated sensation." Burckhardt laid the foundation for Berenson's interpretation of painting as lending "a higher coefficient of reality to the object represented," and giving "a direct effect of life-enhancement" by making us aware of "the material significance of things." Berenson also seems to hold a Paterlike notion of art as a gathering of consciousness into a desperate effort to feel and touch: "In visual art the aesthetic moment is that flitting instant, so brief as to be almost timeless, when the spectator is at one with the work of art he is looking at, or with actuality of any kind that the spectator himself sees in terms of art, as form or colour." Visual sensation is "ideated" into what Baudelaire termed *connaissance* and Pater "a quickened multiplied consciousness," a form of participation or empathy. The fugitive aesthetic moment indicates "the fragility and the precariousness of our condition in a universe that knows nothing of our needs, our pretensions, our claims." The aesthetic moment tells us what science tells us: we are alien from a hostile reality.

Yet Berenson insists that science cannot give us the life-enhancing sense of participation or identification with what it represents, the "ideated plunging into a state of being." The sense of identification is heightened by converting visual to tactile values, giving some of the three-dimensional experiences normally assigned to sculpture: "my retinal impressions are immediately translated into images of strain and pressure in my muscles, of resistance to my weight, of touch all over my body." Thus Berenson's ideated sensations transpose what is seen into a synaesthetic consciousness of grasping, embracing, or walking around the objects. The transposition, however, does not occur unless the painter has "great skill in rendering": "The greater the painter, the less likely he is to be aware of aught else in his art than the problems of rendering." And to render the fullness of the object's being, the painter must have the sculptural and tactile sensibility, the organic rhythm and movement that Aristotle sought in the dramatist. Berenson is reacting against an entirely visual representation of the world; yet while he invokes the notion of methexis, or participation, he holds to the theory of aesthetic distance.

The ideal visual plane—the inviolable distance—in science and art was a magical boundary that made necessary some willing suspension of disbelief, a convention or artifice that was accepted in the laboratory as well as in the theatre; and the dishonesty entered when the artifice was confused with reality, with accuracy of representation. Seen thus, reality is an abstraction, and Marshall McLuhan has made great play with the thesis that our whole culture has been falsified by the visual conception of reality attributable to the invention of movable types. However McLuhan may overstate his case, there can be no doubt that the ideal visual plane or distance established in both art and science gave to each a false appearance of consistency that does not inhere in the earliest and latest periods of art and science. Both the Greeks and the new-wave writers tolerate discontinuities, inconsistencies, and incoherences unacceptable to nineteenth-century arts. Or, to put it otherwise, distance during the nineteenth century was fixed—the focus of art and science was steady. It is hardly so with Greeks and moderns, who, as McLuhan says, exist in an auditory-haptic culture, to an extent non literate insofar as the oral is more important than the written word.

Breaking the Plane: Irony

We do not, however, have to rely on McLuhan, for in the past few decades there has been a persistent abandoning of the "literary" text and a return to what might be called—adapting a word from painting—"action" writing. We cannot read a text by Beckett or Ionesco as we used to read drama. Beckett offers us acts without words, gestures only, and Ionesco's drama arises from babbling. The humdrum cadence of what is heard on Paris streets is the only structure in Queneau's dialogues, and the suspicious small talk in Nathalie Sarraute's novels is aliterate. As assassins of style these writers have moved beyond culture. In their own ways they are all performing a coroner's inquest on rhetoric and elocution. The aliterate drama and novel have no codes of propriety, verisimilitude, or genre; they have no established grammar. It is hard to deal with such writing as printed texts; they require no aesthetic distance. In ranging beyond culture this art has recovered a social tongue that has little in common with the traditions of literature.

Our mode of agraphia is prevailingly oral and choreographic. The extreme of agraphic drama is the Happening. One hesitates to make a great deal depend on these fashionable affairs, yet in their own clumsy way they get back to an elemental situation in which literature seems to have arisen. The Greek epic appears to have evolved in a preliterate context, the poet reciting his narrative to musical accompaniment along with some kind of pantomime, mimicry, or perhaps gymnastic. Epical verse seems to have been recited with the whole body. Highly stylized (or formulaic) as the rhetoric was, it remained elliptic, disjunctive, and less consistent than the printed text to be read at leisure and thus open to questions about unity and point of view that do not occur when poetry is recited.

It seems agreed that Homeric poetry originally was spoken or chanted in a ceremonial situation when the hearer, having little consciousness of himself as a person, almost completely identified himself with the events recited. This kind of mimesis was a communal experience resembling participation in the dance, an "epidemic" methexis. The appearance of the alphabetic text inhibits this empathetic state and presents the reader with literature from which he detaches himself, regarding it from a distance; he thinks as he reads, and the critical faculty comes into play. When the reader's sense of his own identity intervenes, the original auditory-motor response is to an extent blocked by aesthetic judgments: Is this character behaving consistently? Does this episode seem probable? The reader no longer identifies himself with what he reads. It has been conjectured that Plato's attack on the arts in *The Republic* is due to the shift from an oral to an alphabetic literature, for the written poem becomes a form of knowledge, and this knowledge is not so reliable as philosophy or mathematics: "all those poets beginning with Homer are only imitators; they copy the images of virtue and the like, but the truth they never reach." If the reader trusts these images, he is deceived, and if he is carried away by the poem or yields to its magic, he loses control of himself and becomes as weak as a woman. So Plato cannot tolerate poetry as either imitation or participation.

Whether or not Plato's distrust of poetry is due to an alphabetic literature, it is clear that an oral-auditory poetry accommodates the inconsistencies and discontinuities that are unacceptable in the written text, which requires a kind of unity and coherence that has been associated with "classical" art and all its ideals of structure and form. Yet one of the truly classic instruments was dialectic, a speaking from two points of view, otherwise known as irony. Irony is itself a kind of double voice, occurring whenever there is a double meaning, which was inherent in the auditory resonance of early drama or dialogue: irony occurs when the character hears one thing, and the audience hears something the character does not hear. There is a gap between what the speaker says and what the hearers understand. Irony is the collision between two points of view. Socrates, that master of philosophic irony, appears at the moment when oral literature had not yet been arrested in an alphabetic text. He said that the written word is not "living," therefore not the truth; and the Socratic dialogue brings to bear upon any question double, often unreconciled, points of view. The deepest irony allows for more than one possibility; the situation remains open to doubt and scrutiny. Plato's quest for total knowledge, his obsession with the One, is, in effect, a repudiation of the double meanings of irony, a refusal of drama in behalf of philosophy. Insofar as drama is a dialectic or dialogue, it is a basic form of irony, which allows opposites to coexist.

One of the most complicated ironies in literature is the double meaning in what is said by Othello and Iago. Ordinarily irony is put in the mouth of the hero only: Oedipus curses the one who has brought a plague upon Thebes. He does not see the meaning of what he says, though the audience does. Here Tiresias is the questioner who is not a victim of irony. But the situation is different in *Othello*, where the hero at the start of the play innocently refers to the vices of his blood. The audience understands what Othello does not, that this barbarian will be destroyed by his vices to which he is blind. Then Iago, the tempter, who corresponds to Tiresias in *Oedipus*, asks, "Where's that palace wherein foul things sometimes intrude not?" Iago, of course, is a liar with an intently evil purpose; but the irony is that this liar and traducer does not himself see the truth of what he says—though the audience does. Iago, like the hero Othello, is speaking a truth that he does not himself understand. He is as blind to what he says as Othello. Iago is never more horribly ironic than when he speaks as moralist: "O beware my lord of jealousy." He is most honest exactly when he least intends to be honest, and the audience sees that the devastating truth is in the mouth of Satan. Thus the irony appears on both sides of the dialectic: in the mouth of the hero and the mouth of the villain. Both speak accountably without knowing that they do so, and irony becomes a bewildering echo-effect.

The irony in writers like Ibsen and Hardy is not open as it is in *Othello* or Socrates, for Socrates is really in doubt, and the blindness of Othello reverses itself upon Iago. But the so-called irony in Hardy or Ibsen is closer to cynicism because there is no double view. The characters are victims condemned to disaster in a world where deterministic laws leave nothing open. Jude, like Tess, is the sport of gods who play out their game with wretched men. This is not irony but a disguise for fatality in a closed world of nineteenth-century mechanics. We cannot even call this irony Euripidean, however similar it may appear; for Euripides knows that the gods scandalously and arbitrarily cast men down to destruction, but he also knows that one does not safely mock the gods, for piety is necessary and man is not divine. Plays like the *Bacchae* and *Hippolytus* leave the question of piety disturbingly open.

Such irony springs from a certain indeterminate view. When Homer speaks of Hector he shifts his point of view, breaking the plane of his narrative to look at things from the Trojan angle. This impartiality reappears in Shakespearean drama, where the tormenter and the tormented are held together inconsistently from opposite angles. Thus Shylock asks his wrenching question: "If you prick us, do we not bleed?"—a question that dislocates him from the comic plane where he should fit neatly if he is to be despised. So also, Othello's fate is not determined until the last moment, for there is play in the system; he has his chance to see, though he chooses blindness. The Moor's drama is a form of Socratic dialectic, a discovery rather than a demonstration like Hardy's dealing with Jude and Tess.

Too many so-called ironic effects in the well-made play or novel are demonstrations in which Q.E.D. was predetermined before the action started. If there is irony, it is dead irony, signifying despair or abuse, the irony of a static text, thought through before it was written and after it is read. A living irony is impure, like a living dialectic, in the sense that it remains open to possibilities, to all the uncertainties of lived experience. Otherwise irony is a judgment passed upon characters who have no freedom to choose and are seen from a single, fixed, and consistent point of view. An oral-auditory literature need not be unified in this way, remaining open to shifts in tone, in sympathy. It is illogical that the brutal Achilles should suddenly be touched by pity, and there is little in the epic to suggest that he is capable of learning through suffering.

The quest for ironies in poetry has of late been eager— and labored. How much has modern verse been injured by "metaphysical" discords accessible only on the printed page, where we can discern seven, or more, types of ambiguity? Eliot charged Milton with writing a dead language while his own verse was sometimes written in a language so alphabetic as to require notes on bills of exchange and Hermann Hesse and Tarot packs. Heavily burdened as Milton may have been by alphabetic cargo, his epic has greater acoustic resonance. In spite of Eliot's care for the spoken cadence, a great many of his pages must be looked at. The poetry of incantation is more readily heard in the flamboyant musicale of Wallace Stevens. Browning remains another analphabetic poet in the oral tradition, his verse in certain cases reducing itself to the sublinguistic level of grunts or bestial expletives and the cacophanies so alien to the cultured language of Tennyson. Browning's persons are dramatic precisely because they are presented in an ambiguous focus and lack the consistent "development" that was expected by the Victorians. They are creatures who exist only when the poem is read aloud, for their character is apparent in the inflection of their speech: they talk their way into being. We do not visualize them as we do Tennyson's tapestry figures. And Browning's speakers are wont to use a mode of direct address, breaking the ideal aesthetic plane of the poem by an appeal to the reader as unflinching as the soliloquy in Elizabethan drama or the Greek choral-comment. Oral verse has always allowed an irregularity in "style." Homer intrudes his passage on ploughing with mules, and Aristophanes shifts from bawdry to lyric. Sometimes there is parataxis—a breakdown in grammatical coherence, the "abbreviated rhetoric" of Browning's verse or Hamlet's reproach to Gertrude:

> For who that's but a queen, fair, sober, wise,
> Would from a paddock, from a bat, a gib,
> Such dear concernings hide? Who would do so?
> No, in despite of sense and secrecy,
> Unpeg the basket on the house's top,
> Let the birds fly, and like the famous ape,
> To try conclusions, in the basket creep,
> And break your own neck down.

Such impassioned speeches, like Macbeth's strange passage on pity striding the blast, escape the logic of the written text; they violate the aesthetic distance as Milton does in the dramatic moments in *Lycidas*.

This violation of aesthetic distance is itself an irony—
an abrupt shift in point of view, or break in the ideal
plane—as it is used in the theatre by the Greeks, by the
Elizabethans, and by Brecht and the moderns. The
proscenium theatre established an ideal plane, or distance, between the stage and the audience, a dramatic
stereography as artificial as it was limiting. The drama
was a world seen—confined—behind this ideal plane, like
the view through a window in painterly perspective, imposing a visual coherence on the scene. Classical drama,
with its unity, and the well-made nineteenth-century play
were distanced by this convention. But in the oral-auditory theatre of old comedy there was a moment when the
chorus, suspending the action, faced the audience in a
parabasis to speak directly in the voice of the author. The
mediaeval theatre did not bother about either unity or
consistency, freely mingling comedy with sacred legend
and using many of the modes of direct address that were
transmitted to the Elizabethan theatre in the form of
soliloquy or prologue or interpolated episodes. Shakespeare enjoyed the full advantages of a theatre that ad-
mitted the discontinuities and illogicalities revived in the
modern theatre by Brecht under the name of "alienation
effects." A Shakespearean play acted in the round, using
plots and characters that were often formulaic, was not
seen from any single consistent or fixed point of view;
the stage accommodated itself to far and near, here and
there, and the discontinuities of vision that might be
called non-Euclidean.

Such acoustic drama, by breaking the plane, gives its
own kind of illusion more ambiguous or ironic than the
illusion of the picture stage. Shakespeare's heroes can
refer to the fiction of their own theatrical performance, as
when Richard III and Iago confide to the audience that
they are not what they are, or when Hamlet puts on his
antic disposition to play the role within the role. The very
figment of imitation is used ironically when the prologue

to *Henry V* prods the audience to judge the deficiency of the stage:

> ... But pardon, gentles all,
> The flat unraised spirits that hath dared
> On this unworthy scaffold to bring forth
> So great an object. Can this cockpit hold
> The vasty fields of France? Or may we cram
> Within this wooden O the very casques
> That did affright the air at Agincourt?

The illusion of Shakespearean drama is in minding true things by what their theatrical mockeries are: Agincourt will be enacted by four or five ragged foils disposed in ridiculous brawl. Such theatrical insolence destroys imitation for the sake of creating a higher illusion, a negation of negation that leaps outside the limitations of the stage by ridiculing its techniques.

The tactic has been termed "metatheatre," drama where characters make no attempt to conceal their theatricality.[13] An insidious figure like Iago vaults outside the aesthetic plane to ask directly, "And what's he then that says I play the villain?" inviting the spectator to appraise the medium in which he is working. Shakespeare heightens dramatic consciousness by publicly scrutinizing his method just as the modern scientists or playwright examines the validity of his technique. Ionesco's playlet *Improvisation* employs the irony of calling attention to the fake theatrical chairs, tables, walls, and properties, thus involving playwright, actor, and audience in a metaphor that goes by the name of drama, a play-in-the-making as Pirandello calls it, or a process, to use Whitehead's term. The same maneuver, requiring a complex and self-conscious participation instead of a spectator-view, occurs when Rauschenberg mounts alarm clocks in a "painting," which is a quite different kind of observation from the pre-Raphaelite study of "nature."

The classic instance of renaissance metatheatre is Calderon's *Life Is a Dream,* where the hero is drugged until he confuses the shifting planes of reality. The psychedelic experience is repeated in *Midsummer Night's Dream*, a play within a play. The morning after her midsummer madness, Hermia discovers that illusion is a facet of reality: "Methinks I see these things with parted eye, When every thing seems double." The charitable but nevertheless ironic double vision of metatheatre enables Theseus to take a dramatic view of the interlude played by the rude mechanicals, for he recognizes, like Shakespeare, that "The best in this kind are but shadows, and the worst are no worse if imagination amend them." The Theseus imagination endows the playlet with a validity over and above the absurdity of the performance. This double vision is a mode of irony insofar as it recognizes the gap between what is seen and what is meant or what is understood.

The ironic double vision of metatheatre is like the indeterminacy principle in modern science, allowing the same "fact" to be measured by two different scales of observation. It is not the naïve single vision of nineteenth-century observation, so accurate and so literal in its precision. It has something in common with the spectacle presented in a Roman theatre in 1637 when a crowd onstage was seemingly in a theatre, and the characters in this theatrical theatre point out to the audience seated in the theatre itself that theatre is illusory—an audience seeing a theatrical action where an audience is seeing a theatrical action, etc. Before Pirandello and Ionesco worked through this double vision to its last skepticism about method, the renaissance itself had discovered the fallacy of the objective or detached view of a world from which the spectator was excluded. Mannerist and baroque illusions destroyed the aesthetic plane and drew the spectator into the painting, into the ambiguous visual worlds spread on the ceilings of churches like S. Ignazio, a fantastic architecture to be seen from a fixed point of view but not isolating the beholder, who is enraptured.

The most ironic use of metatheatre is Brecht's, with its insistent skepticism about theatrical method, its demand that author, actor, spectator be constantly aware of the illusion created. Brecht intends that neither audience nor actor should submit uncritically to what is being enacted. There must be at every instant an awareness of all the fallacies of distancing. Brecht calls this demolition of the aesthetic plane an "alienation effect" which, unlike baroque, will not invest in the spectator's emotions. In the older drama spectator and actor were alike hypnotized or victimized by an illusion of the aesthetic plane, but in epic theatre "the audience can no longer have the illusion of being the unseen spectator at an event which is really taking place." The actor will destroy aesthetic illusion by reading aloud the stage directions before he begins to act, and both he and his audience are ever aware that he is playing a role. The "alienation effect" makes impossible any illusion of objectivity common to art and science in the nineteenth century: "The stage's inaccurate representations of our social life, including those classed as so-called naturalism, led it to call for scientifically exact representations; the tasteless rehashing of empty visual or spiritual palliatives, for the noble logic of the multiplication table." Brecht's "alienation" is an instrument for *involving* the audience.

Refusing the logic of continuity, Brecht would have the epic playwright treat certain scenes as self-contained theatrical feats so salient that they are, ironically, raised above the level of the play. Such discontinuity destroys the "assumption that there is a fourth wall cutting the audience off from the stage and the consequent illusion that the stage action is taking place in reality and without an audience." When the old aesthetic trance is broken on both sides of the spotlights, the critical activity can be brought to bear upon drama while it is being played. Under the former necessity to distance, art was injured by any open examining of its methods. But, again,

Brecht's drama amounts to a heightened awareness of the limitations of method. So Brecht steps outside the old limited initiative of trusting a certain method and, like the modern scientist, devotes himself to a critique of his methods. The great contribution of the Brechtian theatre is the principle that art can be intelligent; it can operate without any willing suspension of disbelief, without invoking any false magic: "An old tradition leads people to treat a critical attitude as a predominantly negative one. Many see the difference between the scientific and artistic attitudes as lying precisely in their attitude to criticism. People cannot conceive of contradiction and detachment as being part of artistic appreciation." The old detachment was uncritical; Brecht's detachment, or alienation, is an act of skepticism, an awareness of alternative readings. Like the new scientist Brecht makes his scrutiny of method a facet of the creative process, an instrument for plural approaches to reality. Brecht's alienation effect is not the old distancing of the spectator from the artistic world as it is "observed," but is, instead, an acute consciousness of the need to appraise the method by which the world is observed or represented— and *not* to trust method or medium.

In forbidding the audience any empathetic identification with the play or any naïve belief that the play is the world accurately observed, Brecht is returning to the Shakespearean premise that "the best in this kind are but shadows," a certain kind of mockery. Shakespeare never accepted the notion of artist and audience as spectators only; he violated the aesthetic distance, keeping relations between actor and audience, drama and reality, flexible, shifting, inconsistent, not only in soliloquy, but in many topical passages diverted frankly toward the pit, or the vaudevillelike direct address of Hamlet's scenes with the players and the gravedigger. Shakespeare, like Aristophanes, was always exploiting the presence of his audience: in Hamlet's jokes about the English, or about Shakespeare's own company, the antics of his fellow actors. His characters, known as Practisers, akin to the old Vice in morality plays, confide to the audience how they are about to manipulate others, giving a puppetlike quality to the performance.

Accepting these Shakespearean discontinuities, the drama of Brecht is characteristic of what has happened everywhere in recent science and art, both of which violate the old premise of necessary distance. The scientist now admits that he enters into his observations: Heisenberg says that "method and object can no longer be separated. The scientific world view has ceased to be a scientific view in the true sense of the word." In painting the distance has been violated ever since cubists began to use collage, intruding fragments of actuality into the painted surface, inviting us to regard the juxtaposition of newsprint and pigment in a composition that refers to the nonaesthetic. The naturalistic documentation of the novel has been extended toward the nonaesthetic in Gide, Dos Passos, *chosiste* fictions, and Capote's reportorial technique. The distance between life and art is no longer fixed or definable even as minimal; which is to say that art as art seems dated. There is participation as well as observation.

Visual World and Visual Field

The genre most given to observing is, of course, the novel, that most alphabetic of all literature, existing on the printed page to be read by the eye only. The novel, springing into being with technological innovations like typography, paper-making, graphic arts, and marketing, developed so fast that it was a thriving genre long before there were theories about form and method in fiction. When Fielding, unencumbered by rules, tried to define the novel, the best he could do was to name it a comic epic poem in prose, a category that left everything in doubt. Fortunately the novel had a healthy, undisciplined growth before critics got at it; its vitality, looseness, and abundance in its epic phase allowed the disorderly, at times slovenly, treatment by Smollett, Sterne, Hugo, Thackeray, and Dickens, most of whom had small concern about any ideal fictional plane or distance. An appropriate description of such narrative is Smollett's prefatory remark to *Ferdinand, Count Fathom:* "A novel is a large diffused picture, comprehending the characters of life, disposed in different groups, and exhibited in various attitudes," and clustered about a central figure. This definition reminds one of the cartographic perspective in the first stages of renaissance painting, which surveyed from some unspecified height or distance a terrain that was not in coherent perspective but, instead, an extensive tract with groups of figures engaged in some activity serving for a pictorial theme. Point of view was not a problem. Practice and episode preceded theory.

As the nineteenth century went along, questions about proper form in the novel became consequential—the kind of questions that previously led, rather unhappily, to notions of unity in the drama. Thus many canons of dramatic unity were foisted upon prose fiction, which was often treated by theatrical formulas of plot, character, and setting. Meanwhile great novelists like Stendhal, Balzac, Flaubert, George Eliot, Zola, and finally Henry James were becoming increasingly interested in method until modern criticism has made the novelist oversensitive to his form. However James may protest that novelistic "form is to be appreciated after the fact," many of his tentative proposals about the art of the novel reduce themselves to the needs for prestructuring by point of view.

The very term derives from orthogonal perspective and indicates how deeply the novel has been a visual genre. Then, too, during the nineteenth century the novel was supported by illustration in the text itself, letterpress being only supplemental to the graphic features in Dickens's early work. How are things to be seen—from what angle; and how can point of view give cohesion to fiction? These became pressing matters, and sensitivity to point of view has never been better expressed than in James's preface to *Portrait of a Lady*:

> The house of fiction has in short not one window, but a million—a number of possible windows not to be reckoned . . . But they have this mark of their own, that at each of them stands a figure with a pair of eyes, or at least with a field glass, which forms, again and again, for observation, a unique instrument, insuring to the person making use of it an impression distinct from every other.

Or, as he says in his preface to *Wings of the Dove*, the novelist must "proceed by 'centers,' " each center of observation creating its own perspective, its "discriminated occasion." Only from a center can the novelist achieve the form whose mark is fictional economy: "There is no economy of treatment without an adopted, a related point of view." James's metaphors derive from Alberti's theory of perspective: they are renaissance in origin, and painterly. From a certain fixed point of view, at a measurable distance, the picture becomes a world observed coherently and all relations become intelligible.

James restates his Albertian view in prefacing *The American*:

> By what art or mystery, what craft of selection, does a given picture of life appear to us to surround its theme, its figures and images, with the air of romance while another picture close beside it may affect us as steeping the whole matter in the element of reality? It is a question, no doubt, on the painter's part, very much more of perceived effect, effect *after* the fact, than of conscious design—though indeed I have ever failed to see how a coherent picture of anything is producible save by a complex of fine measurements.

After James fine measurements became even finer as the analysis of point of view in the novel led to an awareness of not only the angle from which things are seen *within* the confines of the narrative, but also the angle from which the author himself sees his narrative, whether it be a vision with (*avec*) his characters immanently, a vision behind (*par derrière*, predetermining, foreordaining), or a vision outside (*au dehors*, neutral, indifferent).[14]

These subtleties are all related, however indirectly, to the fiction of the observer in science. The vision *avec* has been relatively infrequent and marks, as in Robbe-Grillet or Nathalie Sarraute, an existential reaction against the older customary notion that the writer manages his story. Ordinarily the author, like a scientific observer, is outside by definition, or at least behind. For this reason Roland Barthes has labeled the traditional novel a lie, a dead static account of what happened: the very figment of the imperfect tenses and the impersonal "he" is a mask for finality before the novelist begins to write, and even the first-person "I" of the novel is often a mere persona. The pretence that the author is an agent who "sees" from a certain point of view gave rise to the most preposterous of all theories, the fiction of authorial silence, the exclusion of the writer from his work, Flaubert's attempt to vanish behind the ideal plane of his story. Wayne Booth has dispelled this myth: the author has many voices which he cannot silence, however he tries to remain "objective." The most attentive realism assumes that some things are more real than others, and every realist is impersonal in his own tone. The basic question is not what is observed but where the writer focuses his interest, his eye; how he modulates his observation over certain areas. After all, the observer fixes his own angle of vision, and there are numberless observers. So the novelist cannot silence himself, cannot exclude himself from what is observed any more than the scientist can.

Flaubert deceived himself about his impassibility, his

indifference, his distance. He made every effort to accomplish his "elocutionary disappearance," like Mallarmé. "The less one feels a thing," he writes, "the more fit one is to express it in its true nature." He intended to be unmoved by his characters and plots: "I believe that great art is scientific and impersonal. . . . The man is nothing, the work is everything." Such impersonality culminates in Zola's proposal that the novelist is a stenographer who forbids himself to judge. "Thus he disappears." Curiously enough, Zola also granted that art is nature seen through a temperament—a side of his theory that appeared in his art criticism, where he is almost romantic: "that which I seek above all in a painting is a man, not a picture. . . . Like everything else, art is a human product, a human secretion. . . . I don't care a fig for realism . . . I don't care a fig for more or less exact observation if the powerful individuality which brings the picture to life is not there." And so he goes on, in *Mon Salon*. The pretense of impassibility was carried over to our day by Ford Madox Ford, whose "perfect" novel is supposed to abide by the principle that "The author must not, by taking sides, exhibit his preferences. He has to render, not to tell." The distinction is specious.

The theory of impassibility, or "seeing from a distance," is a problem helpfully treated by psychologists who make a distinction between the visual world and the visual field, a difference much to the point in the art of the novel.[15] The visual world, the world of things "out there" in Newtonian space, is an abstraction that can only be thought but cannot be seen. We actually see in a visual field, which is quite unlike the visual world we "know." The visual field shifts with the movement of the eye, and it has a single sharp focus at the center of the (roughly speaking) oval area of perception. We know that we live in a visual world, yet it is a three-dimensional construct of things arranged stably and logically in a space that is alien to our sensations. The visual world cannot be perceived all at once, yet it can be thought into existence.

The constructs of renaissance painting are a visual world with Euclidean or Newtonian constancy rather than a visual field. Geometric forms do not tally with what we see in a visual field, which changes in size, contour, and color as it is perceived by the eye. Furthermore, impressions of color, contour, motion, distance, and depth are modified by light. We experience through the senses a variable clustering of visual fields, and when a painter or writer tries to fix or stabilize these fields by imposing a rational form upon them, he falsifies the data of vision, translating the evidence of his senses into structures intelligible enough but alienated in the guise of thought. There is no constant shape or size or scale to the world as perceived, but only as it is conceived.

Therefore the painter or novelist who attempts to "see" the world steadily and whole from a fixed point of view is setting an artificial angle and distance between painting and painter, painting and beholder, novel and author, novel and reader. Holding a point of view is a tactic in a visual culture that requires consistency above all. Is this attempt to confirm a visual world as we find it in the "reassuring" structure of the Balzac novel a result of the need for security in a middle-class society—a society that seeks to confirm by its art and science the stability, rationality, and reliability of its regime? Realism may be a way of supporting a social order.

Flaubert suffered more than most novelists from the mania for impersonal vision, for assurance that facts are reliable, that they be seen at a proper distance, held in the plane of his "pure" fiction: "Art must rise above personal emotions. . . . It is time to endow it with pitiless method, with the exactness of the physical sciences." Dickens and Thackeray did not have this anxiety about purity or distance. They both, in their own way, felt free to intrude—to erupt, in Dickens's case—into their fictions. Dickens operates in a visual field, not the visual world as the psychologists define it. There is no inviolable point of view in Dickens, who breaks the fictional plane, addressing his reader shamelessly by exclamation, exhortation, maxim, and invitation—all the tactics of confiding and confessing. Thackerary's moralizing is as intrusive as Dickens's plunging headlong into his own wildest melodrama, exulting, taking lyrical flights, shuddering at his own horrors, hating his own villains, fondling his own benevolent and innocent creatures. The exclamatory and abandoned mode makes Dickens a novelist to be read aloud in the family week after week.

By contrast Flaubert is creator of a world to be seen rather than heard. Not only seen, but seen from a held point of view, a distance of science. *Salammbo* was a result of his painfully accumulated evidence, his impersonal accuracy, his learned scenography. His reconstruction of ancient Carthage is a museum composition, an archetypal tapestry novel, the researched fiction fabricated into a fake archaeology—an instance of art aping science. As in laboratories, the conditions are entirely controlled. After fabulous industry Flaubert was ready to document his details with the relentless attention of a pre-Raphaelite study. Though the story is romantic, *Salammbo* is an inventory of Carthaginian data, an extreme instance of the typographic art that converts literature to information, an ensemble that is quantitative rather than qualitative.

Take the passage where Hamilcar enters the temple of Moloch:

A candelabrum completely covered with chiselled flowers was burning at the far end, and each of its eight golden branches bore a wick of byssus in a diamond chalice. It was placed upon the last of the long steps leading to the great altar, the corners of which terminated in horns of brass. Two lateral staircases led to its flattened summit; the stones of it could not be seen; it was like a mountain of heaped cinders, and something indistinct was slowly smoking on the top of it. Then farther back, higher than the candelabrum, and much higher than the altar, rose the Moloch, all of iron, and with gaping apertures in his human breast. . . . Ebony stools were ranged round the apartment. Behind each of them was a bronze shaft resting on three claws and supporting a torch. All these lights were reflected in the mother-of-pearl lozenges which formed the pavement of the hall . . .

The scene is held in consistent perspective: "at the far end," "upon the last of the long steps," "two lateral staircases led," "on top of it," "much higher than the altar," the lights reflected along the lozenges—the spatial arrangement is as specific as it is in paintings by Millais and Holman Hunt.

Georg Lukacs has dealt with the "sham objectivism" that made Flaubert at times, like the Camden Society architect, "a special kind of scientist" more concerned with precisions than anything else.[16] The archaeological stage-setting results in a stylization that is "neither scholarship nor art." The distances are false because the writer constructs a visual world instead of recovering life as it was lived in a visual field. The accumulation of fragments of the milieu arranged in a consistent perspective produces only a costume piece where the fabrication is a substitute for experience. As Lukacs says, the authentic novel accepts the fact "that any reflection of objective reality is necessarily relative," and the relativity of lived experience causes a certain "incommensurability of its detail." The details in *Salammbo,* like those in pre-Raphaelite painting, are all-too commensurate. The deeper the retreat into archaeology, the more the fiction is immobilized and petrified into a studio construct. The arts of the later nineteenth century were all in one or another way affected by studio artifice, that is, by visual artifice. There are a good many studio effects in Stendhal's novels, which likewise are artifacts, but the studio effects in

Stendhal are not so visual as the studio effects in *Sa-lammbo*, Huysmans, or Art Nouveau, Rossetti, and Pater. Stendhal is still able to work in a romantic field of experience where the details are incommensurate, where the distances are uncertain or variable.

Besides, the archaeological novelist is seldom able to keep his distance in any case, since the past he sees is a creation of the present: all history is modern history. Instead of being historical, the most minutely documented historical novel is alienated from history; it is "a world of exact costumes and decorations, no more than a pictorial frame within which a purely modern story is unfolded." The Carthaginian data in *Salammbo* are pseudohistory (alienated history) for the core of the novel is its sadism (or post-romanticism), which unconsciously reveals itself in the pages about torturing captives, barbaric warfare, and the cruel death of Matho. If the Carthaginians were sadists, they could hardly have seen themselves as sadists, as does Flaubert or his reader. Which is to say that Carthaginians were not decadents. Flaubert has veiled his own poisonous reponse to his century behind the antiquarian foreground; so his history turns out not to be history at all, but aestheticism.

Insofar as the past is past, history is inaccessible with its incommensurate detail. All other history is a figment or a construct, a representation of the presence of the past. The distance from which history is seen is itself the essence of history, just as the distance from which facts are observed in a laboratory is itself an inherent value in laboratory findings. History is a quest, perhaps, rather than a finding on the basis of any reliable evidence. Whether he will or no, the historian, the novelist, the scientist participates, and the act of imitating (mimesis) is affected by the degree of the observer's participating (methexis), his distancing. The specious observation is often the one that excludes the observer's awareness that he is involved in the observing, in the mimesis. The antiquarian novel pretends to isolate or insulate itself from time, and it cannot. Its purported accuracy is fraudulent. The novelist is not impassible after all, for as Nietzsche said, behind every observation is an eye.

Flaubert's impassibility breaks down in *Bouvard and Pécuchet,* a book that moves outside his own system by parodying the scientific impersonality and neutral distance. In these pages Flaubert spits out his bile that was secreted by the detached method he professed. Bouvard and Pécuchet expend their fortune and their lives in one scientific experiment after another, proving what Homais had already proved in *Madame Bovary,* that science is a mode of madness. Having ruined their farm by agronomy, they venture to remedy their plight by studying chemistry, which leads to physiology, then medicine, astronomy and geology, archaeology, history, theories of magnetism, phrenology, and pedagogy. Their encounter with literature is a refutation of Flaubert's own method in *Salammbo:* they find that documents don't help, and that Scott, Dumas, and Balzac are inaccurate. They even conclude that "syntax is a fantasy and grammar an illusion." So they reject historical and realistic fiction as a "heap of bric-a-brac," which, of course, is Georg Lukacs's opinion of it. Bouvard and Pécuchet are the Don Quixotes of their century, for if Cervantes dispelled the romantic illusions of his day, Flaubert (less sympathetically) here dispels the illusion of bourgeois science with its clichés of objectivity.

Since Flaubert is speaking directly to us in *Bouvard,* the tone is not that of *Salammbo.* Satire is a mode of direct address and as such keeps some of the resonance of oral-auditory literature, not only in *Bouvard* but also in Dickens, in Thackeray, even in Jane Austen's quiet voice. The satiric novel has vocal inflections that are silenced in documented fiction where the author pretends to stand outside or apart, where things are only "seen." Nobody would think of reading *Salammbo* aloud; but the weary

(111

sardonic voice of Flaubert is heard speaking throughout
the most refined and destructive of his books, *Sentimental
Education*. The sight of Mme. Arnoux's foot rouses in
Frederic a suspicion that she will at last give herself to
him; but that would be a nuisance— "and partly from
prudence, partly to avoid tainting his ideal, he turned on
his heel and began to roll a cigarette." Flaubert's judgment is corrosive. If the novelist is truly impassible, this
judgment is silenced.

Color and Geometry

To this point it has been suggested that the
objectivity of art and science was associated with a tyranny of the visual originating in the renaissance perspective that set a distance and represented from a spectator's
point of view a stereographic spatial area as artificial as it
was limiting. But that is not the whole truth about the
visual culture McLuhan attributes to the Gutenberg revolution, for John Ruskin knew that there is a visual culture
based not upon geometry or stereometric space but rather
upon color and light. The difference between these two
sorts of visual experience is crucial. The visual art that is
spatial required an isometric, commensurate, rationally
unified world, whereas the visual world that is colored or
chromatic (*colorito* or *cromatico* as Fellini has it) is a
heteromorphic, incommensurate world giving a quite dissimilar kind of illusion. The world of color or the world of
black-and-white (*cromatico*), values of light, interested
Ruskin far more that the world of space: "Everything that
you can see in the world around you, presents itself to
your eyes only as an arrangement of patches of different
colours variously shaded." This is Turner's world, which
is both colored and chromatic, and Ruskin in rejecting
geometry as the basis of vision justified the impressionist
experience. The impressionists are the revolutionaries in
nineteenth-century painting. Their art is visual in a new

and unrationalized way, and they destroyed the coherent
perspective that had been founded on Alberti, mathematics, and isometric space. It is a visual field instead of
a visual world.

In painting there was a continuing opposition between
Ingres and Delacroix, and both were visual. Ingres drew
and Delacroix colored. Essentially this is the conflict between Nazarene or pre-Raphaelite art with its realism
based upon drawing, and colorists or luminists such as
Turner, Constable, and Whistler. These latter created a
visual field that does not derive from a typographic culture as McLuhan describes it. McLuhan is speaking of an
art that cannot tolerate discontinuities or disrelationships
because it has the visual logic of a Euclidean system;
Ruskin, the impressionists, and most modern painters are
given to a visual art that is non-Euclidean, the colored or
chromatic art open to all the incoherences and topological distortions the modern scientist finds in reality. The
renaissance perspective coordinated visual experience
spatially; it is harder to coordinate chromatic experience.
Seurat, in the closing days of impressionist experiments,
tried to do so, attempting to impose upon chromatic
modulations the hard geometric discipline of renaissance
drawing. His effort to translate color to a spatial design
and mathematic proportion is a last attempt to systema-
tize the chromatic method of impressionism. Some impressionists had invoked spectrum analysis, but Seurat
reverted to Euclid, and his painting has unique tensions
within it. These tensions had appeared earlier in Nicolas
Poussin, colorist and geometrician.

The chromatic art of the impressionists easily slid over
into auditory effects: witness the last harmonies of Monet
and Whistler, where geometric perspective does not matter. In his late coloristic technique, Monet salvages the
auditory values that had never been really excluded from
the culture McLuhan considers visual. Undeniably renaissance design meant geometry—symmetry, balance,

equation, ratio, closure—but these proportions were also a harmony, and music was a correlate of the visual mathematic of these closed systems. And while the later impressionists were painting their harmonies, the symbolists were giving their own meaning to music, redeeming it from renaissance mathematics. Although Mallarmé referred to the poem as a constellation, he also considered it a vibration, a *disparition vibratoire*. There was always a tendency in symbolist verse to evaporate the seen into the heard. Meanwhile Swinburne was writing an auditory verse, and his cloying melodies have some of the diffused coloristic and chromatic effects of the impressionists.

Among the impressionists Monet recovered most fully what Ruskin called "this colored world of ours" by an empiricism of the eye alone. As usual, Ruskin was at odds with himself about the primacy of color and drawing, first arguing that Locke was correct in thinking "bulk, figure, number, situation" the primary qualities of things, then changing his mind and arguing that

> The perception of solid Form is entirely a matter of experience. We *see* nothing but flat colours; and it is only by a series of experiments that we find out that a stain of black or grey indicates the dark side of a solid substance, or that a faint hue indicates that the object in which it appears is far away. The whole technical power of painting depends on our recovery of what may be called *the innocence of the eye;* that is to say, a sort of childish perception of these flat stains of colour, merely as such, without consciousness of what they signify, as a blind man would see them if suddenly gifted with sight.
>
> (*The Elements of Drawing*, I)

Ruskin has returned to the visual field; his point is simple: we have trouble mathematizing color, less trouble mathematizing space. His emphasis on color as the primary vehicle of painting is a recognition that renaissance three-dimensional composition and the spectator-view are limited and artificial approaches. He also notes that colorist painting "will always show a slight tendency toward flatness." His axiom that "We never see anything clearly" is a rebuttal of the spatial dogmas about "finishing" details in a painting. He might be talking about Monet's water lilies when he says that "every object will cast some of its own colour back in the light that it reflects." Shadow, he suspects, is "a more important element than the substance": "The man who can see all the greys, and reds, and purples in a peach, will paint the peach round, and rightly altogether; but the man who has only studied its roundness, may not see its purples and greys, and if he does not, will never get it to look like a peach; so that great power over colour is always a sign of a large general art-intellect." He might be referring to Cézanne. Urging that "colour always disguises form," he endorses the impressionist tactic of broken pigment or discontinuity of tone: "do not mix the purple on your palette and lay it on so thick as to overpower the red, but take a little thin blue from your palette, and lay it on lightly over the red, so as to let the red be seen through, and thus produce the required purple."

Here the problem of color becomes very complicated, for it involves light as well as hue, and also an apprehension of space that is quite different from the isomorphic space of renaissance vanishing-point perspective. These problems of light and space cannot be solved by geometry unless they are treated by other modes of perspective such as those used in the tradition of Byzantine-Romanesque art, where space is discontinuous, and flat, and often an aspect of light. Quite unlike vanishing-point perspective, which organizes scenes from a single "outside" point of view and rationalizes the composition into an isometric geometry, the space created by a Byzantine dome seems irrational, both flat and curved, as in Hagia Sophia; it shifts, rotates, expands upon mosaic surfaces that glitteringly incorporate light into curvatures; it is space in part created by the contour of the fabric itself, and the figures on these surfaces, even if they are held in the static plane of the gold ground, foreshorten themselves so that their appearance changes as the beholder moves. And the dome gives resonance to music and word. The compartmented spaces within Hagia Sophia are not only solid but also flat, and as in much modern art this Romanesque composition accepts a principle of interruption or juxtaposition instead of continuity. The pilgrimage church in France is a succession of bays, isolated but homogeneous, and these discontinuous units are an order of haptic and acoustic space, not only thought and seen but heard and felt within the nave at Vézelay, the plastic expression of a culture phrased in the formulaic *Song of Roland* with its static, isolated *laisses*, each like an assonanced icon, and its flat pattern of color. Like Homeric poetry, the *Chanson* is constructed by a sequence of rhetorical stereotypes chanted almost liturgically: "High are the hills and dark the valleys." It is a verbal mosaic.

This golden, rotational, auditory space is a field of metamorphosis that Newtonian space hardly accommodates. The hill with two shining trees and the four bright steps which Roland mounts is a topology closer to modern geometry than to the isomorphic space of renaissance perspective. There is resemblance, also, between these Byzantine pictorial formulas and the figuration in Van Gogh, whose tormented cypress trees belong in an icon and whose ravines wrench Euclidean space into contradictions where depth is flattened and curvature is pulled toward the surface. Byzantine space, like the cloisonnism in Gauguin, employs a non-Euclidean logic comparable to the mathematic of Lobachevsky or Reimann, postulating conditions where more than one line can be drawn parallel to a given line at a certain point or where no line can be drawn parallel. These interrupted dimensions were not accessible to the old stereography; they require a poetic of space explored by Gaston Bachelard: the coexisting, multiple, disjunctive spaces of the cave, the corner, the shell, the drawer, the carapace—spaces that are haptically known or even heard, not simply seen in uniform perspective. This fieldlike non-Euclidean space was rediscovered in the neo-Byzantine planes of color into which Cézanne analyzed Mt. Ste. Victoire; then the cubists synthesized this pictorial geometry into compositions that were tactile as well as pictorial, for the very pigment was interrupted by passages of alien texture (*collage*).

Such multidimensional, polysensorial space, essentially Byzantine, complicates our perception of the world and is a basis for the field-experiences in novels like Claude Mauriac's *The Marquise Went Out at Five,* an area-study of what is happening and what *has* happened in the Carrefour Buci at a certain hour. Present and past are flattened into a montagelike surface configuration resembling the superimposed perspectives in op art, where space derives from light and color, where the geometry is not only spatial but luminous. In such fields, references among forms, contours, times, places, and figures are all open and reversible; the composition is created from inside as well as outside the situation. Mauriac's novel brings ambiguous vector effects into relations between far and near, now and then, inward and outward. It is topological fiction. As in Byzantine art, there is no one perspective; there are only perspectives. By contrast, Flaubert's *Salammbo* is a naïve historicism, a mere literary reconstruction establishing, like renaissance painting, a visual logic of continuity and coherence where none existed for the Carthaginian.

The formulaic-auditory multidimensional space, and its resonance, survived, also, in the gothic cathedral with its multilateral extension, its stained-glass windows which were mosaic adapted to fenestration. The fluid, linear spaces of the gothic nave are not drawn toward a vanishing point, and the gothic light and atmosphere almost dissolve the delicate structure of the stonework. In mediaeval painting, too, light is an absolute; light was Logos, identical with the essence of things, since God was light.[17] The gold ground symbolizes the Light that creates; it is pictorial texture, substance, and essence. Mediaeval light is uniform and penetrating; it is transcendent; it does not fall from a given source; it is the very form of objects; it is space and being as well as color. Form, color, light are synonymous. Gothic light is a neo-Platonic radiance, for things do not exist unless they participate in the light of the One, the effulgence of Being. Since the gold ground symbolizes ontological light, no distinction appears between matter and spirit. The shadowless gold transposes color to space, which is flat and boundless; there is no deep perspective since figures are locked in their gold ground, as in mosaic. Because things exist insofar as they are lighted, there are no cast shadows; figures are not modeled, and there is no chiaroscuro. The flat perspective of gothic stained glass is also ontological in that the figures are identical with the color pattern of the window, without plasticity. Color is light, and light is being, as Dante knew.

The renaissance changed all this by its new perspective, for with the perspective-observer view of things, it was necessary to designate the source from which illumination falls; and light falling from a local source casts shadows. At the heart of the renaissance Leonardo wrote about light as distinct from color, raising the problem of chiaroscuro, which became involved with the theory of perspective, cast light, and angle of illuminating. This use of local light radiating from an assigned source appears in later manuscript illumination (which is not really illumination in the gothic sense, but painting). Cast light begins to appear sporadically in late-mediaeval painting, in Conrad Witz, in Gruenewald; then at last scientifically, in La Tour, as evidence of the the secularizing of a culture increasingly concerned with local appearances, with evidence, with exact observation, with a new kind of logic. Already in Dante's Hell there is a protorenaissance local light, quite different from the transcendent light of Paradise; the infernal chiaroscuro is a secularizing of the world—the world revealed in the dubious light from a candle, not from God who is Being. Instead of universal transcendental light there is now only local irradiation, which can be extinguished, which changes the appearances of things according to the angle from which light falls and according to its intensity. This secular light is contingency. And objects continue to exist even when light is withdrawn.

Furthermore the play of light from a local source means that illumination becomes an aspect of spatial design: light is subjected to space. Thus enters the problem of chiaroscuro, the modulation of light over the contour of things. Light becomes a different value from color, which dims into variable hues. Light is now merely "lighting"—a theatrical effect. When the lighting dims or is put out, objects are "there" in another sort of being. They are separable from the light that falls upon them, so that Locke's distinction between the primary (mathematical) qualities of things and their secondary (sensuous, especially colored, touched, or heard) qualities becomes necessary. After Locke, objects are real only so far as they can be reduced to abstract or scientific dimensions and physical properties derived from measurable spatial schemes devised by the mind. Reality becomes a mathematical order, whereas the painterly world is reduced to a visual illusion in which figures emerge, change, and vanish as the source of local light shifts. In La Tour's candlelight painting light has phenomenal value only, but space is a constant. And if space is to have any reliable or constant structure, it must be seen from a fixed angle. What could be drawn seemed real; what was lighted or colored was a transient impression. The academicians were always insisting that drawing, not coloring, was primary.

Given this angle of vision, this set distance, the painted

representation was provably accurate or, in modern phrasing, objective. The painter or eventually even the writer like Flaubert could state the facts to be seen by anyone taking the same point of view. As Huxley says, the strongest claim for the validity of scientific truth is that anyone can verify for himself if he attends to the evidence. Artistic and scientific methods of observing give reliable information about local conditions, always provided the spectator remains at a given angle of vision. Point of view becomes a needed artistic and scientific premise if representation is to be exact.

In the long run this specified approach is a very confining vision, and it was left, paradoxically, for the most visual of all nineteenth-century arts—impressionism—to discover its limitations. Impressionism was an intently local kind of art: the haystack seen changing its semblance hour by hour under sunlight. Impressionism is the later phase of a painterly art that arose within gothic, when cast shadows first appeared and there was a new sense of the local quality of phenomenal light, affecting color. The perception of the reality of what is local and individual and conditional came with gothic art and thought. It was evidence of a secularizing and protoscientific attitude clear enough in Grosseteste's speculations about light; and as gothic developed, the architect dispersed fabric and space in atmospheric light while the painter became aware of the modulations in the changing light of nature. Impressionism is the final expression of this secularizing of painterly vision. Significantly enough, Monet chose the façade of Rouen cathedral as a major motif, for late-gothic structures are premonitory of the vision that reduces the world to a flickering illusion, dispelling the material into chromatic nuances, losing geometric spaces amid transient hues.

Yet there is a difference between gothic light and impressionist color: Panofsky suggests that high gothic obeys a principle of transparency, light permeating the gothic nave as it penetrates the gothic window. High gothic is light *through,* not light *on.* The gothic principle of light through, or transparence, persists belatedly in Tintoretto, Greco, and Rembrandt, whose color and light are almost a roentgen vision of objects. In this sense they are, like Turner, inheritors of gothic light rather than protoimpressionists. Impressionists, relying on the secular lighting of the renaissance or cast illumination, began by studying light *on,* continuing the method of La Tour. But sensitive as they were to "this colored world of ours," they soon found that their broken color amounted to a prismatic diffusion of light, so they had to abandon the old chiaroscuro. As it dims into shadow, light also refracts, changing hue as it falls on an object at a given moment from a given source under given atmospheric conditions. Thus the refractions and vibrations led them to another mode of vision grounded in light, not color, and they found that they could reach their harmonies only by returning to the gothic light *through.* The ultimate impressionist technique is almost that of the X ray, which is a secular variant of the mediaeval idea that light is essence. When Monet painted the lilies at Giverny, returning to the gothic transcendent light, he unexpectedly reached an intersection between artistic and scientific techniques. And in writing his chapters on mountain gloom, mountain glory, and Turnerian light, Ruskin in effect discovered the transparencies of the last impressionism.

The course of impressionist painting perfectly exemplifies Edgar Wind's theory that whenever any art tries to purify its use of a certain medium the art passes over into the area of another medium (Focillon called this interference). Trying to see things as they "are" when a certain light falls on them, impressionists invoked the prismatic analysis. They broke up their palettes into touches of pure pigment in a program that put them in the vanguard of a realism wholly given to the evidence of the eye. Above all others they reveal the consequences of isolating the visual experience from the plastic, tactile, auditory. Their painting depended almost entirely on exclusions: they treated reality solely as it was seen, to the disregard of formal composition. As a result they recovered the empiricism the renaissance had falsified by its mathematical theories about space, perspective, and drawing. Even more than renaissance painters the impressionists staked everything on optical evidence. In so doing they found that color is form, that light is space. Then in spite of all its intentness on accuracy, impressionist painting, purified to primary color, became increasingly subjective until the fully exploited medium led across the border from objectivity to symbolism, a color so sensitive that it could be heard in the harmonies of Monet's abstractions, where the world is secondarily derived from the play of light, where color exists almost by hypothesis alone.

The impressionists discarded sculptural and geometric space in behalf of an optical reportage so limited that at times it was nearly theoretical. The plastic and tactile values they jettisoned were not recovered until their experiment had been pushed to its extreme and the pigment itself became a texture to reintroduce, in the guise of impasto, the lost dimensions. These plastic and geometric dimensions in renaissance painting had been, in any case, only an artifact, for there had been a dissociation of sensibility whenever the painter used color and line on a two-dimensional surface to establish a third dimension. And there was also a dissociation of sensibility when the impressionists isolated the optical from the other senses. This dissociation was healed when the post-impressionists began to smear pigment, which became a vehicle for the actual presence of the plastic or third dimension. Such exploitation of the medium led to cubist collage and to action painting, reintegrating the pigment with the representation, the visual with the haptic and tactile.

The history of the arts suggests that no movement is ever consistent with its own principles, and impressionism, one of the most empirical developments in western painting, could not abide by its own retinal doctrine. As soon as the quest for visual accuracy slid over into abstract color composition for its own sake, the impressionists, in the teeth of their own method of "objective visual observation," abolished their observed world, translating it into monochromatic pure harmonies. In some comparable way the scientist, using his own kind of observing, ended by abolishing the physical world in favor of a system of abstract laws of "force"—the mysterious immaterial energy behind this world of things. And the marble, chiseled images of Parnassian verse transformed themselves, at their purest, into the invisible Beauty of symbolist poems, just as the archaeological descriptive passages of Tennyson's *Idylls* transformed themselves into the languid music of Swinburne's harmonies. So too, the fussy specifications of pre-Raphaelite painting, frozen into strained designs, evolved through Burne-Jones's decorative arrangements into the abstractions of Whistler's nocturnes. The local became transfigured into the abstract. The impressionists and other realists at last emptied their world of things until there was nothing left to observe—only formulas for abstract color and tonality.

Yet the eye for the local remained sharp in Degas, that radical empiricist who operated in his own metatheatre. Influenced as he was by photography, that most optical of techniques, Degas proves that a fixed angle of vision does not always give a coherent, consistent, or unified view of things, as renaissance painters presumed it did.[18] Degas is the *reductio ad absurdum* of the Albertian theory that a given point of view structures the world logically. Degas's angle shot, as theatrical as the *di sotto in su* of mannerism, reveals how discontinuous space can appear within the visual field. His painting-from-the-wings is a travesty of the renaissance spectator-view; it is a complex of visual fragments that break the aesthetic plane as freely as Shakespearean drama. When Degas sees ballet girls rehearsing or women bathing, he draws the spectator into the action with the imperative, almost distorting, focus of the naked eye, which has its own gravitational pull, eccentric and arbitrary. This retinal artifact, the arrested glimpse, is topological, a field-effect that brings a sense of participating as well as observing, for we are inside and outside at the same moment. Degas studies the existential space that Gaston Bachelard calls "lived," the space that has no preestablished or even reliable scale, a transient arrangement or provisional geometry standing in isolation; it does not lead to generalities, propositions, or laws. We lack a mathematic to close this optical assemblage into a system. If Degas's pastel color is a unifying harmony, his unfilled aching voids have a tactile pathos. Thus Degas returns to the superpositions and juxtapositions of the Lascaux paintings, and the effect is not dissimilar—a kind of sympathetic magic. His attention to the evidence is poetic, not scientific. By the naïve foreshortening of the eye itself Degas rebels against the academic synthesis of form and affirms the empiricism of vision without context. The situation is posed but not rationalized.

Treating his scenes as excerpts from process, Degas clears the way for action painting, which finally closes the distance between painter and beholder. He is far more concerned with the act of perceiving than with what is perceived; at least he senses that what is observed is shaped by the retina of the observer. The form is determined by the attention brought to bear. Degas allows all relations within his visual field to remain unrevised. Unlike the later Monet and Seurat and the divisionists, Degas strikes us as being nontheoretic, since he stays so close to his optical data, refusing to draw conclusions about structure and reality. We have the evidence without the law; and the evidence suffices, making irrelevant any theorem that might be phrased about space, distance, or design. He sees the world *en passant*. For Degas there is no such thing as space: there are only incommensurable spaces or arrangements locally seen. In one of the best commentaries on Degas's work Pierre Francastel states that this "fragmented and closely seen vision" modifies the frame in which the painter was taught to establish his world, scenographically.

Again, such episodic vision links Degas with Shakespearean theatre, where a single scene is allowed to stand out above the level of the play in an isolation or emphasis that gives the action an erratic and powerful attack. Degas and Shakespare are both willing to sacrifice unity of composition for dramatic accent. There is no official order behind this theatrical vision, which authenticates the local, momentary appearance as it is seen from an unpremeditated angle, an artistic act of good faith. In somewhat the same way Shakespeare presents Shylock in successive discontinuous moments as monster and man, untroubled as playwright about any consistency of character. The vivid impression is more valuable than the logical perspective.

Something of this disjunction, immediacy, and local distortion is carried over into Dickens, who cared as little as Shakespeare about consistency, and whose novels are a succession (rather than a sequence) of highly charged theatrical episodes. The immediacy in Degas and Dickens often brings about a grotesquerie: the figures in each are caricatured, deformed by the sharp angle from which they are seen. This distortion is theatrical, a tactic of the metatheatre where Dickens and Degas employ the play-within-the-play and are aware of the role-playing of their figures. Degas catches the Vicomte Lepic stepping off the curb: we cannot say that he is posed; yet he is obviously posed, and Degas is calling attention to the fact that this episode, photographic as it looks, is an artifice. Thus the painter outdistances his own studio effects. So also Dickens, enjoying to the full his own casting, invites inspection of the role-playing of his characters; and his villains, especially, are as conscious as Richard III of their own melodrama.

Degas does not conceal that he is painting a picture; Dickens does not conceal that he is writing a novel. Both break the plane as Shakespeare broke it in the prologues in *Henry V* calling attention to the absurdity that the audience will not see the battle of Agincourt but a mockery of this action. By stimulating this participation of the reader or beholder, Dickens and Degas get outside the closed aesthetic system of their day, the false distancing that was supposed to make the work a duplicate of what is observed. Ibsen, with his realistic theatre, never moves outside his own theatrical code, which is "closed" and to be seen from a distance that forbids trespass—and yet he puts into the mouths of his "real" characters all the problematic questions in which he is interested, a subterfuge ignored by Dickens. Ibsen is there all the while addressing us; but it would spoil his drama were he to call attention to his illusion. He must pretend to be absent. But when we look at a painting such as the "Café-Concert at Les Ambassadeurs," we are alerted at once that Degas is the one looking at these puppet-girls seen beyond the neck of that cello and the hats of the women in front rows. Neither Degas nor Dickens is shackled to the objective. They are not absent.

IV

Alien Worlds

Pathos of Distance

THE NOTION OF DISTANCING, or holding up the mirror to nature, presupposes in both art and science the fiction of an absent observer, which is to say an alien or detached spectator; and ever since the renaissance it has fostered "externality illusions." A pretentious means of expressing this situation is to use the terms "alienation" and "reification," terms which recur as a theme in recent criticism, especially socioliterary criticism represented by Roland Barthes and Lucien Goldmann. Actually this criticism is not new at all, for in his obscure and blundering way Wordsworth, acknowledging his debt to Coleridge, wrote a passage in *The Prelude* that anticipates the reaction against the idea of objectivity or the isolation of the observer from what is observed:

> . . . But who shall parcel out
> His intellect by geometric rules,
> Split like a province into round and square? . . .
> Who shall point as with a wand and say
> "This portion of the river of my mind
> Came from yon fountain?" Thou, my Friend! art one
> More deeply read in thy own thoughts; to thee

> Science appears but what in truth she is,
> Not as our glory and our absolute boast,
> But as a succedaneum, and a prop
> To our infirmity. No officious slave
> Art thou of that false secondary power
> By which we multiply distinctions, then
> Deem that our puny boundaries are things
> That we perceive, and not what we have made.

(*Prelude,* II)

Nietzsche, too, was one who reacted against "our meddling intellect" that "mis-shapes the beauteous forms of things" by science—and Wordsworth adds by Art, also. For Wordsworth, like Nietzsche, sought participation, and knew that there is no such thing as objectivity, which became a *deus ex machina* of art and science after the renaissance. When Nietzsche used the term "pathos of distance" he was not referring to this sort of estrangement, but to the distance between the hero and the herd. Yet the more significant pathos of distance is that between the artist or the scientist and the world he observes, the world from which he is by definition excluded, the world which is only a cultural illusion, a world he reifies. Roland Barthes says that for more than a century the artist has found himself face to face with the Form that has been posited before him like an object, the *Littérature-Objet;* and Style, "like a vertical and solitary dimension of thought," has become the writer's "thing," a splendor and a prison. Consequently all literature became a version of an *écriture policière,* subservient to the ideal of Order. Thus the artist aped the objectivity of the scientist, but in his own way: for as the scientist hypothesized the inviolable order of Nature, the artist hypothesized the inviolable order of Art. And both were alien worlds. Nietzsche was wise enough to know that "there is no such thing as science without assumptions," and he warned, rephrasing Wordsworth, "All seeing is essentially perspective, and so is all knowing."

Just as significant is the connection Nietzsche makes between the scientific intellect and asceticism: "In the physiological sense, science is closely allied with the ascetic ideal; a certain biological impoverishment is necessary to both." Nietzsche regards asceticism in the artist as a betrayal of art, and he links the ascetic ideal with the bad conscience of modern man—with his coated tongue and sense of guilt—a symptom of his dishonesty. He resents the dishonesty, also, of the scientist's externality illusions, the fetish of objectivity, and puritanism inherent in scientific discipline. Thus bad conscience and guilt are side effects of the distancing of the world in art and science, an aspect of what Ernst Cassirer calls the tragic isolation of the self that occurred as soon as man erected a boundary between himself and the world. As soon as man recognized outside reality as apart or other, he suffered an incurable wound of being estranged from an order that could only be thought. When he "reified" or distanced his world, he faced the penalties of the meddling intellect.

The Marxist critics have, of course, made great play with the theme of reification. Lucien Goldmann has contrived an entire sociology of the novel as the genre which expresses the alienating effects of a society that produces for the market, where commodities have an autonomous magic value, of themselves. Thus the hero of the novel becomes a problematic figure because he is of necessity distanced from the world in which he lives. But the artist himself is also a problematic figure, often as alien from the world of Art as the scientist is from the world of Nature. The cameo world of the Parnassians, the enameled marble forms of Gautier, the remote domain of symbolist Beauty were all as alien as the system of abstract law erected by the neutral scientist. Marble, onyx, enamel are transformed into an autonomous or reified world of Art. So Huxley, by some kindred magic, supposes that a "condition" of carbonic acid, water, and nitrogenous compounds are "the phenomena called life." The most daring of all scientific books, Ernst Haeckel's *Riddle of the Universe* exemplifies the nineteenth-century ability to reify the world in abstract form, to misplace concreteness, in Whitehead's term. Haeckel rejoices that the mysteries of reality have steadily vanished before our understanding of nature until only a single one remains: the identification of substance. But this problem is only a logomachy, says Haeckel, for the "real physicists" have found that substance is nothing but the laws of force, the supreme, unalterable, verifiable scheme of matter and motion. Nature is an abstract system of forces, a construct derived from facts. Like the symbolists, Haeckel treats things as hieroglyphs for some insubstantial reality beyond themselves. Haeckel's vision of the ultimate substance is a fetishism as blinding as the inviolable and dangerous Beauty of Herodias, remote and alien. By a kindred fetishism Taine discovered that the ultimate laws of literary history—race, environment, epoch—are absolute forces:

> Such are the grand causes, for these are universal and permanent causes, present in every case and at every moment, everywhere and always active, indestructible, and inevitably dominant in the end, since, whatever accidents cross their path, being limited and partial, end in yielding to the obscure and incessant repetition of their energy; so that the general structure of things and all the main features of events are their work, all religions and philosophies, all poetic and industrial systems, all forms of society and of the family, all, in fine, being imprints bearing the stamp of their seal. ("Introduction," *History of English Literature*)

Usually the distancing of the world in abstract artistic form induced in the poet a sense of guilt that the scientists did not feel. Tennyson, harried by his ideals of Beauty, faced up to the guilt inherent in artistic distancing when he wrote "The Palace of Art" in 1832, the romantics being hardly cold in their graves. Attracted to the artificial Beauty of Keats's pseudomediaeval verse, Tennyson tells how he built a citadel in which to dwell "at ease" apart from the world. His palace is an architectural pastiche filled with stained-glass ornaments, gothic corridors, and paintings and tapestries in the pre-Raphaelite mode of the *Idylls*, a museum of Art with green and blue arrases, images of the Virgin, the vales of Avalon, angels, houris, weeping queens, and the silver sound of great bells over the mosaics and floral motifs. Amid this Arthurian apparatus the poet sits apart "contemplating" the world from an Olympian distance. But uncertain shapes haunt the corners—"phantasms weeping tears of blood" and nightmares—and he is saddened by thinking of the iron face of Nature:

> The hollow orb of moving Circumstance
> Rolled round by one fixed law.

Shadowed by his sense of exile, he finds the palace a tomb in which he hears, far off, the tread of Others. Driven back into the world by his burden of "sin," he leaves his "new land" almost as Hans Castorp is called down from his magic mountain.

Tennyson's poem is a boundary between the politics of the romantics and the social imperatives that at last give Prufrock his own bad conscience. Wordsworth and many others had been shaken by the French Revolution, but the melancholy of the Victorians with their need for social involvement brought into literature the intimation that art had become marginal. This was a malaise that did not afflict the eighteenth century for the most part, an age of innocent aestheticism enjoyed by dilettantes such as Horace Walpole, Thomas Gray, and other antiquarians who lived fussily but untroubled in their Dellacruscan or bardic world. Gray's mediaevalism is different from Ruskin's; the Victorian study of the gothic brought a compulsion to reform the English way of life. In sum, the abiding problems in Ruskin and Arnold are how to relate art to life.

The turn from the romantic to the Victorian is basically

due to the increasing sense of guilt inherent in writers as different as Dickens, Mill, George Eliot, Browning (at moments), Melville, Poe, and Baudelaire and other French decadents. Often this awareness of guilt disguises itself—for example, in Arnold—as a quest for culture, or it takes the form of not being at home in the world as it does in Dostoevsky's underground man or Oblomov or Kafka's paralytics.

One might trace the malaise about art back to Hamlet's vain effort to relate the aesthetic to the moral life: when he hears the player, he asks what Hecuba is to him and feels his own inability to respond morally to his cue. Yet he makes the preposterous supposition that a moral monster like Claudius will be guilt-stricken by a theatrical representation designed to catch his conscience. The heart of one of Hamlet's mysteries is the conflict between his exquisite aesthetic sensibility and his puritan conviction that drama—the well-played role—does not suffice in the moral life. Perhaps he comes close to some resolution in the last act, when the gravedigger teaches him that no matter what role we play we all come to the dust that stops a bunghole; so it does not matter whether or not he duels. Whatever may be Hamlet's failure to adjust art to morality, he phrased the problem that lies behind the aesthetic of the nineteenth century. The romantics were often rather naïvely persuaded that art was life: the acts put on by Stendhal's heroes do not always work, but Byron was carried away by his roles; and Shelley at times confused poetry and politics. The post-romantics discovered that life can be transformed by art but knew that art is not life. That was their affliction.

Essentially the question is one of aesthetic distance, the perspective requiring poet, painter, and beholder to waive their involvement with what is presented in artistic form. The penalties for detachment did not fall with full weight until the decadents tried to live in art forms; they could not evade the diffused and largely unassigned sense of guilt that penetrated art itself. Oscar Wilde's rather shoddy novel, *The Picture of Dorian Gray*, discloses what the scientist did not admit, namely, that it is impossible to be merely a spectator. Wilde himself discovered in writing *De Profundis* the truth of what he proposed in his novel: "I treated art as the supreme reality and life as a mere mode of fiction." By bitter experience he learned the pathos inherent in artistic distance, a pathos already felt by such romantics as Benjamin Constant, one of the first to use the phrase "art for art's sake." Stendhal was continually aware of the difficulty of translating life to art.

Although Tennyson's poet is driven back from art to life, one of the marks of nineteenth-century poetry is the recurrent metaphor of the horizon, the voyage, the distance, the beyond—far, far away, as Tennyson has it. The need for distance or detachment takes contradictory forms: the detailed spectator-observation of nature, excluding the observer in the interest of accuracy, or else the flight into the distance, over the far horizon. Lamartine sought *nouveaux rivages;* Baudelaire embarked not only for Cythera but on the voyage that led over more perilous horizons, toward the Ahab experience; Mallarmé fell silent before the awesome *Azur.* If the spectator-observation is overprecise, this horizon distancing is as vague and indefinite as possible. The dim distance was a *Sehnsucht* among the romantics—or a skylark flight or an Icarus propulsion toward an ideal; often among post-romantics it was only an escape. Yet the painstaking attention bestowed on the foreground by the observer is no less an evasion or an escape, for it is a symptom of repressing the self, a mark of alienation no less decisive than the Icarus-flight or the voyage. The contradictory forms of distancing—either the neutral attention of the spectator or the flight to dreams beyond nature, the visions that are believable only if they are remote enough— are alike a way of alienating. One of the most curious ways of distancing is found in Stendhal, whose heroes, like Fabrizio, seek security behind a prison wall that isolates them from reality but enables them to indulge their dreams.

Tennyson's Ulysses ambiguously symbolizes both heroism *and* escape as the voyage across the horizon. Sometimes the Tennysonian distancing is an evasion symbolized by vagueness of background, the dissolving landscapes and seascapes of the *Idylls* resembling the soft focus of a cinematic fadeout, or the "blue distance" in renaissance painting. This technique of vague distance endows the painting or poem with an arty dimension that may seem almost mythical; and painters like Carrière specialized in a soft-focus realism. In Tennyson the misty background implies a fallacious notion that whatever is artistic has to be indefinite, suggestive, ineffable, larger-than-life; this particular Tennysonian method is a pathos of distance that still serves as a surrogate for myth in some of Eliot's poems where one catches music from a farther room or the song of mermaids who no longer sing to us. It has been damagingly associated with Jungian archetypes, and is surely one of the fraudulent devices of nineteenth-century art: whatever can be clearly seen or known is not "big" enough for art, which must escape to the imprecise.

The closing scenes of the *Morte d'Arthur* have the pseudomythic soft focus of Bergman's more ostentatious films, a decadent evaporation or vanishing, the twilit atmosphere of Maeterlinck's plays or Yeats's Celtic visions. The black-stoled, sacral queens place Arthur's body in the barge that sails away "like a dream" into a Whistleresque dissolve:

> . . . Long stood Sir Bedivere
> Revolving many memories, till the hull
> Look'd one black dot against the dawn.
> And on the mere the wailing died away.

The distancing is temporal as well as spatial, for Tennyson turns from the present to either the "far future" or the romantic—that is, the archaeological—past. The *Idylls* echo the noise of old battles rolling mightily by a winter sea, but the hero of "Locksley Hall" dimly envisions the wonder that will be. A frail, dissipating hope is in Tennyson's sense of a world-whisper coming across the faint horizons beyond nature, life, death, tranquilizing his fears and doubts by tremulous illusions:

> Moreover, something is or seems,
> That touches me with mystic gleams,
> Like glimpses of forgotten dreams.
> ("The Two Voices")

The glooming horizon before Ulysses is a more uncertain utopianism than the romantic vision of man's Promethean future. Baudelaire knew that his invitation to voyaging brought a risk of plunging into the gulf before one discovered the new world of *calme et volupté*. And Mallarmé was terrified by the vacancy of the indifferent sky.

Thought as Fetish

Much of the yearning for distance was what T. E. Hulme called spilt religion. Long ago Malinowski argued that the religious life does not depend upon the existence of gods but rather upon a sense of the difference between the sacred and the secular; and F. M. Cornford said that when a culture loses its confidence in its gods, the sense of the sacred is transferred first to philosophy, then to science. The shift from religion to philosophy to science as sacral can be traced in ancient culture as the chthonic gods, then the Olympians, yielded to Plato's Forms, then the Forms to the devout atomism of Lucretius, whose nature teems with life. The supplanting of religion by philosophy and philosophy by science amounts to substituting one myth for another: from the myth of the gods to the myth of the Idea, then to the myth of *natura res gubernans* which is not so secular or amoral as would appear. This shift seems to have recurred when the anthropomorphic Christianity of the Dark Ages yielded to the philosophic phase of Aquinas's scholasticism, then to the scientism of a Newtonian world. The myths of the old orders, in fact, could not hold together the Elizabethan world picture, which barely reconciled Christianity, the new philosophy, and the new science. It was a world picture that did not survive the Newtonian physics with its myth of the spacious firmament.

Anton Ehrenzweig has drawn some conclusions: under the old religious and humanistic world order, man found the center of his universe within himself, acknowledging his responsibility for his own condition, recognizing the existence of his own sin or guilt or blunders.[19] The premise of the religious or tragic view was a homocentric compulsion that brought man face to face with himself either in the Christian notion of original sin or in the tragic notion of the flaw in human nature. But with the coming of renaissance science, man began to evade himself by displacing these compulsions into the world outside, where they no longer seemed to be moral or spiritual laws but laws of a necessity inherent in nature. That is, he objectified his own imperatives in the illusions he called science. He reified his world, reading into natural law (which was at first a mathematical-physical cosmos) the "forces" within himself. His compulsions now put on the mask of thermodynamics, the Newtonian laws of motion. If this is so, then Edmund in *King Lear* makes the proper comment: "An admirable evasion of whoremaster man, to lay his goatish disposition on the charge of a star."

Ehrenzweig puts the question in his own way: "Could it not be that the scientific reification process derives its element of *external* guilt and compulsion from some *internal* guilt and compulsion?—that we project a deeply repressed guilt feeling (based on the internal compulsion of the superego) into the external world?" Is the scientific notion of external causality a myth that enables us to escape from our own urgencies, which are transferred to, or projected upon, the laws governing nature? Thus the scientist may meet himself in alienated guise in the iron laws of matter and motion, a *deus ex machina* in very neutral form. Nietzsche warned what happens when the law of causation fails and we are left, again, face to face with ourselves; at this moment we are forced back upon a tragic view of life.

Unlike most scientists of his day Huxley was tinged with feelings of unconscious guilt, which phrased itself in his plea for studying science as a moral discipline. He asserts, illogically, that there is an ethic inherent in natural law, and he speaks like a puritan in urging that we must obey the decalogue as written by that nineteenth-century Mosaic figure, Darwin; otherwise there is retribution. The laws of substance, causation, inertia are universal and "true for all time," and they must be "riveted" in the mind. Huxley says that "blind faith" is the one unpardonable sin—for scientific skepticism is "the highest of duties"—yet he never doubts the "definite order of the universe," which cannot be infringed. Furthermore Huxley feels great malaise about the misery arising from the struggle for existence within society and between societies, since the price to be paid for economic survival is a necessary wretchedness of the poor, which must be kept within tolerable limits. His scientific objectivity scarcely veils his bad conscience.

These feelings of suppressed guilt are far more apparent in Hardy's *Jude the Obscure*, a novel of radical alienation in a world viciously hostile to man. Jude is hired to drive away birds feeding on the harvest: "They seemed, like himself, to be living in a world which did not want them." Jude's world is a place where man faces his own most antagonistic drives in external form. "All around you there seemed to be something glaring, garish, rattling, and the noises and glares hit upon the little cell called your life, and shook it, and scorched it." Jude is "predestinate." His dim sense of guilt and responsibility is transferred when he gives Sue Bridehead the kiss that changed their lives. "Is it," he asks, "that the women are to blame; or is it the artificial system of things, under which the normal sex-impulses are turned into devilish domestic gins and springes to noose and hold back those who want to progress?" Sue protests she is not to blame: "The universe, I suppose—things in general, because they are so horrid and cruel." In Hardy's world "there is something wrong somewhere." Not nature only, but society itself has become a sadistic mechanism for torturing people with the guilt they once assigned to their own mistakes or sins. The very idea of sin—perhaps the very idea of blundering—has become irrelevant in Hardy's world, where misfortune is "there" as a built-in necessity.

Tragedy, we say, has somewhere behind it a sadistic wish to see man destroyed—or a masochistic wish to suffer. For the most part (until Euripides, perhaps) the Greeks tempered this sadism by assuming that man through his own blundering is at least half to blame for his failures. Hardy's sadism is the untempered malignity of a scientific law disguised as a myth projecting man's guilt into an artificial system of things, a tyranny he invents to scar himself without needing to bear the responsibility for being scarred. Masochism becomes sadism; the sense of guilt is unassigned and diffused. Hardy turns the world into a penal colony by alienating himself from himself, meeting his own self-hate in the iron laws of nature, an externality illusion, or reification, as disastrous as it is evasive. The distancing is quite false. It is, after all, *Hardy's* nature. The deceptiveness of this illusion had already been mentiond by Blake, who wrote "tho' it appears Without, it is Within."

Nietzsche made the same point when he accused the scientist of inventing the pretentious lie of our civilization: "Our whole attitude toward nature, our violation of nature with the help of machines and the heedless ingenuity of technicians and engineers, is *hubris*." By *hubris* Nietzsche meant that under the pretense of observing nature we impose upon it our own impulses in alienated or reified form, the guise of scientific law; thus we fall victim to our self-deception. The scientist unguardedly displaced his rejection of himself into the artificial system of things that hits upon the pitiable cell called our life.

A psychologist would say that appeal to the iron laws of nature is an overestimation of what is external. It is not a commitment to reality so much as an estrangement from reality. The objective world of mechanistic nineteenth-century science and realistic art, and the distant inviolable world of Herodiaslike Beauty posited by the symbolists, are essentially hostile worlds. Or, stated conversely, our own aggression expresses itself in alien, reified form in myths of worlds outside, or beyond. If there is not aggression, there is at least a precautionary attitude reflected in Huxley's admonition that nature's discipline is the unexpected blow she deals us unless we study her laws. This is a revised Calvinism: if we are knowing enough, we can avoid the penalties so arbitrarily dealt out, and we can be saved by science instead of by grace.

The notion that man meets his own nature in alien form outside himself is the basis of Ludwig Feuerbach's critique of religion. Feuerbach took God to be only man worshiped in a projected image of himself, and he believed that man betrays himself whenever he contemplates himself in such estranged guise. There is a pathos of distance in man venerating a god who blinds us to our manhood. Blake approximates the Feuerbachian thesis in "The Everlasting Gospel":

> Thou art a Man, God is no more,
> Thine own Humanity learn to adore.

This would seem to be the Shelleyan thesis in *Prometheus Unbound*, the belief that man is divine. Blake, however, differs from both Shelley and Feuerbach because he is more concerned with the humanity of God than with the divinity of man. Blake is not really deicidal, though Shelley and Feuerbach are. Yet all three are fearful of man's alienating himself from himself.

It is paradoxical that such alienation of man from himself should have been one of the consequences of romantic idealism, for the romantics were those who so strongly affirmed the reality of selfhood, making consciousness an absolute. Yet at the same time there was a romantic tradition of thinking or feeling the world into existence; that is, they had their own way of reifying insofar as the world was identical with their idea of the world. Their world was the self in distanced form. At the height of the romantic idealism Schopenhauer took the world to be "my representation of the world"; to cease to represent the world was to annihilate the world. Insofar as the romantics thought or felt their world into existence their solipsism was not unlike the feat of the scientists who established the laws of nature by projecting their own logic into the world in alien and reified form. There is, after all, a certain resemblance between the so-called imperialism of the romantic vision of man as Prometheus and the imperialism of the mind as phrased in the iron laws of matter and motion, a positing of consciousness outside the self in a reality that is supposed to be "other."

Marx treated this kind of idealism as a variety of fetishism, the overestimation of thought erected into a system which then appears to exist outside the head, in reality.[20] Hegel was the great philosopher of such imperialism of the mind, for the substance of Hegel's world was Hegel's own reason: what could not be thought did not exist, and what existed was a construct of Hegel's mind imposed outside himself. Hegel's romantic imperialism was total, for the very existence of an object was an affront to his mind, and the "otherness" of things had to be denied by thinking them into being. To think of an object is to subdue its otherness by subjecting it to consciousness, thus establishing its reality. In Hegel, above all other romantic idealists, consciousness is an absolute. Hegel read history as the liberation of man's mind from the bondage of the world. In the first or Oriental phase of history spirit was immersed in matter, lacking the energy to release itself; the Greeks began to detach the Idea from the material in which it was submerged; the Romans established the realm of universal law, the *imperium Romanum* embodying the politics of the spirit; the Christian-mediaeval thinkers attained the realm of the eternal ideal; and the Germanic peoples reconciled spiritual and secular in an empire of Thought manifest in the State, objectifying the Ideal in the moral and political life. This is Thought at the zenith. Hegel makes a conquest of reality by the very act of cognition, which is also an act of appropriation. He gives final sanction to the Cartesian thesis that only what can be thought exists.

Marx referred to Hegel's system as "egoism raised to the level of thought," or "alienated science thinking itself," a simpler way of saying what Hegel himself wrote in his *Philosophy of Art* in a passage showing how mechanistic science and symbolist verse were extensions of this romantic imperialism:

> The universal demand for artistic expression is based on the rational impulse in man's nature to exalt both the world of his soul experience and that of Nature for himself into the conscious embrace of mind as an object in which he rediscovers himself. He satisfies the demand of this spiritual freedom by making explicit to his *inner* life all that exists, no less than from the further point of view giving a realized *external* embodiment to the self made thus explicit. And by this reduplication of what is his own he places before the vision and within the cognition of himself and others what is within him. This is the free ration-

ality of man, in which art as also all action and knowledge originates.

Long since, poetry and the other arts have returned from the Hegelian world of absolute thought, and the immodesty of scientific systems has been rectified by Wittgenstein, who answers Hegel, in effect, by stating, "Just as the only necessity that exists is *logical* necessity, so too the only impossibility that exists is *logical* impossibility." Matthew Arnold, also, when he visited the Grande Chartreuse, rebuked a century that had so recklessly imposed its ideas upon the world and then identified these ideas as reality:

> You give the universe your law,
> You triumph over time and space.

Romantic freedom was often a way, like scientific law, of conquering the world outside by thinking it into being, an aggrandizement that makes reason totalitarian and symbolizes man's spirit as the world outside. Keats called it, with good cause, the egotistical sublime. The romantic imperialism is inherent in Coleridge's notion of the shaping imagination of the poet, which creates another world by a will that diffuses, dissipates, in order to establish a realm of its own. Or, as Marx might say, the world is one's idea in reified form. The idea becomes a fetish.

The fetishism, the imperialism, reappears in Mallarmé's perfect poem, existing as pure Thought, an essence that can be envisioned only by a process of elimination—discarding from the Poem all that is "prose," that is, all reference to things. The perfect poem is the final ellipsis: what cannot be stated but only suggested. The Being that is pure is empty, exempt from the Chance that obscures the daily world, from the *Hasard* to which ordinary existence is subject, from the contingency that always attaches to the actual. The poem is an act of contemplation so distanced that objects cannot even be named. Mallarmé cries, "These last months have been terrifying. My

Thought has thought itself through and reached the Pure Idea." The ineffable, unwritten Poem, hypostatized as an absolute contour or constellation, has the Beauty of Nothingness, silent and alien from poet and reader. Mallarmé has thought himself into a realm where the poem reveals itself in a Being that is total estrangement. Such is the paradox of symbolism at its extreme, a poetry that started by using the object as hieroglyph, then finally obliterated or subtracted the object by absolute Thought, the supreme Hegelian art. Thought thinking itself is the suicidal poem, a structure of alienated language.

This reification of thought was only a heritage of the enlightened rationalism transmitted by Holbach and Godwin to romantics like Shelley. As heir of the *philosophes,* who were given to Cartesian rationality and faith in the reality of thought, Shelley illustrates this phenomenology of mind, which has little to do with the other materialistic side of his thought; he was both Platonist and materialist. At the height of his apocalyptic vision Shelley inhabits an indestructible order erected by his own conceptions, for the poet's mind creates its transcendent realm from thoughts each containing within themselves, as he says, the principles of their own integrity. Willing his ideas into existence, Shelley resists the tyranny of history by the tyranny of his ideas, achieving, like Hegel, an absolute freedom from Man:

> . . . free from guilt or pain,
> Which were, for his will made or suffered them.

He asked his friend Hogg: "What do I love? Do I love a person, the embodied identity? No! I love what is superior, what is excellent, or what I conceive to be so." As he admits in "Epipsychidion," love is a quest for his own idea embodied outside himself:

> In many mortal forms I rashly sought
> The shadow of that idol of my thought.

Shelley's imperialism of mind afflicts him with the romantic agony of attempting to structure the world as a mirror of his own consciousness. "Thou demandest what is love? It is that powerful attraction towards all that we conceive, or fear, or hope beyond ourselves, when we find within our own thoughts the chasm of an insufficient void, and seek to awaken in all things that are, a community with what we experience without ourselves." The community is not a union with what is outside the self, but devotion to an image or fetish created in one's own likeness, a "soul out of our soul," a being whose nerves "vibrate with the vibrations of our own." It is a monologue which demands not a response but, rather, an echo; and such romantics have been rightly called ventriloquists. This egocentric humanism is what repels Robbe-Grillet from every form of romantic or heroic tragedy, which demands from the world what the world does not give, and which leaves the self in tormenting isolation: "I call out. No one answers me. Instead of concluding that there is no one there, I decide to act as if there *were* someone there, but someone who, for one reason or another, will not answer." So the sound of our own cries at last stupefies us into believing we can be redeemed by the urgency of our own solitary voice. Shelley's solitary cries sounded to him like affirmations. His political idealism is a mode of ventriloquism, and his Promethean vision of the future is a mythology that at last leaves him alone with his dreams, enchanted by utopian distances.

Marx himself resorts to this utopian distancing, demanding from history the apocalyptic future on which he founded his own mythology. His vision of the final proletarian revolution and the instituting of a classless society after a phase of crude communism is as desperate and melodramatic as Shelley's democratic idealism. For melodrama is a category of thought inherent in the nineteenth century not only in Shelley's romanticism, but also in the Marxist dialectic, in Hegel's historical method, in

Tennyson's poetry, in Hardy's novels, in Ibsen's plays—
everywhere. Melodrama is another way of imposing ideas
on the world or creating a fictitious world of abstract
forces—good and bad—so that the characters are not
people but allegorical figures who conform to the preconceived scheme of action. That history can become melodrama by the imperialism of the mind is clear enough in
Shelley's lyrical drama; curiously enough, Marx distances
history in the same melodramatic way. The actors in this
Marxist melodrama ("the expropriators will be expropriated") are "collective personifications"—capitalist and
worker facing each other in a total ideological conflict
that brings in a new social order. The world is recreated,
as it is in Shelley's Prometheus melodrama. Shelley's figure of Demogorgon knows that Jupiter the tyrant must
unwittingly bring about his own fall by a "necessity" implicit in the world order. In the same vein Marx predicts
that the capitalist regime "brings forth the agencies for its
own destruction." Marx and Shelley are both intoxicated
by the urgency of their own solitary voices.

This melodramatic aspect of Marx's thought is symbolic and unhistorical, a romantic-rationalist prophecy
with a strong moral imperative behind it, like Shelley's
vision of the freedom to which man is destined when love
triumphs. Marx prophesies a moral reconstruction once
man understands the nature of the tyranny that has enslaved him: "From that moment new forces and new passions spring up in the bosom of society; but the old social
order fetters them. It must be annihilated. It is annihilated." Marx is at no greater pains than Shelley to
designate what happens during this moral overturn, except to indicate that it comes with an enlightenment—the
imperialism of mind. The utopianism of Shelley and
Marx, their mythology, is a way of escaping from time, a
distancing of what is not clearly understood. Their vision
of the future alienates them from history, just as Tennyson alienates himself from history by his vision of the "far
future."

Marx and Keats

Yet there is a less utopian, a less imperialistic, side of Marx's thought, for he is properly called a materialist, and if he resembles Shelley in his apocalyptic mythology, he resembles Keats in his materialism and his half-tragic understanding of the human condition. This is the side of Marxist thought that is not alienated, and the reciprocity between Marx and Keats, unlikely as it seems, is a kind of countermovement against the distancing so common in the nineteenth century.

Especially in his early essays Marx distrusted abstract thought; he has a Keatsian sense of "real things." Marx shares with Keats a belief that experience must be rooted in the senses, in nature, in history, in what is empirically known. In what could be a refutation of Hegel's idealism, Keats wrote, "Axioms in philosophy are not axioms until they are proved upon the pulses"; and Marx defines an idea as the outside world reflected in the mind. He knows, like Keats, that we estrange ourselves by rationalism, this being the theme of "Lamia," a poem that parallels Marx's attack upon Hegel's substituting thought for living. Although it is argued that Keats was gradually led to distrust poetic experience because it is not philosophic enough, he nevertheless regards Apollonius as chill, "a reasoning self-sufficing thing, an intellectual All-in-all." For Keats and Marx, as for Gautier, the world exists; it cannot be thought away or reasoned into being. Marx notes, "The fact that man is an embodied, living, real, sentient, objective being with natural powers means that he has real, sensuous objects as the objects of his being, or that he can only express his being in real, sensuous objects." Keats has his own way of saying this: "O for a life of sensations rather than of thoughts." In thus rephrasing the Hartleian psychology Keats repudiated the egotistical sublime.

Unlike Hegel, Keats and Marx derive thinking from existing, not existing from thinking; they invert the Cartesian maxim to read *Sum, ergo cogito,* or, as Ortega said, thought is a feature of our biography. Life for Keats and Marx is a dialogue carried on between the self and what is beyond the self, the *Umwelt* and the *Mitwelt*—the poet exists "partly on sensation, partly on thought." If this dialogue takes place, then a thing of beauty can be a joy forever since it is capable of exciting fresh responses. Marx stated that a being who fails to acknowledge what is outside himself is not a natural being, but estranged. Perhaps the closest parallel to Marx's epistemology is Keats's notion of negative capability in the poet who "has no identity" insofar as he is always "filling some other body—the sun, the moon, the sea and men and women who are creatures of impulse." The selflessness of this sympathetic identification, closing the distance between observer and observed, is illustrated when Keats writes that if a sparrow pecks about the gravel, "I take part in its existence and pick about the gravel." This experience is different from Shelley's identification of the skylark with himself, for Keats is identifying himself with the bird, not the bird with himself.

The capacity to extend one's existence into the existence of others is an act of the dramatic (not melodramatic) imagination, and Shelley himself once endorsed the Keatsian notion of negative capability by stating, "A man to be greatly good, must imagine intensely and comprehensively; he must put himself in the place of another and of many others; the pains and pleasures of his species must become his own." Yet as poet Shelley is seldom imaginative in this sense of surrendering himself or identifying himself with others, which is dramatic imitation as Aristotle understood it, a representation of reality instead of an affirmation of one's ideas only. Keats, not Shelley, had the tolerance of the dramatist, who can exist amid "uncertainties, mysteries, doubts, without any irritable reaching after fact and reason" to impose his vision arbitrarily. The man of achievement, Keats remarks, "especially in literature," has a "capability of submission" or "humility," a "neutral intellect." One thinks of Eliot's impersonal poetry; but Eliot was asking the poet's surrender to his medium, whereas Keats was asking surrender to "the Earth and its contents as materials to form greater things." Keats is closer to Wallace Stevens than to Eliot.

Certain novelists had this negative capability, notably Turgenev, who is among the great accepters able to exist amid uncertainties and doubts without irritable reaching after reason; his fiction thrives on the evidence furnished by men and circumstances in all its incoherence and inconclusiveness; his impartiality is more humane than the fictitious objectivity of the scientist. In a character like Bazarov he illustrates the irritable reasoning that gripped the idealist and scientific mentality in trying to think the world into being. Yet he holds Bazarov in the same focus with the other characters of the novel, and in so doing suggests the relevance of Keats's remark that men of genius "have no individuality, no determined character" because they can give themselves, like Shakespeare, to creatures as different as Desdemona, Caliban, Iago, Edmund, and Miranda.

Doubtless Nietzsche was justified in saying that the artist does not tolerate reality; yet Keats and Turgenev master reality without escaping from it or annihilating it by imperalism of the mind. Their art is an encounter with people and things, an address to what is outside the self, a concession to their existence without capitulating; for, as Keats says, the earth is the material from which he forms "greater things, that is to say, ethereal things." His poetry is an act of transcendence or rebellion that resists the world without rejecting it. Camus speaks of art as a creative rebellion that transforms without destroying, and Keats compares the poem to Adam's dream: "He awoke and found it truth." This dream is what Wallace Stevens calls the countergeography that the poet erects amid the geography in which he lives: "The real is only the base, but it is the base." The ethereal Keatsian dream is generated by things as they are, by sensations, the pulses, the sea, and the lives of men and women; it is a transcendentalism that has little in common with the transcendentalism that attained the ideal by negating or denying the actual. Carlyle, for example, keeps insisting that nature is only an appearance, a phantom, that matter is spirit, that things are mere transparent symbols. This nugatory transcendence rejects the empiricism with which Keats or Stevens or Turgenev begins.

From the experience in the flesh arises Adam's dream, the wild surmise, the aesthetic revelation like an epiphany. From the warm human pastoral, aching, is born the cold pastoral of abiding beauty. From the heard melodies come the unheard. So, also, Marx believed that only by plunging into history could man control history; only by being a member of a community can man realize his social being. By committing himself to history man revises history; by participating in the present, one insures the future: only through time is time conquered. Unlike Hegel, Marx saw that men create the state—the state does not create man, a fallacy of political idealism. Here again one must recognize the complexity of Shelley's romantic politics, for his *Philosophical View of Reform* is thoroughly Marxist in its materialism, its commitment to history, its justification of revolution. The insurrection in this document is quite unlike the visionary politics of *Prometheus Unbound;* it is not utopian, and however he may prefer negotiation, Shelley recognizes the right of the oppressed to wage a class war to change the existing situation.

The notion of transcending history by participating in it is close to the tragic notion of transcending suffering by suffering, and Marx's myth of the class war has certain tragic overtones. He insists that man is accountable for his own enslavement. Something of the same half-tragic sense of man's responsibility for his plight had appeared in Shelley's *Prometheus Unbound,* since Jupiter the tyrant is a figment of man's own mind, an image that will be dethroned when man thinks differently. Marx accuses man of being enslaved "through his own infamy." There is some tragic flaw bringing into Marxist mythology a note of human guilt, deficiency, or delusion, which must be faced, resisted, and transcended. Marx discerns man's ignominy, stupidity, and self-deception, which can hardly be thought out of existence as they are in Shelley. Following the Greek proverb *pathein, mathein,* Marx sees that "to be sentient is to suffer, to experience. Man as a sentient being is a suffering being, and since he feels suffering, a passionate being. Passion is man's faculties striving to attain their object. He is a being for himself, and as such has to authenticate himself in existence as well as thought." Or, as Keats said in his ode, to think is to be full of sorrow, perhaps despair. Marx does not transfer the pain to a Prometheus-image; man has suffered in history.

The sense that life is authenticated by suffering is stronger in Keats, who asks his brother, "Do you not see how necessary a world of pains and troubles is to school the intelligence and make it a soul? A place where the heart must feel and suffer in a thousand diverse ways . . . it is the text from which the Mind or Intelligence sucks its identity." He writes to Reynolds, again, that life is a mansion of many apartments, only the first of which he has so far entered: when we are young, we step into the infantile or thoughtless chamber, where we linger until we begin to think; then we no sooner enter the chamber of fancy than we are enchanted by pleasant wonders, intoxicating; but the heart sharpens the vision of man, showing that "the world is full of misery and heart break, pain, sickness, and oppression—whereby this chamber of

Maiden Thought becomes gradually darkened." Beyond, doors open to the dark passages to be explored if we are to validate ourselves in being as well as in thought. Marx's description of this validating is not so poetic; he simply notes that "consciousness is from the very beginning a social product, and remains so as long as men exist at all."

Since life determines consciousness, there must be a dialogue between the world and the self, a dialogue in which there is an I-Thou contradiction, or an I-It dialogue, as when Keats addressed himself to the sparrow or when Wordsworth entered into relation with the tree, the field speaking to him of something past. Keats entered this dialogue with the Elgin marbles, with the stony urn, with things that always spoke to him. Without this dialogue between man and things, man and man, living is an abstraction. It was often an abstraction for Shelley the poet, who in spite of his materialism was prone to confuse reality with his idea of reality. In this idealizing transcendence only the monologue is possible.

Pathos of Consuming

However, if Shelley venerated his thought, he did not fall victim to that other kind of reifying against which Marx rebelled—commodity fetishism. In his early essays Marx extended Feuerbach's notion of alienation, applying it to both Hegelian idealism and to the market. He argued that in both philosophy and economic life man is estranged from himself: first, because he worships himself in alien and unrecognizable form by presuming that his ideas are reality, and second, because he is controlled by the mechanism of production and exchange he has invented. The tyranny of the idea and the tyranny of the commodity are alike a result of man's tendency to reify, to deny his humanity by projecting it outside in alien forms that appear to be real, as when he equates his existence with what he owns or consumes. Marx took this materialism to be a loss of freedom.

The virtue of the romantics was their affirming the hegemony of the self, its incorrigible freedom. If at times Shelley, like other romantics, alienated himself by supposing that only his ideas were real, he did not fall victim to the sort of alienation common among the Victorians who revered prosperity. Macaulay, rejoicing in England's abundance, exclaimed, "The shopkeepers are richer." To make a fetish of the commodity is to obliterate the self by the Mammonism Carlyle so detested, and a great deal of Victorian literature is an incoherent attempt to salvage some of the personal identity that had dissipated among things.

In explaining commodity fetishism Marx pointed out that at first sight an item on the market seems to be a simple thing; yet in economic theory it transforms itself into "a very queer thing" abounding in mysterious values. If we take it as something useful, it is not mysterious at all: it is a product of labor, an artifact made from natural substances by man's industry. But as soon as it is thrown on the market to be exchanged, it loses its obvious meaning and becomes sacred or symbolic, endowed with charismatic importance, "changed to something transcendent." A kindred change occurs, Marx says, when light falls on an object, altering its appearance. When sold and bought, the commodity is transvalued into an image of social well-being, whatever its use may be.

By metamorphosis "commodities as use-values now stand opposed to money as an exchange value," and they become, numinously, symbols of prosperity, property, respectability, pleasure, or an evidence of productivity, which is taken to be an end in itself. The mystique of productivity was seductive. Carlyle, who despised *laissez faire* and the market, ardently preached that the ills of his time could be remedied by producing commodities: "Produce, produce," he cries. "Were it but the pitifullest infinitesimal fraction of a product, produce it in God's name." No matter if it be imperfect, shoddy, or needless, producing justifies itself as a sign of self-expression, duty, obedience, and all the obligations Carlyle denoted by the term Work.

As one of the most compulsive writers of an inner-directed age, Carlyle read into the very act of producing the moral imperatives which he hoped would cure England's Mammonism. He never asked whether production was itself a symptom of Mammonism, a brand of commodity fetishism. Consequently he hailed the Captain of Industry as a modern hero who can redeem us from the ills of our dismal existence, leading us out of the slough of materialism by producing things. Carlyle was, of course, writing in an era of a scarcity economy, and to this extent his solution is relevant: people did need goods. Yet he reveals the moral and psychological involvements of commodity fetishism. Driven as he is, he has the manic tone of Nietzsche; but he is utterly un-Nietzschean in his lack of the Dionysiac, or erotic, impulse. He shows only the self-tormenting spirit of Nietzsche, and in his frantic command to produce is heard a Calvinist law of duty. Carlyle is one of the most joyless writers of his age, urging us to express "the force that is within us" but wholly deprived of Blake's exuberance. His expressionist psychology derives not from Eros but the superego, converting Labor to Obedience, an urge that frustrates and represses. Activated by an impulse closer to hate than to love, Carlyle's morality of work is a version of despair, the opposite of Blake's energy, which is delight. This hysteria to produce is not creation but a blind activity like subjection, if not slavery (recommended for Negroes in one of Carlyle's ugliest essays).

Here is commodity fetishism moralized. Marx draws his own moral conclusion, namely, that under the spell of this magic the producer loses control of his social relations: "The product dominates the producer," and the worker is penalized by the anarchy of the market. Though Marx was concerned with the oppressed laborer, he also saw what commodity fetishism did to the middle class, corrupting it, making it philistine, as Arnold saw when he said that culture is not having something but being something. Commodity fetishism is a middle-class mode of reifying the world and alienating the person from himself. If the worker was alienated from the product of his work, the "capitalist" was estranged from himself by the goods he bought.

Insofar as existence is scaled to consumption it is a starved life, a self-defeating strategy of desire. As consumer, man loses himself amid possessions that become progressively useless, therefore alienating, as prosperity grows. One of the archetypal consumer personalities in fiction is Undine Spragg in *The Custom of the Country*. Edith Wharton's most destructive heroine, a figure who suggests that in middle-class society man is essentially a producer and woman essentially a consumer, is a Medusa who devastates her own life and the life of every man she meets by conspicuous consumption. She is a respectable Becky Sharp; her adventures are more limited in range than Becky's because they are only a market operation whereas Becky had the larger picaresque vocation of exposing all the frauds in *Vanity Fair*. Edith Wharton's novels are probably the most telling documents to support the theory being worked out by Lucien Goldmann on the sociology of the novel, a literary form he finds deeply influenced by the nineteenth-century economics of producing for the market. The fictional world in which Undine exists marks a consumer-phase of culture in which goods become autonomous and the person tends to disappear. Edith Wharton is already heading toward the *roman sans personnage* as written by Kafka, by Camus, by Nathalie Sarraute, by Beckett, by Robbe-Grillet.

A subtler and more complicated study of the strategy of desire is Flaubert's Emma Bovary, who reveals more inwardly than Undine Spragg the alienating effects of commodity fetishism. Emma is stupid, gross, and sordid, but she had romantic dreams of happiness—like the wistful yearning of Lamartine for *nouveaux rivages*—and she seeks a fulfillment of these dreams, which are not altogether illegitimate considering the leaden banality of her environment. At first Emma's dreams have a certain pathos; then she seeks to realize them by marketing satisfactions, by consumer pleasures. That is her downfall, for her dreams can never be realized by the coarse enjoyments at her disposal. The romantics dreamed of another world "beyond," and Emma at first alienates herself by such dreams. But if romantic dreams are alienating, even more so are the middle-class luxuries Flaubert so detested. Emma is estranged by consumer pleasures which can never content her, which debase the dreams to vulgar sensations. Frederic Moreau in *Sentimental Education* is another character caught between outdated romantic visions and consumer gratifications, though Frederic is less rebellious, less desperate, than Emma, less susceptible to injury, better able to compromise his way out.

One is tempted to say that Emma seeks whatever poetry there may be in consumer pleasures, the glamor of elegance seldom, if ever, felt by Balzac's characters, devoted as they are to the five-franc piece. Balzac's people exist in the marketplace, but Emma is a more human and depressing victim of the strategy of desire than anyone in Balzac, even Cousin Pons. Balzac studied the mentality of the exploiter and pitied the victims; but Emma is not innately an exploiter, however she exploited others, and she is her own victim. By nature she is simply a creature of uncontrollable middle-class cravings. The irony is that Emma is a middle-class girl trying to escape from the middle class by satisfying her desires; but her desires are devalued middle-class desires, which make mere elegance seem romantic. She is betrayed by the delusion that consumption can be happiness.

This is the sadder since Emma was temperamentally

capable of pleasure, seeking to abandon herself to Eros in a society that had banished Eros. Her body was the only endowment with which she could have met the demands of Eros—love in the flesh, or lust, might have been fulfillment. But her lust was perverted by her dreams, which unhappily were dreams of crass satisfactions, and she was led to worship idols of the middle class that stifled her and estranged her from her flesh. Emma was a petty-bourgeois Venus without any of the inhibitions that make the *bourgeoisie* prudential. She had the naïve or infantile sexuality that is repressed by the entrepreneur, who looks mean by contrast. Though she was incorrigibly foolish and self-deceived, she never seems as contemptible as the atrophied Homais, who symbolizes the desexualizing of the self by technology. Emma was willing, even eager, to surrender herself, to be possessed; yet she could not give herself fully to quasi-romantic scoundrels like Rodolphe and Léon, both as cautious as Homais. And Bovary, stupider than Emma, could not even dream.

Had Emma's dreams been only of passion, her rebellion might have amounted to a kind of heroism; at least she would have been true to her deeply erotic nature. But her romantic dreams were contaminated by her vulgar appetite for the ornate, her lower-class hedonism. The pathos in this perversion of desire is clear when Emma goes to the ball at the chateau, which glimmers before her eyes in a fantasy that is corroding, not liberating. As she enters, she is enveloped in warmth, perfumes, and the odor of truffles. "The silver dish-covers reflected the lighted candles in the candelabra, the cut crystal covered with light reflected from one to the other pale rays; bouquets were placed in a row the whole length of the table; and in the large-bordered plates each napkin, arranged after the fashion of a bishop's mitre, held between its two gaping folds a small oval-shaped roll." The lobsters, the quails, the fruit, the steward in silk breeches and white cravat, the porcelain stove inlaid with copper and surmounted by a statue of a woman all suggest to Emma "the complexion of wealth." The scene is a museum of middle-class expense.

So her dream changes, and she is seduced into confusing romance with consumption. The mistake is fatal. She disqualifies herself for romance and enters the long course of degradation that alienates her from herself until she is lost amid the indulgences of her middle-class tastes, which are embodied in the plush rented chamber in Rouen where she meets not a romantic but a merely Bohemian fate. Like one of Ionesco's people, she is finally lost amid furniture:

> The bed was large, of mahogany, in the shape of a boat. The curtains were of red levantine that hung from the ceiling and bulged out down toward the bell-shaped bed-side; and nothing in the world was so lovely as her brown hair and white skin standing out against this purple color, when, with a movement of shame, she crossed her bare arms, hiding her face in her hands.
>
> The warm room, with its discreet carpet, its wanton ornaments, and its calm light, seemed made for the intimacies of passion. The curtain rods, ending in arrows, their brass pegs, and the great balls of the andirons shone suddenly when the sun came in. On the chimney between the candelabra there were two of those large pink shells in which one hears the murmur of the sea.

The setting reminds us of the extravagance of George Moore's apartment in the rue de la Tour des Dames, Paris, in days when Moore gave himself to decadent Beauty: the hangings of red, the terra-cotta figurines, the cushioned seats and heavy canopies, the censers and Turkish lamps. The exotic Beauty of the aesthete is another phase of commodity fetishism, a devotion to luxuries different from Emma's luxuries only because they were *recherché*. Emma's devotion to elegance is an aestheticism *manqué*, commonplace, debased to philistinism.

Léon and Emma lunch by the fireside on a little round table inlaid with rosewood. Emma no longer dreams; she has capitulated to her bourgeois sensorium. As a small-town love goddess she was born for rapture—at least she was enchanted by what she read in novels. But she was too unsophisticated to understand that these raptures must be guarded as dreams. Here Frederic Moreau had an advantage, for he protected his vision of Mme. Arnoux by living with Rosannette, then by pursuing Mme. Dambreuse. The wisdom of Baudelaire and the symbolists was to protect their dream by distancing it into another world. The pathos of her dreaming might have made Emma a quite different heroine; but she ruined herself amid actualities. It has been said that we are all artists in our dreams. Emma's dreams were her capital, which she squandered by yielding to her appetites. Her adventures bring only deprivation; so when Rodolphe and the rest have left her, she is, too late, forced back upon the truth:

> What an abundance of illusions! Nothing was left of them now. She had got rid of them all in her soul's life, in all her successive conditions of life—maidenhood, her marriage, and her love—thus constantly losing them all her life through, like a traveler who leaves something of his wealth at every inn along the road.

There is a difference between Emma and that other small-town Venus, Eustacia Vye, who in Hardy's novel never has the chance to satisfy her consumer instincts by going to Paris. Consequently Eustacia has the privilege of dying a still-rebellious romantic figure, untainted by the Bohemianism that would have been her lot had she been able to indulge her desires as Emma did.

As Emma descends, there appears another less amiable aspect of her disposition, the need to exploit. She turns possessive, if not ruthless, revealing that other psychology of the marketing personality, the drive to own. Venus attaches herself to her prey. Thus Flaubert's novel brings in the theme of exploitation which Marx always associated with the theme of alienation. When the worker is exploited or treated as a machine to produce things, then the product stands over against him as alien, as a loss of his own being. "The worker puts his life into the object, and then his life belongs no longer to himself but to the object." The more he expends himself in his labor, "the more powerful becomes the world of objects which he creates in the face of himself," and the more impoverished is his existence. The worker is distanced from his product, itself his industrial persona, in which, however, he has no part when this product is thrown on the market. This economic distancing due to exploiting the worker has certain resemblance to the aesthetic distancing required in Art for the sake of Art, the impersonal theory of creating that so tormented the poet when he sacrificed himself for his Work (like Mallarmé's Book) standing over against himself as alien. Somewhat like the worker the artist is exploited by the tyranny that establishes Art as an absolute, impoverishing the self. If the worker is dehumanized, so is the writer.

The Ethic of Thrift

The recent reinterpretation of Marx as moralist should not have been necessary, since it is evident from *Capital* that Marx was always an evangelist as vehement as Carlyle, Dickens, or Ruskin, his political and economic theories being largely derived from his ethic, which repudiated the doctrines of leather-tongued liberals. And since his evangelism is so melodramatic, Marx is one of the masters of the grotesque. His theory of the class war leading to an overthrow of the exploiter is one more lurid Victorian fiction, distancing history toward a utopian future, much like William Morris's *Dream of John Ball*. In his preface to *Capital* Marx is at no pains to disguise his melodrama: "I paint the capitalist and landlord in no sense *couleur de rose.* I deal with individuals only so far as they are personifications of class interests." The villain is "our friend Moneybags." All this sounds very like Dickens writing *Hard Times* in 1854, or his *Christmas Carol* in 1843, the year when Carlyle finished *Past and Present* rejecting cash payment as the sole nexus between men.

Marx not only moralizes; he caricatures like Dickens or Daumier or Forain. *Capital* is only now being read as a dramatic action, an allegory of a struggle between forces of good and evil waged within man, who is divided against himself by greed and a desire to appropriate: "Capital is dead labour, that vampire-like, lives only by sucking labour, and lives the more, the more labour it sucks." Is this the vocabulary of political science? It is a language with which Dickens describes Carker with his traplike white teeth. As one of the great mythologists of his day, Marx has an apocalyptic vision of revolution not unlike Blake's: "Along with the diminishing number of capitalists grows the mass of misery, oppression, slavery, degradation, exploitation; but with it too grows the revolt of the working class. The knell of capitalist private property sounds. The expropriators are expropriated." The so-called scientific Marxists have misread the text and the cast of thinking behind it, a theatrical vision that cannot be translated into politics of expediency without robbing it of its moral meaning.

The ethic of Marx's myth is in his sardonic pages on appropriation as a motive that estranges man from himself, causing us to lead a surrogate existence in the affluence that lives for us:

> The less you are, the less you express your life, the more you have, the greater is your alienated life and the greater is the saving of your alienated being. Everything which the economist takes from you in the way of life and humanity he restores to you in the form of money and wealth. And

everything which you are unable to do your money can do for you; it can eat, drink, go to the ball and to the theatre. It can acquire art, learning, historical treasures, political power; and it can travel. It can appropriate all these things for you, can purchase everything; it is the true opulence.

Marx's rather naïve hatred of money echoes what the eighteenth century often said about luxury, and his abhorrence of Mammon places him in the long tradition of those who have seen wealth as evil. Marx's only originality is his perception that money is a symbol of power, a vehicle of appropriation, a means of distancing man from himself. Again Marx is more concerned with ethic and psychology than with economics, for he takes acquisition to be a way to suicide. By appropriating, the "capitalist" creates a domain standing over against himself, impoverishing his own life; so capitalist as well as worker is dehumanized by the system of production. Scrooge is Dickens's image of this trauma, and an array of characters in Balzac—in *Cousin Pons,* in *Eugènie Grandet,* in *Le Père Goriot*—extends Marx's analysis of the alien "capitalist" temperament. One thinks, too, of the poet's impotence and sense of exile before the Beauty of Herodias, symbol of a suicidal Art, inhumane, yet voluptuous.

The alienation of the self by acquisition has been an abiding theme in literature since the renaissance, and the motive of thrift has been closely associated with the acquisitive society that may, or may not, be due to the reformation. In the thrift-motive we again meet the technological mind concerned with economy, precaution, and all the calculation that Valéry identified with method. Marx was fascinated with the thrift-motive, which Weber and Tawney have treated as a puritan syndrome. Whether puritanism is a feature of the "capitalist" mentality or vice versa, a paradoxical "worldly asceticism" marks the protestant ethic, averse as it is to self-indulgence and expenditure, yet eager to lay up treasure (for sufficiency may be a token of grace). Disliking idleness and improvidence, this ethic is originally and steadily congenial to a technological discipline that achieves "methodical control of the whole man." Whether the asceticism of an acquisitive society is due to a protestant obedience to one's "calling" or whether protestantism merely permeated every social activity with devotional attitudes, the business man in any case became "a practical ascetic," and his religion "canonized as an ethical principle the efficiency which economic theorists were preaching as a specific for social disorders." The motives inherent in the reformation (and counter reformation) were cognate with motives in the early capitalism that emphasized thrift—motives that are fully expressed in our technology, devoted as it is to total efficiency. And always behind this puritan ethic is the strange contradiction between parsimonious or ascetic methods in production and the extravagant consumption of our gross surplus of products, on which we must spend lavishly in the name of prosperity.

In his 1844 essays Marx dwelt on the ethic of *laissez faire:* "Political economy, the science of wealth, is therefore, at the same time, the science of renunciation, of privation, and saving." It is, he says, among the moral sciences, and its dictates do not fully reveal themselves until we strip it of its pleasure-seeking mask. Marx sees that the theory of economy conceals a conflict between what is moral and what is enjoyable, between parsimony and superfluity: "Everything which goes beyond the most abstract need (whether it be a passive enjoyment or a manifestation of personal activity) is regarded as a *luxury.*" In its primitive phase capitalism reveals the incompatibility of its two basic drives, toward economy of means and excessiveness of ends. After all, this is one basic conflict in *Lear,* as it is in *Père Goriot;* for when Goneril asks her father why he needs more than five and twenty servants—why even ten, or five, or one—she phrases a maxim on which Taylorism operates. And Lear gives the proper answer, namely, that human life ceases to be human when efficiency is the sole criterion:

> O reason not the need. Our basest beggars
> Are in the poorest things superfluous;
> Allow not nature more than nature needs,
> Man's life's as cheap as beast's.

Lear discovers that according to economy, "Age is unnecessary."

But *laissez faire* is devoted to spending as well as saving, extravagance as well as parsimony, and one of Marx's penetrating comments summarizes the paradox inherent in capitalism from its first days: "Capitalism is destroyed at its very foundation if we assume that its compelling motive is enjoyment instead of the accumulation of wealth," that is, if we assume we should be prodigal instead of frugal. In the conversion of Scrooge from stinginess to charity Dickens epitomizes the polar opposites in the capitalist mentality. Even behind our new economy of expenditure there remains the ideal of efficiency, that primal asceticism, the engineer's thrift.

In principle political economy was, even during the renaissance, given to productivity, enjoyment, abundance, prosperity, and what might be called pleasure; but the psychology behind this principle was a spare puritan urge to save, renounce, and repress pleasure in the interest of prudence, discipline, and security. Already in an era of expanding machine productivity Marx saw the opposition between laissez-faire ideals of thrift and laissez-faire ideals of consumption. Freud designated this opposition by the terms Unlust and Lust. If there is a puritan repression of pleasure, man stands in a hate-relation to his world, and if pleasure means only consuming, man transfers his existence to the things that live a surrogate life for him. Either way he is alienated. Furthermore, consuming is not a truly libidinous act, but an act

(163

of appropriation that can make man, as Marx noted, a tension-ridden being dominated by his property.

As moralist, Marx saw the motive of gain expressing itself in the accumulation of money, an instrument for living outside the self, a reifying or distancing that parallels the distancing of scientific law. He also understood that money represents more than greed or luxury (the old moral connotations); it is an instrument of power—again like science. In fact Marx's originality as moralist arises from his extension of an old ethical judgment into the whole area of economic life, controlled as it was by a new industrial order. He modernized ethics and in so doing discovered that capitalism—that is, an industrial economy—involves certain psychological attitudes toward gain, frugality, expenditure, appropriation, and science. Marx left his psychological analysis of the capitalist mentality in great disorder, but it is at least as important as his myth and his economics and raises many of the questions Freud dealt with. In studying the era of primitive accumulation Marx detects that behind the renaissance magnificence there is a mentality of thrift, a mentality which dominates not only the early phases of an acquisitive society but the later industrial and technological regimes.

Some of Marx's shrewdest analysis of the psychology of thrift is found in his digressions on Shakespeare, for Marx seems to have sensed that Shakespeare, writing in an age of primitive accumulation, furnishes, almost prophetically, a full spectrum of characters who exemplify the attitudes of the so-called capitalist mentality, a mentality that is acquisitive, puritan, prodigal, parsimonious, and technological. We speak of Shakespeare as our contemporary; he is never more contemporary, as Marx knew, than in this scrutiny of acquisitive society with its contradictory psychology, and he projects most of the themes later treated by not only Marx but Weber, Tawney, Freud, and recent social psychologists. Possibly Marx may have found his new ethic in Shakespeare.

The gulf between Marx the conventional moralist and Marx the modern social psychologist appears when he comments upon *Timon of Athens,* a play dealing with "the nature of money" and the withering effects of greed. This drama is almost a morality play, and Marx is less sophisticated than usual in discussing its obvious meaning. With great gusto Marx quotes Timon's set speech on "yellow, glittering, precious gold" that makes black white, foul fair, wrong right. In this savage action Shakespeare strips bare the Shylock theme, detaching it from any Jewish implications and bringing it directly to bear upon the gentile: "What a god's gold, that he is worshipped in a baser temple where swine feed." The association of money with cruelty—which is merely grotesque in Shylock—is openly revealed in *Timon,* an allegory to illustrate Marx's own axiom, "The less you are, the more you have, the greater is your alienated life." Timon learns that possessions are not inalienable; in his society to lose one's goods is to lose one's being. Powerful as the rhetoric may be, *Timon* is a hackneyed fable lacking the refinements of other plays on acquisition and alienation, for which gold and greed are inadequate symbols. Yet Marx's overestimation of this play leads us to reinterpret him as a writer of mythical imagination "nourished on Aeschylus and Shakespeare," in whom he traces the outlines of his own morality and psychology.

Elsewhere and often Shakespeare played finer variations on the theme of thrift, variations that were coarsened by Marx, Balzac, Ibsen, and many later writers. Knowingly or unknowingly Shakespeare treats thrift as a puritan motive to which he is hostile. Thrift, puritanism, and hate are cluster-motifs in Shakespearean drama with subtle and far-reaching associations.

Of course we think of Shylock; yet Shylock is only incidental to Shakespeare's larger rejection of the morality of thrift. In fact when Shylock tells Antonio that thrift is a blessing if men steal not, he only tangles the ethical question, for we are supposed to hate Shylock; and yet the Jew has voiced the postulate on which Elizabethan middle-class enterprise was beginning to prosper. Clearly Shylock is a better business man than either the feeble Antonio, who is negative, ineffectual, improvident, or the wastrel Bassanio. The real question is not economic but moral and psychological: is thrift the same as greed? If thrift is greed, then thrift is funny, or at least contemptible. So far as Shylock is merely greedy, we can laugh him out of existence as a harmless grotesque, a figure surviving from a morality play. But Shylock is thrifty, and with his sober house and scorn of gaiety is a better puritan than anyone in the drama. And insofar as he suggests the power over others that can be gained by acquisition or enterprise, Shylock is a sinister figure to be feared. Meanwhile the gentiles thrive in their own reckless and romantic way. Bassanio thrives, like Antonio, by a kind of luck or fortune that resembles lottery; he falls into wealth not by Shylock's enterprise but, like one of the heroes in a Scott novel, by a risk and venture that has nothing to do with the market. In Belmont gold is a romantic value; yet it is associated with death, as Morocco finds when he opens the golden casket. The moral problem of thrift is faced only on the Rialto, where it is disguised in a good deal of theatrical rhetoric about the unalterable course of laws that cannot be revised lest "the trade and profit of the city" be impeached. The quality of mercy itself seems to be, in the language of the law, a surplus return that is twice blessed: ethical compound interest or unearned increment.

Thrift is a problem for the gentile, not the Jew, since Shylock is quite definitive and honest about the worth of thrift as a basic economic motive. Jessica thrives when she turns gentile by gilding herself with ducats she filches from her father. One of the most baffling psychological responses in the play is the fatigue, the weariness, that afflicts both Portia and Antonio, who are inexplicably sad. Is not Portia's weariness, at least, a symptom that attends consumption? She is fatigued by surfeit; she suffers the malaise of an affluent society. In this play the Jews produce and the gentiles consume. The gentile will to acquire is projected upon the vigorous Shylock, and the gentile prodigality, or wasteful (conspicuous) consumption, causes a depression that bears some of the marks of *ennui,* if not nausea. Thus the drama confuses or evades its own premises, for both getting and spending are romanticized, caricatured, or otherwise disguised by the gentiles.

If Shylock is averse to feasting and music, he is not repressed, as Antonio seems to be. Bassanio is wholly unrepressed, but, then, unhappily, Bassanio is a spendthrift who lacks Shylock's sobriety and prudence. Again like one of Scott's heroes, Bassanio is curiously passive, his success coming by dowry. Antonio is sober enough, but a shadow of a capitalist, an uninsured adventurer whose misfortunes have an air of undeserved bad luck. Antonio evades the risk by which profit is justified; as adventurer, he is a photographic negative of buccaneers like Sir Walter Raleigh. Yet Antonio is not rejected, as Shylock is, although Shylock more truly represents Elizabethan mercantile enterprise than the predatory Raleigh. Shylock's prudence, worldly asceticism, and self-righteous orthodoxy are refused along with his ducats, which betoken his alienated life. In Belmont ducats betoken fulfillment of life by unthinking lavish expenditure. Bassanio's outlays seem morally acceptable *because* they are so imprudent; and this recklessness perfectly sustains Marx's thesis that capitalism is destroyed at its foundation if we take enjoyment instead of accumulation as a primary motive. Shylock accumulates and Bassanio enjoys. But Shylock is a more potent figure than Bassanio; we cringe from his power though we disdain his gold. Shylock's gold is comic, but his thrift is menacing: his power is puritanical, having some of the threat of Calvinist despotism. Conversely, Bassanio's imprudence seems to be a commendable thrift—getting on by happy chance, not by work, saving, common sense, or asceticism.

In any case Shylock's thrift is an innocent—even naïve —motive when compared with other manifestations of thrift and enterprise in Shakespeare. Beside Polonius, Shylock is a wholesome, forthright figure. Hamlet's contempt for Polonius is rooted in his distaste for the thrift that seeks a good marriage for one's daughter. To thrive like Polonius, not dulling one's palm with entertainment or wearing more costly habit than one should buy, is a mean business even if one neither lends nor borrows. The middle-class Polonius, more negligible than usurious Shylock, belongs in a Balzac novel. Also, just as Balzac does not know what to do with Vautrin, who thoroughly understands the thrifty game, Shakespeare does not know what to do with Shylock. But he knows what to do with Polonius, whom we see in an unchanging focus.

Thrift, thrift, says Hamlet about his uncle's wedding, which is furnished with morsels from his father's funeral. Hamlet cannot bring himself to thrive like either Claudius or Polonius. He feels a more fastidious puritanism, recoiling from thrift in every form, whether social climbing or the new game of power politics begun by his thriving uncle. Nor is Hamlet deceived when Claudius's enterprise is disguised in the romantic adventure of Fortinbras; just as Julien Sorel sees the vanity of Napoleonic ambition, Hamlet's disabused mind reads Fortinbras's military heroism as folly: winning an acre that will not hold the slain is not honor but absurdity, a disease of statecraft. Then there is Osric, a knave spacious in the possession of dirt, living by a kind of thrift we see again in superserviceable scoundrels like Oswald, one of the rats whose instinct for being useful is profoundly immoral. Oswald can bite atwain the holy bonds of the family. Rosencrantz and Guildenstern are of the same ilk and do not lie near Hamlet's conscience when they are butchered according to plan.

To thrive by serving: that is the most debasing perversion of thrift. Osric belongs with Uriah Heep. The excess of venom Shakespeare spills over such creatures is like Marx's response to the business man whose "service" is a kind of pimping: "The entrepreneur accedes to the most depraved fancies of his neighbour, plays the role of pander between him and his needs, awakens unhealthy appetites in him, and watches for every weakness in order, later, to claim remuneration for this *labour of love.*" Marx and Shakespeare view this marketing orientation as a loathsome corruption of what is authentic. Polonius is nobody; his existence is only a way of getting on, as Ruskin called it. He is a functionary, a man without qualities. Or, as Marx says, serviceability makes everything venal—even Ophelia. This sort of thriving is often seen in comedy of manners, as in *Love's Labour's Lost,* or in Jane Austen, Thackeray, and Henry James. Here the touch is light, though personages like Boyet are offensive to the outgoing Berowne, who accuses them of kissing away their hand in courtesy. Boyet is a pliable comedy-of-manners type, useful without being vicious, accessible without being dangerous.

The vicious serviceable type is Iago, with his profane self-interest, blind, exploiting all idyllic relations. The gross stupidity of Iago's laissez-faire ethic is in his advice to Roderigo: put money in thy purse. This extreme of puritan thrift is mere literal-mindedness, for Iago knows the price of everything and the value of nothing. His cleverness is myopia in acute form; he is sure that a good woman is fit to suckle fools, that Desdemona is full of game, that her wine is made of grapes. This practicality is worse than cynicism because it is utterly blind to any possibility of another view of things: the facts speak for themselves. One of the psychological overtones in Iago is his joylessness, a brand of puritan deprivation or deficiency. He is lively enough, but his comedy, in spite of its resiliency, does not give pleasure—only sport. Iago remarks to Roderigo: "If thou canst cuckold him, thou dost thyself a pleasure, me a sport." Is it overinterpreting to find this contrast between pleasure and sport a key to Iago's comedy, which is a game played not for pleasure but for the technological skill with which moves can be made? There is something inhibited, disciplined, and parsimonious about Iago's machinations: he goes at evildoing with a consciousness of method, a kind of gamesmanship, though he is stone blind about the reasons why the game should be played anyhow. There is something of the same overesteem of skill in *Dombey and Son,* where Dickens reincarnates Iago's naked self-interest in the person of Carker, who can win at chess though he plays with his back to the board. Iago's sport is an aspect of thrift: a perversion of comedy or play, which should be creative and cathartic. Iago deprives play of its ebullience, diminishes it to a technique, a shrunken puritanical strategy.

Iago's most expedient thrift is knowing how to value himself, an ultimate egoism deprived of all generosity. Iago is a pander, but more nihilistically, he is an entrepreneur in an enterprise that negates pleasure. Iago is frigid. He speaks, but cannot feel, the language of lust, and is more glacial than Lady Macbeth, who has repressed her sexuality. Iago's rationality is a living death, for he stands off—as the scientist was supposed to do—to see what happens, objectively, without any involvement, any need to participate. He is a *voyeur,* and his manipulations of others, making them puppets, is a corruption of drama, which he beholds without being moved. Iago performs gratuitous experiments, unaware of the directions in which they lead. He is the ultimate of irrelevant curiosity, an antiself or negated self, exempt from human experience, unable to touch, share, commune: he can only distance things. He cannot even consume; he can only exploit.

His extreme—almost technological—practicality, his

eagerness for immediate results, lead him to calculations ingenious about means but confused about ends. Thus his methods are blind expedients or opportunism. Iago is not truly Machiavellian, since there is no clear or beneficial intent behind his diabolism. We speak of his motiveless malignity; but there is a motive after all: Iago is disturbed by exuberance, cannot tolerate pleasure. Yet he has a vivid notion of what is immediately useful, though he has no long-range idea of utility. For him the value of a thing is its availability at the present instant. Thus his sense of time is foreshortened, since he sees the next moment so clearly but is blind to the future: "Now, now, even now," he tells Brabantio, Desdemona is being tupped. Strangle her *tonight*, he prompts Othello. This urgency of the instant is an aspect of Iago's compulsion, his enterprise, his efficiency. It is the time-scheme of the meddler, the restless exploiter. There are, in fact, two time-schemes in the play: Othello's barbaric slow and homogeneous time—the time of patience, which he learns to discard—and the punctual, driven, neurotic, and disintegrative time of Iago's commercial impulse to do it *now.*

Iago's practicality is competition without a code, an initiative that enables him to give everything a name and thus exploit it. By using language in a magical way Iago can muster the "facts." Like some advertising agent he specializes in words: virtue is only a name, and reputation is signified by a handkerchief. Othello's exuberant self is destroyed when he invites Iago to name: "Give thy worst of thoughts the worst of words." So Othello murders his wife in the name of a cause he cannot name, but which Iago names. Iago's precision in naming is a technological feat—and also a fallacy of exactitude. Iago can name his own "price," a term denoting the magical accuracy of market operations, with their necessary markup. His anxiety about his price is a sign of his alienation from himself: "I am not what I am." Iago is not what he is almost as the price affixed to a commodity does not reveal what it is. Iago's very existence is a groundless phenomenon like "market value." Yet Iago is able to contaminate every value and virtue by his exact and practical definitions.

Throughout Shakespeare thrift is associated with accurate calculation, distrust of enjoyment, and the asceticism which cannot imagine the fuller meaning of charity, that surplus value causing Prospero, facing his criminal brother, to say there is a rarer action in virtue than in vengeance. The opposite of thrift is generosity, forgiveness, mercy, and the magic of a sea-change—it does not make much difference what we call it. It is, as Posthumus says in *Cymbeline*, a canceling of cold bonds, the contracts on which Belmont and the Rialto acted.

The fiercest expression of the thrift motive, this time in anarchic form, is found in Lear's unnatural daughters, who are aware that thriving means aggression, the will to power. In them the Shylock threat is clearly phrased: if one is really to thrive, one must have no scruples ("Father, being weak, seem so"). Regan's command, with its icy logic, shows her equipped to survive in any open market, the most unregulated, that is. Thrift ends in exploitation—Shylock, Polonius, Iago, then Lear's pelican children. Their ruthlessness is the polar opposite of that other aspect of power which is manifest in Blake and Nietzsche as exuberance. The joyless deity presiding over the Lear-world is the Nature-goddess invoked by Edmund, who hopes to thrive because the gods stand up for bastards hotly conceived in stealth, thus having the energy lacking to decent fops begot lawfully in honest beds. The play is nearly a development of Freud's thesis that hate is older than love, Eris than Eros; and living by this elemental discord raises a tempest that spills nature's germens, makes reason irrelevant, and alienates man from what Freud called reality (as Marx had already noted, appropriation is alienation, and alienation is appropriation).

Possibly the most alarming single remark in Shakespeare is Edgar's lament that we do not mature until we learn to hate, that we would not age if we did not hate:

> . . . World, world, o world!
> But that thy strange mutations make us hate thee,
> Life would not yield to age.

One of the deeper Marxist meanings of *Lear* is the alienation or abuse of power, which dehumanizes and which involves a problem nearly technological in a very modern sense: namely, the dis-relationship between excess and parsimony, between superfluity and efficiency. It is a play of monstrous excess, which "distribution" cannot undo; here the "superfluous and lust-dieted man" exists in a world dominated by a law of ruthless utilitarianism, the final human engineering that makes age unnecessary. The disjunction between overabundance and parsimony is almost symbolic of a society that produces efficiently and consumes excessively, insanely, in the name of pleasure. Is this the reason why in the Lear-world the act of generation, the supreme pleasure, produces menacing children who are pitiless in their will to control? In such a world the gods stand up for bastards, the thankless ones with serpent's teeth; or as Marx said, we acquire poverty as well as wealth under this dispensation. In a very literal economic sense the unsolved problem of the Lear-world is distribution. Luxury and efficiency: the incompatible values of the Lear-world and middle-class society as Marx saw it in its hideous rashness. Both cause estrangement.

Luxury has other meanings in *Antony and Cleopatra,* for this play negates the psychology of thrift. Here luxury is transformed to pleasure; Egyptian lust is transvalued to Elysian delight. In this phase of excess Antony kisses away kingdoms while Caesar wins his empire by prudence and restraint. Caesar represents the puritan character in its most creditable worldly enterprise: cautious without being frugal, ambitious without being ungenerous, sane without being meanly practical, efficient without being inhuman, Caesar is imperial in his own right. Nor, in spite of his affection for his sister, is he repressed or neurotic. By all sober verdicts Caesar deserves to win after Antony returns to his Egyptian dish. Caesar's worldly asceticism versus Antony's prodigality and outrageous, headlong expenditure expresses a conflict within the renaissance, possessed as it was by ideals of policy and power, strategy, magnificence, magnanimity, and abundance. Marx referred to it as "a Faustian conflict between the passion for accumulation and the desire for enjoyment." When enjoyment is the aim, power no longer corrupts. Antony is committed to a waste that is salutary, not destructive, as it is in *Lear*. As hedonist who has no calculus, Antony stands over against Bentham the methodologist.

At the start of this play of rashness, Antony says that kingdoms are clay, turning his back on Machiavellian politics with one imprudent phrase—our dungy earth feeds beast and man alike. The nobleness of life is a love that cannot be reckoned, a foolish irrational abandonment leading him and Cleopatra, at last, beyond the Nile to an Elysium where Dido and Aeneas come to see the pleasure of those who have expended their wealth and their luck. So abundance becomes joy, recklessness becomes virtue, luxury becomes transcendence, and generosity becomes redemption. The presiding deity is Eros, whose creature is Charmian, a fertility image less imperial than Cleopatra but more elemental. Her palm bespeaks the fecundity of the Nile. Antony's bounty knows no winter; it is an expense of spirit that lifts others, as when he breaks Enobarbus's canny heart by sending his treasure after him. Having known the unthrifty Antony, Cleopatra sees that it is paltry to be Caesar. Thus Shakespeare fills out the spectrum of his drama on the theme of thrift with all its adhesions, moral as well as economic and psychological.

The Ethic of Waste

Such unthrifty pleasure is also the basis for an aesthetic, as Marx and Ruskin saw. It has been argued that as Marx first conceived it, communism is an aesthetic as well as an economic and moral revolution.[21] Under a communistic society "the alienated world" of industrial activity would eventually yield to an artistic world where work would become joy—a joy forever, as Ruskin and Morris have it, because the artisan could fulfill himself in his work, making labor humane and creative. Transforming economic life to an aesthetic activity requires the discarding of a hollow technological notion of waste: waste as inefficiency. The puritan premises must go.

A privative and repressive notion of waste is itself wasteful because it leads to frustration. The most satisfying human experience presumes an acceptance of the principle that man is natively a wasteful creature who lives by necessary inefficiencies and irrational expenditure of his energies and talents. Andrew Bradley proposed that if tragedy is the highest representation of human experience, it grants the premise that in the fulfilled life there is always waste—a waste of virtue, noble intention, intelligence, and effort. The technological axiom of equal, or commensurate return for expenditure denies the disproportions in tragic events, which cannot be made to balance. When man is able to realize his nature, there is an expense of spirit that cannot be justified by any equation he can write. Aristotle referred to the tragic hero as one who because of his blunder suffers a misfortune that is *anaxion*—in excess of what might be expected.

Art is a mode of waste, a desire to make something for the satisfaction of making it as well as for its utilitarian worth. As the most imitative of creatures man expends himself in making what is superfluous, and the superfluity

(175

of effort should be in creating rather than consuming. Ruskin makes this principle the basis for his interpretation of gothic, which is not only functional but decorated. Indeed, Ruskin detects the fallacy behind so-called functional architecture insofar as it is focused upon utility rather than upon the uncalculating instinct to "spend in luxury" what will stand as a memorial to our pleasure as well as to our needs. Gothic decoration qualifies the law of parsimony in building.

Every sociologist seems to have recognized the relevance of Daniel Bell's statement: "If one is to deal meaningfully with the loss of self, of the meaning of responsibility in modern life, one must begin again with concrete problems, and among the first of these is the nature of the work process itself, the initial source of alienation. . . . Few individuals think of 'the job' as a place to seek any fulfillment." Technological control manifesting itself in various kinds of management, personnel, and marketing analysis has made work, and even some professions, inartistic. The most sinister response to such technological control is the new cynicism of those who detect that the job can be made a fulfillment if the control is more complete. The proposal now is that the scientific management of the past broke down because its indices did not extend into the wider social context, which can convert human engineering into sociology, a pseudoscience so embracing that conditioning can become, unlike the old Taylorism, total. It is apparent that the new Bohemianism of youth is merely a way of signing off from an economy so very amenable to this total conditioning.

Bohemianism may not be, however, the only or the advantageous response to this threat, for it begins to look as if the most implausible but most genuine refuge or resistance may be the one recognized by Marx, by Ruskin, by Morris, and by their disciples like Lewis Mumford and Sir Herbert Read: namely, what we call art. Subservient as the artist may have been to past societies, to patronage, to the market, it remains prevailingly true that the artist has been very resistant to conditioning. If it is true that our economic life is now a means of alienation, then William Morris said in one sentence almost all that can be said on this score: "The thing which I understand by real art is the expression by man of his pleasure in labour," a pleasure that gives happiness to maker and user. Morris was echoing what Ruskin, his master, wrote in a Victorian-sounding essay, "A Joy Forever": "Now, we have warped the word 'economy' in our English language into a meaning which it has no business whatever to bear. In our use of it, it constantly signifies merely sparing or saving; economy of money means saving money—economy of time, sparing time, and so on." Our post-Keynesian economy of expenditure does not really invalidate Ruskin's judgment, for the idea of abundant consumption is still at odds with the parsimonious and efficient methods we invoke in production and marketing, a situation that causes a kind of social dissociation of sensibility, a conflict between the psychology of man as consumer and the psychology of man as producer or marketer. He consumes indulgently but produces and markets puritanically, a maladjustment as severe as any caused by the division of labor. Thus the problem of work remains unresolved under advanced technologies that are Taylorism wearing a modern mask.

The job will not be a fulfillment until technology is more thoroughly penetrated by the economy of art, which requires an irrational expenditure. The expenditure in art is not, after all, a waste, but a therapy for the alienations that have afflicted even the so-called professions, not to mention business. Ruskin instinctively recognized the human need for "the uncalculating bestowal of the wealth of labour," which produced gothic ornament: "I believe the right question to ask, respecting all ornament, is simply this: Was it done with enjoyment— was the carver happy while he was about it?" Of course the mediaeval carver may not have been happy; yet Ruskin properly identifies "the necessity of the whole man being in his work; the body must be in it." Ruskin anticipates those who are now seeking in art what the clinic does not give, or what art can give better—the humanizing of economic life according to the principle that "art is valuable or otherwise, only as it expresses the personality, activity, and living perception" of the artisan. Earlier, in his "Notes" to *Queen Mab*, Shelley had accepted the same principle that "there is no real wealth but the labour of man." If work is artistic, it is a means of affirming life, not a surrogate for life or an estrangement from life. The technician who offers things in such abundance often distances producer and consumer from himself. Or, as Jung says, "The secret of artistic creation and of the effectiveness of art is to be found in a return to the state of participation." Jung uses the term "participation mystique." But it not a mystique. It is an imperative to offset technological sterility.

V

Participation

Style and Pleasure

A GREAT DEAL of nonsense has resulted from Jung's notion that art is an address to the collective unconscious, that the artist participates in a communal selfhood symbolized by archetypes. The obvious fact is that the renaissance brought into modern culture an indelible sense of individuality—economically, religiously, politically, artistically; and any tenable idea of participating must come to terms with this sense of individuality—which, after all, is estimable. And it is Freud, not Jung, who furnishes an idea of participating without making art a mystique of communal archetypes. Our way to this conclusion will, however, be indirect.

Jung's distrust of individualism appears in his charge that the protestant was an iconoclast who left our world with an alarming poverty of symbols. Yet John Ruskin probably gave a sounder appraisal when he remarked at the opening of *The Stones of Venice* that the corrupt religion of the renaissance found itself facing two adversaries, "Protestants in Germany and England, Rationalists in France and Italy; the one requiring the purification of religion, the other its destruction. The Protestant kept the religion, but cast aside the heresies of Rome, and with them her arts, by which last rejection he injured his own character, cramped his intellect in refusing to it one of its noblest exercises, and materially diminished his influence. . . . The Rationalist kept the arts and cast aside the religion." The effects of rationalism he describes at the opening of *Deucalion:* ". . . by substituting analysis for sense in morals, and chemistry for sense in matter, we have literally blinded ourselves to the essential qualities of both matter and morals. . . . And still, with increasingly evil results to all of us, the separation is every day widening between the man of science, and the artist —in that, whether painter, sculptor, or musician, the latter is pre-eminently a person who sees with his Eyes, hears with his Ears, and labours with his Body."

During our own day there has been a *rapprochement* between the arts and science in that both have returned to thinking with the body, giving cause to hope that the old rationalism has worn itself out, or is doing so. Thinking with the body is craft, and the difference between craft and technology can be defined by the pleasure that accrues from work serving (again in Ruskin's phrase) as "expressions of the mind of manhood by the hands of childhood." Of late technology has been touched by the joy of finding in its solutions the play of intellect that satisfies man's need to invent. Pier Luigi Nervi has said that today, "Even within the realm of the most rigorous technology, the mind remains and will remain completely free and able to express, interpret and manifest its most profound and mysterious creative forces."[22] Furthermore in the most advanced technologies there is a return to the craftsman's empiricism, the kind of thinking with the body that was done by Leonardo, whose mechanics were an aspect of his sensuous experience, the sensitivity of his eye and hand.

Such advanced technology differs from the technology

that was directed toward an ideal of efficiency leading to privation and repression, and Nervi himself is at moments bound by the puritanism of this archaic technology when he endorses a functionalism that is nothing more than "the invention and study of the necessary methods to achieve a defined goal with maximum efficiency." When the urge to efficiency is dominant, functionalism is likely to be a product of limited initiative, and pleasure is likely to be diminished in the interest of parsimony. Yet always in the background of this functionalism was an irrationality inherent in the Benthamite calculus and the hedonism of *homo economicus,* who carefully controlled his methods for producing a wasteful surplus, useless satisfactions, marketable though they were.

The aesthete was one of the least fortunate of technologists, since his maximum efficiency in manipulating his medium did not have even a market utility; the usefulness of art was questioned, but not the usefulness of industrial products. Pater's exercises in style illustrate even more clearly than industrial technology a conflict between pleasure and parsimony. Desperately grasping at any exquisite sensation, "any stirring of the senses, strange dyes, strange colours, curious odors," trying incessantly to feel pulsations, Pater suffers the anguish of the artist who failed to reconcile the hedonism of his end with the asceticism of his means, an efficiency almost pathological in its dread of surplusage, its methodical calculation. Although he claimed that his moments were valuable "simply for those moments' sake," his art shows the same disrelation between puritanism of means and hedonism of ends as was inherent in economic life. Pater's dealing so scrupulously with his instrument is the technological anxiety that Marx would term skill fetishism.

The conflicting principles in technology and aesthetics are what give Art Nouveau its singular fascination—a mode or style that fuses pleasure with puritanism. This aesthetic exploitation of a medium is a functionalism that differs from our neofunctionalism (post-Bauhaus) because it is devoted to Art—and thus to decadence. The finely decorative line of Art Nouveau is a quasi-functional last phase of aestheticism, consciously given to ideals of Beauty. The spare, severely puritan designs of Mackmurdo at their most functional cannot conceal the aesthetic devotion to Beauty that was phrased in Oscar Wilde's maxim, "It is through Art, and through Art only, that we can realize our perfection; through Art, and through Art only, that we can shield ourselves from the sordid perils of actual existence." Wilde was temperamentally a hedonist and technically a puritan. He explains that "emotion for the sake of emotion is the aim of Art, and emotion for the sake of action is the aim of life, and of that practical organization of life we call society." The most functional contours of Art Nouveau are symptoms of alienation from a middle-class society that had denied Beauty.

Art Nouveau was frankly erotic: witness its seductive rhythms, which are usually organic and often sexual; but within it lay a restrictive parsimony no matter how decadent or indulgent its sinuosities. The frail structures of Art Nouveau are created by elimination, reducing exuberance to a formula. Aubrey Beardsley's purged but voluptuous vitality shows the tension between aestheticism and asceticism, the flamboyance and repression in the *fin de siècle* style. The organic liveliness is fastidiously phrased, with a technological economy that is at odds with the licentiousness of the artist. A puritan coquetry gives Art Nouveau forms their odd and fragile salaciousness, their feminine compliance. This delicate and abandoned design is at once participation in organic life and withdrawal from organic life. One reason for the charm of Art Nouveau is that it has not committed itself entirely to technological deprivation. Yet it is thoroughly intended, intimately and constantly controlled, and above all firmly *seen*. It sublimates fleshliness by "style."

Economical as it was, the *Yellow Book* style has none of the bleak functionalism of engineering because it was in part a reaction against the commercial and mechanical, and its ambiguous forms still belong to an alien world of Beauty. Howbeit, Art Nouveau derives from the sundry arts-and-crafts movements, and William Morris phrased a creed for those who hoped to make art a way of life, a means of participating instead of withdrawing or alienating. When Morris asked for an art "which is a happiness to the maker and the user," he attempted to reintroduce pleasure into work and design. His proposal bears directly upon two of the most influential interpretations of art, Marxist and Freudian, both insisting that art must be pleasure, direct or sublimated.

Lionel Trilling has suggested that inherent in the drift of literature from Wordsworth to Dostoevsky was the rejection of what Freud calls the Pleasure Principle; he suspects that the devaluation of pleasure is to an extent due to our repulsion from consumer-directed art. A great deal of nineteenth-century art was marketable—not only the miscellaneous journalism of the realistic novel but also the lushness of Tennyson's poetic Beauty. One reason for the ugliness of modern art with its exhibition of the disgusting and repellant is that we have learned to "dread Eden." We have good cause to dread the Eden furnished by the last century, and consequently we have, as Trilling says, been disposed to elect un-pleasure, the ego-instincts or death-instincts that are suicidal.

Our pleasures have often been undependable because they have been merely consumer satisfactions. Here we need a distinction that Trilling might have made, between pleasure and fun, a kind of pleasure to be bought. In the generous Freudian sense of the term, pleasure is not a salable commodity, but fun is. We buy fun, not pleasure, although we have come to think of pleasure as a cruise, a meal, a ticket to the game. The elemental difference between pleasure and fun is indicated in Valéry's remark about consuming literature: in artistic enjoyment the consumer must produce; he must share the artist's imaginative activity. Artistic pleasure is a valid brand of surplus value, a disproportionate but earned return upon the consumer's investment. Fun is supplied for the price paid. It is prefabricated, a convenience of our technological abundance. Such marketable satisfactions are often, in the current phrase, pseudoevents, prearranged exhibitions, and concessions to the image we seek. In a perhaps unconscious revulsion against our devalued pleasures we have turned from a synthetic Eden toward hate, despair, and destruction as more authentic responses.

Pleasure, then, solicits participation, and Ruskin and Morris thought of art as a way of participating more fully in life. The notion of art as participating, which the Greeks denoted by their term methexis, has since the renaissance been secondary to the notion of art as imitation, or mimesis. For centuries the Aristotelian canon of mimesis has been given an unwarranted emphasis in a culture subscribing heavily to the scientific axiom that reality can be observed by an action excluding the observer. The belief that reality is out there to be seen accurately led in one way or another to the conviction that scientist and artist must regard reality impersonally from a detached point of view. But this devotion to the external, whether in science or art, is a form of puritan repression. The scientific method once promised us Eden, yet by its very exercise excluded us from Eden. Does not this detachment explain what Gabriel Marcel terms "the dialectical correlation between the optimism of technical progress and the philosophy of despair which seems inevitably to emerge from it"? Pleasure was doomed by a method that put man "at the mercy of his techniques." It has been pointed out that the dominant modern technique, propaganda, requires participation; but it is not the fulfilling or creative participation of the arts. In short, art and science have alike been mechanisms for repressing the self and preventing engagement insofar as each has accepted the validity of a detached point of view; both were ways of displacing experience upward into the eyes, as Ferenczi says, or postulating it at a certain distance.

Wordsworth wrote sadly of this alienation of experience as the prison house closes upon the boy who only at moments, gropingly, feels the organic sensibility that originally made him one with his world in an experience only partially optical. For Wordsworth felt his highest raptures as hallowed and pure motions of the senses, a complete bodily response or "plastic power" penetrating nature and also absorbing it into his sensorium as evidence of his being:

> There is creation in the eye,
> Nor less in all the other senses; powers
> They are that colour, model, and combine
> The things perceived with such an absolute
> Essential energy that we may say
> That these most godlike faculties of ours
> At one and the same moment are the mind
> And the mind's minister.

> (Fragment of a poem)

Wordsworth could extend his consciousness over a whole area of awareness that in science is confined to mere observation. His mode of participating rather than observing is one of the strongest validations of romantic art. Norman O. Brown would call it a libidinous acceptance of experience. Wordsworth's expansion of consciousness through his animal movements, his appetites, his sense of the rhythms in a landscape is not induced by experiment; it is a generous faculty for identification.

Blake had the same appetite for participating:

> . . . you walk
> In Heavens & Earths, as in your own Bosom you bear your
> Heaven

And Earth & all you behold; tho' it appears Without, it
　is Within,
In your Imagination, of which this World of Mortality is
　but a Shadow.

Here Blake is speaking of pathetic fallacy, as Ruskin
called it, a question Ruskin did not settle because he, too,
was at times convinced that art should be an accurate
representation of what one sees. Yet Ruskin granted that
our most admired poetry is filled with this fallacy, which
is an instinct for participating instead of observing, as he
explains in a letter to his father (June 2, 1852): ". . .
there is the strong instinct in me which I cannot analyse
to draw and describe the things I love—not for reputation,
nor for the good of others, nor for my own advantage, but
a sort of instinct like that for eating and drinking. I
should like to draw all St. Mark's, and all this Verona
stone by stone, to eat it all up into my mind, touch by
touch." This appetite is a release of pleasure as Wordsworth felt it when he spoke of the poet as committed to
"the grand elementary principle of pleasure, by which he
knows, and feels, and lives, and moves," there being nothing standing between him and nature, which to him
was

> An appetite; a feeling and a love,
> That had no need of a remoter charm
> By thought supplied, nor any interest
> Unborrowed from the eye.
> ("Tintern Abbey")

Many romantics had this strong, if sometimes tortured,
desire to participate. D. H. Lawrence is thus a belated
and tormented romantic lamenting the death of great
Pan: "The idea and the engine came between man and
all things, like a death. . . . He found that all things were
related by certain *laws*. The moment man learned to abstract, he began to make engines that would do the work
of his body." Echoing Nietzsche, Lawrence charged the

mind with creating its own horrors, substituting rational principle for spontaneous response: "Knowledge is always a matter of whole experience, what Saint Paul calls knowing in full, and never a matter of mental conception merely."

However it may have been devoted to pleasure, aestheticism put art at the mercy of literary techniques. However he was committed to *volupté*, the decadent writer used an idiom that distanced his world. Gautier, Mallarmé, and Pater alike refuse Eden, making their art a version of renunciation. Lawrence was repressed, but he never rejected Eden in behalf of the blank white page. The chill and sterile figure of Herodias, whose virginity is sacral, is born of aloofness and refused pleasure. The perfection of symbolist art is language fetishism, "the glamor of syntax" not so very different from "the precision of science" painfully achieved by Flaubert, who tried to work on the assumption that "the less you feel a thing the more you are likely to express it as it is." Thus he sets about writing novels by absenting himself.

The emphasis on imitating rather than participating leads to overvaluing what psychologists call a good Gestalt—the precise Form, the acceptable Image. Anton Ehrenzweig has studied this problem of good form in the arts, basing his analysis on William James's recognition that there occur certain interruptions in consciousness, perceptions that are formless or non-Gestalt. These perceptions, which do not fit the pattern of the "surface mind," are a "focusing away" toward what is inarticulate or inaccessible to the idiom of reason. Wordsworth was familiar with such interruptions in consciousness, moments of recognition when:

> . . . bodily eyes
> Were utterly forgotten, and what I saw
> Appeared like something in myself, a dream,
> A prospect in the mind.
>
> (*Prelude*, II)

In these suspensions, he tells us:

> . . . my brain
> Worked with a dim and undetermined sense
> Of unknown modes of being.
>
> (*Prelude,* I)

At such moments Wordsworth is a shaman, and his symbolism is more elemental than the aesthetic symbolism in French poetry, where the *correspondances* are more heavily indebted to the syntax of the daylight mind. Yet both Wordsworth and the symbolists validate Ehrenzweig's opinion that the most potent forms of art have a double rhythm set up between the aesthetic control, giving "form," and the inarticulate recognitions breaking through in unintelligible phrasings from submerged experience. Traditional rhetoric is a disguise or censor imposed, often with indifferent success, upon these intimations of the less rational consciousness, a tariff wall erected against eruptions from obscure depths. A canon of style or form is like an artistic ego or superego whose function is to protect the work against unlicensed perceptions. (Nietzsche remarked that a weak culture hates a strong art.) When a major style is born, the aesthetic canon may not entirely control, much less repress, the intimations of non-Gestalt experience.

Ehrenzweig notes that the mania for style and styles during the nineteenth century is testimony that the age dreaded the Dionysiac in spite of its neopaganism. The aesthetic consciousness that gave Parnassians and decadents their care for style was symptomatic of the tensions that persist in T. S. Eliot. In asking that the poet have control of his medium Eliot served poetry well. Yet his exploitation of his medium does not account for the double rhythms set up in poems like "Sweeney among the Nightingales," where there is a breakthrough (surely unconscious) of impulses Eliot resists. Here Eliot is contrasting the sterility of the Sweeney-world with the hero-

ism of the Agamemnon-world. Both Sweeney and Aga-
memnon are victimized, but Sweeney is in a meaner
situation. While Sweeney sits in his hothouse, Rachel née
Rabinovitch, a vulgarized Eros figure, tears at the grapes
with her paws, a sardonic comment on the debased fertility rites that offer only unsacramental fruit served by a
waiter. Our modern love feast is degenerate enough, and
Rachel is profane. What Eliot does not seem to have
recognized is the full duplicity of the Rachel image, a
Lilith-goddess who really *is* an abiding if disreputable
and dangerously savage fertility principle: she *is* the
maenad who embodies the orgiastic bacchic danger—to
Eliot as well as to Sweeney. Eliot does not seem to know
what Euripides knew only too well in the *Bacchae,*
namely, that the authentic fertility rite is unspeakably
barbaric, bestial, terrifying. But in Eliot's poem, Rachel,
like Sweeney, is a primitive reality who seems more acceptable in classic guise or at mythic distance than when
she can reach us with her paws. The implication that the
Greco-Christian is nobler is a way of repressing Eliot's
own fear of the profane impulses he must distance lest
they break through without disguise. The fact is that the
sacramental feast is still as savage as it ever was: mur-
derous, like Rachel, who appears without the censorship
imposed by theology. Sweeney is likewise ambiguously
used: as a figure to be dreaded, scorned, pitied, and admired. Inherent in the poem is a cultural paradox, for if
Eliot really seeks fertility, he must not condescend to
Sweeney or Rachel. He appears to understand this in
"Mr. Eliot's Sunday Morning Service," where the fertility
principle in all its grossness is embodied in Sweeney's
drenched figure, not in the pustular young priests.

The power of the poem is, of course, due to its ambiguity, which illustrates how inarticulate experiences can be
masked or disguised by focusing consciousness in a clear
and narrow field. As Ehrenzweig says, self-conscious art
tends to give maximum Gestalt formation and thus drain

off the inarticulate, which is too alarming. Eliot's attitude toward Sweeney is an example of what Yvor Winters terms a reference to a nonexistent plot, motive, or meaning. The Rachel née Rabinovitch plot is never clearly structured in the poem, though it is actually the major theme of the action. Winters's own attack on modern poetry is an extreme instance of rejecting what is formless, since he seeks to exclude from a poem whatever does not derive from "formulable logic." He finds many poems defective because they cannot be paraphrased. But what Winters rejects as nonexistent is only too existent: the unarticulated and inarticulate perceptions are precisely what raise a double rhythm in a strong poem such as *Lycidas,* with its formal rhetoric and its unstructured motives, its invisible action. So too the power of *Paradise Lost* arises from the tremendous pressure of Milton's unacknowledged erotic impulses against a highly artificial rhetoric, the poem gaining its "nonexistent" or unformulated plot from the dangerous and shameless meanings Milton projects into his Eden.

It is not wholly perverse to associate the aesthetic anxiety about style (a good Gestalt) with the repression that occurred in nineteenth-century science, which established natural laws. E. H. Gombrich has said that canons of style are often negations, and that the chief function of taste is to avoid what is vulgar. One of the worst cultural snobberies is having a proper stock of motifs and images, the academic mode of rejecting what is unexpected or shocking. That is, paintings often imitate preceding paintings in the name of art. Gombrich finds that one of the most damaging of repressions is realism, since realism is a process of matching rather than making. The art that imitates "real" things existing outside is an art that reifies; and when reality appears as given, not as taken, then painting is merely matching. Making begins with the "minimal image" presenting itself, as it does in primitive art, as relatively "thing-free."

Ehrenzweig, who worked with Gombrich on the problem of realism in painting, links the thing-free image with the eiditic vision of the child: "What is called 'Eiditic' vision is the flexible vision of children, primitives, or artists, and significantly also of twilight vision. Then phenomena of distortion . . . invade the visual field as a whole." Eiditic vision was basic to Bauhaus training, for students were asked to inspect an object intently, then to draw it after it had been removed. This method allowed Gestalt-free incursions that prevented the drawing from being a mere matching of what was observed—which drawing had mostly been since the renaissance had focused perception narrowly and clearly on the model.

The link between painting and science was this tendency to treat nature as given at the expense of nature as taken. This type of realism or reification is like telling a dream by giving it secondary elaboration, that is, verbalizing the inarticulate images of the night vision and thus making them amenable to logic. The illustrative realism of Meissonier's painting is like a secondary elaboration that dispels the dreamlike quality of the dream. Meissonier fixed his vision of historical episodes with extreme precision, but his illustrative accuracy destroys the historical dimension simply by rephrasing the past as present—yet pretending it is historical. To record history with this precision is to falsify history, which must be taken, or imagined, before it is recorded; otherwise it is a dishonest anachronism, like Flaubert's *Salammbo*. In other words, history cannot be created from its data alone, and Meissonier's paintings are only the sum of their data; they are lacking in the dream of the past. All true history is dreamlike simply because it is not present. The data of historical study can only be used to sustain or rectify our dream of the past. Berdyaev means this, apparently, when he says that history can be apprehended only from within, and this apprehension depends on our own consciousness.

(191

The pseudohistorical novel, by transcribing its data, does not recover the past but necessarily makes history contemporaneous with its own archaeological composition. Paradoxically enough the better history is found in Ruskin's chapters on gothic. His dream of the past was doubtless not what the past actually was; yet his vision of gothic, for all its disagreement with the facts, does have the imaginative dimension lacking in Meissonier's painting, the sense of history that is taken and not merely given. All history must be romantic so far as it is taken, if only because the past is gone. History is always the meaning history has for us. There is, then, some truth in Ruskin's view that we must imagine a gothic cathedral, since we *see* a gothic cathedral as nobody was able to see it when it was new. When the dreamer tells his dream, he inevitably falsifies it by accommodating it to the grid of his waking mind; there is a fissure between the dream and the telling, which is necessarily archaeological. Literary antiquarianism is a retold dream, for there is always the fissure between surface and core. Besides, it is usually easier to construct a good Gestalt from archaeological data than from experience lived in the present.

In spite of all the theories of perspective the renaissance painter had to treat nature as taken, not as given; he could not avoid the distortions that sprang from within himself. Instances abound where a rigorous use of perspective produces a structure so obviously artificial as to be almost grotesque: Mantegna's "Dead Christ," for instance. It has been said that renaissance perspective is both geometry and myth. The painter's mathematic did not, after all, construct an "objective" vision of the world any more than did Newtonian physics. The willful foreshortening, the chiaroscuro, the arbitrary angles of vision, the narrow formal focus cannot hide the distortions of depth-perception The world view of orthogonal perspective and Newtonian mechanics is an obviously synthetic view arbitrarily imposed upon data furnished by experi-

ence. Whether he will or no, the artist must participate—
however he may resist or repress by objectifying or styliz-
ing his world.

Grotesque and Numinous

Resistance that expresses itself as rejection, precaution, or even hate can, in some cases, take other forms
than being objective. The hate-impulse can become artistic in caricature, and the denial of Eden in the modern
arts has often expressed disgust and repulsion in the form
once known as grotesque. Yet the grotesque is one of the
most uninhibited manifestations of play and thus is
adaptable to love as well as hate. It has been a constant in
the arts from Homer's Thersites, Aristophanes's figure of
Socrates, mediaeval demons, Goethe's witches, to Hugo's
Quasimodo and Browning's Caliban; from comic and
tragic masks, Pompeiian mosaics, Italian capriccios, to
Fuseli's nightmares and Van Gogh's landscapes. If modern art means anything, it means distortion, disorienta-
tion, and comic or savage formlessness. Writing his
preface to *Cromwell* in 1825, Hugo found the grotesque,
a "new form of comedy," everywhere. "It creates the
abnormal and horrible," mingling body and soul, the
beast and the mind, in our "third civilization" so unlike
the antique and the Catholic. Goya, Dickens, Daumier,
Dostoevsky, Kafka, and T. S. Eliot are all highly charged
with the projective energy of the grotesque, animating
their figures and scenes with their own irrepressible agi-
tation. Like Picasso, they retreat from likeness.

Ruskin's discussion of gothic is deeply committed to
the grotesque, and his admiration for mediaeval art is
partly due to his dislike of the good Gestalt the renaissance tried to impose upon painting. "The Renaissance
frosts came, and all perished." The grand mistake was
supposing that art and science were the same things:
"The sciences ceased at once to be anything more than

different kinds of grammars,—grammar of language, grammar of logic, grammar of ethics, grammar of art; and the tongue, wit, and invention of the human race were supposed to have found their utmost and most divine mission in syntax and syllogism, perspective and the five orders." If the action of science is knowing, the action of the arts is changing and creating.

In contrast to Burckhardt, Ruskin felt that renaissance theory "encumbered the artist with every species of knowledge that is of no use to him," the system of perspective and classic legend, while it left him increasingly ignorant of crafts in which the Dark Ages were skilled. The pride of science ended in academism and conventions that were debased into mere good taste. Ruskin's great contribution was his rebellion against academic formulas: ". . . whatever subject had to be treated, the first aim . . . was to subject its principles to a code of laws, in the observation of which the merit of the speaker, thinker, or worker, in or on that subject, was thereafter to consist; so that the whole mind of the world was occupied by the extensive study of Restraints. The sound of the forging of fetters was heard from sea to sea. The doctors of all the arts and sciences set themselves daily to the invention of new varieties of cages and manacles."

In the grotesque renaissance, as he names it, Ruskin saw the artist liberating himself by play, "for a healthy manner of play is necessary" in the arts. "True grotesque" is the play of a strong mind, a breakthrough of the unconscious, but at the threshold of reason:

> The grotesque which comes to all men in a disturbed dream is the most intelligible . . . but also the most ignoble; the imagination, in this instance, being entirely deprived of all aid from reason, and incapable of self-government. I believe, however, that the noblest forms of imaginative power are also in some sort ungovernable, and have in them something of the character of dreams; so that the vision, of whatever kind, comes uncalled, and will not submit itself to the seer, but conquers him, and forces him

to speak as a prophet, having no power over his words or thoughts. (*Stones of Venice,* "The Grotesque Renaissance")

Though he uses the moralistic language of his day, Ruskin is referring to the upsurge of non-Gestalt perceptions bringing a double rhythm into art forms. Turner's paintings, which Ruskin described as imperative dreams, are a grotesque use of color.

Goya's graphic art is an encounter between the intelligible and the unintelligible as Ruskin describes it: ". . . whenever the human mind is healthy and vigorous in all its proportions, great in imagination and emotion no less than in intellect, and not overborne by an undue or hardened preeminence of the mere reasoning faculties, there the grotesque will exist in full energy." The powerful grotesque in gothic and renaissance is evidence that "Nothing is more mysterious in the history of the human mind, than the manner in which gross and ludicrous images are mingled with the most solemn subjects" in defiance of genre. The potent comic distortion of grotesque is "perception and invention" in the guise of burlesque, horror, abnormality; and the whole body is in it.

Along with Dickens, Browning is among the great grotesque artists in language, image, and temperament, for the body is almost brutally present in the best of his poetry. Seldom is the double rhythm felt more strongly than in "Two in the Campagna," where the most refined and tenuous of moral experiences, the desire to surrender to another self, is figured in the sexual image of beetles blindly groping for honey-meal inside a small orange cup, an upsurge of phallic need into the sentimentality of Victorian love. "Caliban upon Setebos," that devastating Feuerbachlike attack upon theology, is phrased in the grotesque organic sensations of the beast sprawling in the mire, tickled by efts running in and out his armpits

> . . . while above his head a pompion-plant,
> Coating the cave-top as a brow its eye,
> Creeps down to touch and tickle hair and beard,

> And now a flower drops with a bee inside,
> And now a fruit to snap at, catch and crunch.

Caliban is the authentic Sweeney, not distanced among nightingales or classic landscapes. Browning's instinct to deform, distort, disfigure is more sadistic than Dickens's impulse to caricature, more empathetic in its muscular strain. Browning has all the fleshly sensibility of D. H. Lawrence, but in bizarre form.

A lurid wasteland poem is "Childe Roland to the Dark Tower Came," a nightmare vision of what the machine did to the English countryside; here is a Tennysonian idyll converted to grotesque. Whatever Browning may owe to that chapter he read in Lairesse or to a tapestry he saw or to the landscape of the Val d'Arno, his vision is one of the most direct breakthroughs from the unconscious; the traditional mediaeval quest-theme is translated into the barbarous elocution of the dream. Unconsciously Browning is doing what Eliot later did in poems on our dry land, and Browning's art is the more illusive because it is more inarticulate, resembling the ghastly comedy of Kafka:

> As for the grass, it grew as scant as hair
> In leprosy; thin dry blades pricked the mud
> Which underneath looked kneaded up with blood . . .
> What bad use was that engine for, that wheel,
> Or brake, not wheel—that harrow fit to reel
> Men's bodies out like silk?

The grim rankling blotches, the soil breaking into boils, the cleft palsied oak like a mouth gaping at death belong in the landscape of Kafka's "Penal Colony." Even the language is subliterary:

> It may have been a water-rat I speared,
> But ugh! it sounded like a baby's shriek.

Roland is embarked on a senseless quest that caricatures the official notion of risk, a notion basic to laissez-faire enterprise, a notion that justifies profit. But here risk leads Roland to a cul-de-sac; like Captain Ahab he is committed to a suicidal venture, but in a scene more desolate than the oceans over which Ahab sails. Browning has written an antipoem that reduces to absurdity the heroic and classic risk of Tennyson's Ulysses. His nightmare has emptied a middle-class myth. "Childe Roland" is a poem of hate—unconscious hate becoming creative by means of the grotesque. It releases impulses Browning himself would hardly acknowledge. The disguise is no more successful than in *Lycidas*. This art is as expressionistic as Ensor's hideous carnivals or Van Gogh's writhing vision of Provençe. Browning's "nonexistent plot" is his rejection of the industrial order. The poem is not imitation but a nearly manic projection, a sinister mode of play.

There is, in fact, a deep congeniality between Browning and Nietzsche, who thought of art as a manic or uninhibited play, an ecstatic projection and a way of participating. Even Nietzsche's politics are ecstatic, a sinister play, and his Great Blond Beast is an eruption of the grotesque into social thought. Art and politics are for Nietzsche acts of methexis, a grotesque vitality that abandons precaution; both are epidemic. Even Blake with his devotion to energy and exuberance did not feel so strongly as Nietzsche that art is epidemic or contagious. Nor did Tolstoy, for although he called art infectious, he would put it to utilitarian purposes like social reform. Nietzsche boldly called art a joyful and powerful play that does not imitate nature but raises over against it the triumphant absurdity of man's experience. The tragic vision is a conquest of the oblivion man faces in his universe; it is equipped for suffering.

Unlike tragic man, the scientist or theoretic man "believes that the world can be corrected through knowledge and that life should be guided by science; that it is actually in a position to confine man within the narrow circle of soluble tasks." Only the artist can accept the terrifying, which science dispels by illusions about reason, knowledge, intelligence. Such optimism presupposes "an eye such as no living being can imagine, an eye required to have no direction, to abrogate its active and interpretive powers—precisely those powers that alone make of seeing, seeing *something*. All seeing is essentially perspective, and so is all knowing." So Nietzsche discards the figment of the objective observer emotionally aloof from nature. Scientific neutrality is Nietzsche's "pretentious lie of civilization," a refusal to acknowledge the person concealed behind the mask of the spectator. When this illusion is shaken, when we must drop the observer's mask, then science cannot face the consequences of its own conclusions; then the tragic artist takes over. The scientist ignored Nietzsche's axiom that "Man would rather have the void for his purpose than to be void of purpose."

As a rebel who cannot accept nature as he finds it, the artist is in the grip of impulses which the surface mind tries to discipline by logic, a logic that causes repression, alienation, and reification. Nietzsche's epidemic artistic impulses correspond to the non-Gestalt depth perceptions, the form-free interruptions in consciousness. Nietzsche interpreted Greek tragedy as an Apollonian serenity hiding the realm of Dionysus, the choral impulse to participate in joy and terror. He was one of the first to see that Greek classicism was a precarious resistance against the titanic menace of the satyr.

Thus Nietzsche's main theme is the enduring conflict between theoretic and tragic man, the rationalistic and artistic view of the world. It is a conflict implied in the title of F. M. Cornford's book, *From Religion to Philosophy*, tracing the course of Greek thought as it gradually formulated a scientific account of the natural orders, thus banishing primitive notions of fate (*moira*) and the gods and replacing these anthropomorphic forces by Ionian thought, which reached "a very simple and clear model of the structure of reality from which the super-natural has all but disappeared." Ionian science avoided any "circuit through the unknown" and substituted a closed system of physical necessity.

This cycle of thought, banishing deities and invoking a new magic of necessity, began all over again after Sir Isaac Newton furnished his mathematical mode of reality avoiding any circuit through the unknown. The following generations forgot what Newton himself and other great scientific minds knew, that their discoveries were, to them, a kind of play, the free exercise of a mind driven by curiosity and eagerness that resembles the Dionysiac spirit. The Newtonian system lost its half-prophetic won-der when it hardened, as natural law, into an entirely theoretic world view. Whitehead said that the great de-fect of eighteenth-century science was its failure to pro-vide for the deeply felt experiences of man or to tolerate the sense that nature is organic. It was left for Pope and the deists to salvage the intimation that nature is an or-ganism, a being whose body is nature and whose soul is God. Then later Wordsworth more fully recovered the sense of something interfused in nature, its "haunting presences" and numinous organic life.

The numinous kept returning in various ways among Greeks and moderns—in Euripides, who was not a mere rationalist; in James Thomson as well as Wordsworth; in Thomas Hardy's deeply troubled animism. In the *Bacchae* Tiresias warns the Thebans that we cannot ration-alize about the gods, who are as old as time and who are not argued away. So also the numinous returns in the last pages of Zola's *Germinal* when Etienne departs from the Black District hearing underground, chthonic tongues the middle class could not silence: "An overflow of sap was mixed with whispering voices, the sound of the germs expanding in a great kiss. . . . In the fiery rays of the sun on this youthful morning the country seemed full of that sound." These are the subterranean voices

Oedipus heard at Colonus. Whitman heard them in his democratic vistas. The oracular voice of Egdon Heath is more somber: "The place became full of a watchful intentness now; for when other things sank brooding to sleep the heath appeared slowly to awake and listen. Every night its Titanic form seemed to await something; but it had waited thus, unmoved during so many centuries, through the crises of so many things, that it could only be imagined to await one last crisis—the final overthrow." On Egdon Heath the winds sing through clenched teeth, and Eustacia Vye, "absolute queen here," is a figure waiting to be possessed by maenadic rites. D. H. Lawrence would have provided the rites.

Hardy and Lawrence have a tragic sense of life that comes, as Nietzsche said, when the bland illusion of causality has been pushed to its limits, and science, turning upon itself, bites its tail. Then the "deus ex machina, the god of engines and crucibles," yields to the artist who faces a chasm of oblivion. This is the moment when Hardy, living in an Alexandrian age, was seized with awe, for the law of causation suspends itself in his novels; the disastrous coincidence seems fated. Behind the flimsy causal mechanics of Hardy's plots there is always the forbidding presence of an unnamed and unnamable fate playing out its saturnine game with Tess and Jude, with Clym Yeobright and all who believe they can reason their way through life. At times the same numinous fatality tinges Ibsen's plays, where infections and nervous disorders seem as destined as Oedipus's incest. The very laws of causality bring inexplicable results, frightening "benighted souls" who are forced to recognize that their sanity is "ghostly." Amid the "catastrophe" of modern life causation seems to be only a figment of logic, and we are forced back at the farthest limits of science to art.

The most ghostly form of sanity is "thought guided by a thread of causation," which gives only an illusion of knowledge, the representation of nature that comes from scientific observation. The wisdom of the artist is a mode of participation, and behind the official optimism of science Nietzsche heard the chorus of satyrs, creatures afflicted with a terror that is also ecstasy, not sickness. Nietzsche asks whether there are not neuroses of health, and he takes art to be such a neurosis: a participation neurosis. The notion was already in Blake, who read into the sunrise his raging desire. The sons of Albion have blinded themselves by the single vision of science, have closed the doors of perception in Newton's sleep. But the bird that flies is "an immense world of delight" and the vegetative universe opens like a flower expanding to eternity. One of the most sterilizing effects of seeing nature with the mind alone is that art imitates by copying what is outside: "No Man of Sense can think that an Imitation of the Objects of Nature is the Art of Painting." Thus Blake scorned the academicians: "A Man sets himself down with Colours & with all the Articles of Painting; he puts a Model before him & he copies that so neat as to make it a deception: now let any Man of Sense ask himself one Question: Is this Art?" Such copying represses the energy that is delight. It is a form of science, and for Blake "Science is the tree of Death. Art is the tree of Life."

Freud's Aesthetic

The revolution in the recent arts and in recent science is basically due to the fact that the notion of art and science as imitation has been displaced by the notion of art and science as participation. Nietzsche's prophecy has been fulfilled to the extent that science has been pushed to the far limits of inquiry where it becomes an almost artistic activity; as Heisenberg says, the observer is involved inextricably with every observation he makes. Freud stands at the critical phase of this revolution, since he was led, however unwillingly, from his scientific objectivity to a validation of art as a way of participating. Few moderns have had more profound effects upon criticism than Freud, and few have been so at odds with themselves about the value of art and the nature of the artist and his relation to reality. But Freud's indecisions and confusions are indispensably helpful. As scientist he was unalterably committed to the reality-principle and held steadfastly to the notions of nineteenth-century science as an observation of, and concession to, the world out there; and as aesthetic critic he fell victim to the notion that art is imitation, though in his own indirect way, for he condescended to the artist as one who offers us the false representations he calls fantasy-satisfactions. These fantasies were, however, a result of the artist's frustration or repression, which caused him to sublimate or distance life and reality by his special kind of illusion. In general he reveals the paradox that appeared in Plato, who repudiated art but was one of the most poetic of philosophers. Freud repudiated art officially but is admittedly one of the great mythologists of our day. And his inconsistencies about art are more illuminating than others' clarities.

Whatever the incompatibles in Freud, he at last, like Marx, accepts an aesthetic view of life and sanctions art, if unknowingly, as an effectual therapy. Stranger still, Freud's implication that art is a mode of participating in reality is an answer to the charge so often brought that his psychoanalysis leaves the patient isolated from the society in which he exists. Freud has only himself to blame for this confusion, since he never resolves his view of art, which has within it two opposing interpretations— art as imitation or evasion of reality, and art as commitment to reality. Although he never says as much, he actually sanctions a view of art held by Ruskin and Morris: namely, that art is not primarily mimesis but methexis, a neurosis of health and a release from repression.

In short, Freud's recurring attacks upon art as a narcissistic fantasy gratification, a self-indulgence, do not represent his position. As scientist he was caught in the dilemma characteristic of his age when the pleasure-principle seemed to be in conflict with the reality-principle. Like Huxley and the rest he trusted science and officially turned to science, not art, for therapy. And his understanding of science was that of his day—the scientism convinced that reality is actually "out there" and can be "accurately" described or observed. Freud's premises as scientist are those of a naïve realism: man is a spectator. Anything that hinders our perception of reality and adjustment to it is damaging, and man is always in danger of heeding his need for pleasure instead of acceding to the demands of nature. To this extent Freud is liable to the charge that he set up a false boundary between what is subjective and what is objective. Freud's distrust of art is as puritanical as Plato's; for the fantasies of art, pleasurable enough, are more injurious than our dreams—they enfeeble our waking life, convincing us that we do not need to come to terms with actuality. Officially Freud treated art as one of the auxiliary constructions we seek in order to deceive ourselves; it is not pleasure but a substitute for pleasure. For him art was ero*tic* but not dedicated to Eros. Everyone is familiar with Freud's depreciation of the artist as one who evades reality and encourages us to evade it. With spartan rigor Freud tells us that the test of maturity is an ability to face the world as it is—that is, as it is known to the scientist.

As therapist, therefore, Freud was devoted to the positivistic or rationalist tradition of science, quite at odds with the "poetry" in his thought. Freud's distrust of the accessory constructions of art is apparent in his various statements that the conscious self must be trained to accept the necessities of external reality and must thus renounce "temporarily or permanently" not only sexual but sundry other quests for pleasure. The artist is not a "reasonable being" but a "pleasure-seeking animal" encouraging us to feed on the "meagre satisfactions" of illusions that leave us starving. Freud repeats the charges brought against the poet by Thomas Love Peacock.

In passing it might be said that realism and naturalism could be defended by Freud's own appeal to science. Why did Freud overlook the experimental novel and its impersonal observing? He might have exempted Zola from his contempt, for the naturalists intended to bring to the novel the precision of scientific method with its full attention to the reality-principle. Is it not likely that Freud's own sensitivity to art led him to feel the deficiencies of realism? Did Freud unconsciously recognize that the fallacies of naturalism were also the fallacies of the scientific method?

In any case Freud's most supercilious pages on the artist can hardly be used against the experimental novel as Zola tried to write it, and Freud was obviously thinking of another kind of artist, a neurotic who is driven by clamorous instinctual needs for honor, fame, riches, and love, gratifications of which he is deprived. This kind of artist (so far as he exists) knows a path leading to such gratifications; he has a talent for modifying his fantasies (originating in "prohibited sources") and recasting his desires in art forms that attach a pleasure strong enough to earn our indulgence until we accord him what he lacks. The passage is Freud's most cynical; yet he knew well enough that art is an erotic act, not a *substitute* for an erotic act. In fact, he admits that art is a half-way region between reality and fantasy since the emotions it provokes are real. Notwithstanding, he revives Plato's unintelligent warning that we must guard against Homer's charms, the lies that have a magic to make us weaker than women. Like Plato, he fears that poetry is addressed to "the inferior part of the soul," whose nobler activity is the calculating rational faculty; by measuring and numbering we rescue ourselves. As scientist Freud agrees with Francis Bacon that poetry is mere feigning, satisfying the mind with shadows when the substance is not obtained.

This distrust of fantasy-satisfaction is inherent in the dour culture of those who rely upon science to control life. It is a dated attitude, though at times it has a half-tragic dignity, as when Bertrand Russell pleads for the stoicism of disinterested or objective regard of reality: the very aim of education, Russell says, echoing what Huxley once wrote, is "the endeavour to make us see *and imagine* the world in an objective manner, as far as possible as it is in itself, and not merely through the distorting medium of personal desire." The distorting medium of desire: would it have occurred to Dickens that desire is a distorting medium? Or even to Shelley and the encyclopedists and libertarians? Or to Blake? So Russell repeats, "The kernel of the scientific outlook is the refusal to regard our own desires, tastes, and interests as affording a key to the understanding of the world." Russell fears that this may sound like a truism. It is a truism, whose triteness conceals what he did not perceive: objectivity is not only detachment but dehumanization, alienation, and, as Nietzsche saw, self-deception. Freud the scientist is Freud the puritan, the therapist enforcing discipline to the demands of a limited truth, a restricted vision. To this extent his effort was directed toward Unlust rather than Lust.

He argues, of course, that scientific restraint, this puritan realism or precaution, eventually and indirectly affords happiness; as he says, a great many of the most rewarding satisfactions accrue from sublimating quests for pleasures that must not be released in their primary form. Freud's notion of civilization—and its discontents—is based on his conviction that man must control his archaic drives.

Nobody would quarrel with this view. The question, rather, is whether Freud believed that the only adjustment to reality can be the scientific method. Here again Freud agrees with the realists, who reacted against "romantic mythology" and half-deistic beliefs that nature's "holy plan" is trustworthy. The realists began to see nature as it "is," hostile, but not to be ignored. Realistic art with its grim view of things was a reeducation of sensibility not unlike the reeducation science was enforcing. Freud's view of education was intimately associated with the many nineteenth-century examinations of education, involving an idea of the two cultures, art and science, each with its pedagogy, each with its attitude toward nature.

Freud's prohibitive view of education is strangely similar to Huxley's; that is, we should "learn the laws which govern men and things and obey them." It is only fair to add that Freud had little of Huxley's admiration for nature. Rather, like John Stuart Mill, he was unable to find in nature any moral imperative, whereas Huxley urged us to fashion our affection and will into an "earnest and loving desire" to move in harmony with physical laws. Huxley endows nature with quasi-moral jurisdiction of a kind that makes Hardy's Egdon Heath a tragic force. Yet Huxley and Freud both warned that unless we learn the discipline of science, we fall victim to the tyranny of nature, which is a blow without admonition. Far better than Huxley, Freud knew that nature is hostile, that man's oldest relation to reality is hate. The essay on "Formulations Regarding Two Principles of Mental Functioning" is curiously close to Huxley's recommendation of what education should be, and there are overtones of Baconian methodology in each; for as the "pleasure-ego" strives only toward direct gratification, the "reality-ego" strives to protect the self against injury. This precaution, nevertheless, does not in the long run nullify pleasure but only guards it by means of the conquests achieved through science.

Science, not art: for positing a hate-relation toward nature leads Freud to value science above art as a safer and sounder economy. Thus he can affirm, as did Huxley, that education is a victory won by substituting the reality-principle for the pleasure-principle. The artist cannot make this conquest because of his "peculiar" way of reconciling these two principles, turning from reality when "he cannot come to terms with the demand for instinctual satisfaction," then in his fantasy-life allowing "full play to his erotic and ambitious wishes." We are foolish to "concede" any sober justification of these illusory constructs. In another devastating passage in his essay "A Weltanschauung" Freud indicates that he respects philosophy and even religion above art. Of the three, only religion can be "taken seriously," for art, benign and innocent as it is, seeks mere illusory effects; only when the artist is "possessed" can he invade reality. Philosophy is more helpful, but only because it uses the same methods as science.

In general Freud takes a position not far from John Stuart Mill's, for he sees man engaged in a struggle with his own nature as well as against nature. Mill examined the scientific method in its Benthamite guise, and as an unhappy utilitarian he concluded that "All praise of civilization, or Art, or Contrivance, is so much dispraise of Nature." Yet Mill questions the premise tacitly accepted by Huxley and Freud, that nature is identical with reality. Mill sees the natural order as inhumane and immoral: ". . . in sober truth nearly all the things which men are hanged or imprisoned for doing to one another are nature's everyday performances." If man is to triumph over his natural instincts and nature, he must rely on "an eminently artificial discipline," which is moral, not natural. Though we must obey natural law, we should not guide ourselves by this law, but by our self-imposed ideals of culture which counter our instincts.

Freud is even more dismayed than Mill about the evil in human nature, posing, again like Plato, the task of mastering man's lawless, wild-beast self. With nearly tragic perception Freud senses that guilt is inherent in human experience: there is no such thing as an innocent sexual act for man, and Freud's fear of self-deception seems to be as great as Sophocles's fear of blundering into disaster through blindness. Freud detects, like Nietzsche, the "pretentious lie of civilization," and seeks an ethic of honesty, repudiating what Plato called the lie within the soul. Freud's psychotherapy, like Marx's economics, is a moral science; man's inability to make the right choices is a tragic and also a medical problem. But then again, it was for the Greeks also.

Yet this tragic view of human irresponsibility is to an extent negated by Freud's scientific optimism, and Philip Rieff has pointed out that as psychoanalyst Freud hoped to cure our self-delusions, our blindness, our pathological human condition. If guilt, discord, and disease are capable of being treated scientifically, then what began as tragic conflict ends in a "comedy of knowledge." Freud remained the rationalist, and his potentially tragic view was circumscribed by his scientific method. We must ask to what extent this method was committed to the detached observation of reality required by the old scientism, which was itself illusory, privative, and repressed. A satisfactory notion of art—which he did not develop— might have saved him from the limitations of his method, which reifies, alienates, and leads toward hate, not pleasure. In attempting to revise Freud, Norman O. Brown has appealed to a Dionysiac notion of the self; but we do not necessarily need a Dionysiac self so much as a revision of our notion of science. The trouble is not that Freud failed to surrender to the Dionysiac, but rather that he had a nineteenth-century faith in science.

Modern scientists such as Whitehead have rejected the notion of science as the observing of "reality" in a physical order controlled by the laws that were only figments of reason projected into things: "Matter-of-fact is an abstraction arrived at by confining thought to purely formal relations which then masquerade as the final reality."[23] Mistaking the abstraction for the fact is misplacing concreteness. As therapist Freud failed to recognize that *the* scientific method is only a special way of symbolizing reality, that the scientific conception is, in Wittgenstein's phrase, "founded on the illusion that the so-called laws of nature are explanations of natural phenomena." Since these laws structure reality only within their own logic, the meaning of reality must exist outside this logical scaffolding.

As moralist, however, Freud sensed the tragic meanings of man's condition: we are up against the unknown as were the Greeks in their world, where oracles spoke obscurely. Man's struggle is not only against his own nature, but also against the uncertainties at the boundaries of knowledge, the fatalities we do not comprehend even by science. Nevertheless in holding to a simple faith in science, Freud betrays a certain *hubris* in his confidence that we can know the reality-principle. His responses were sensitive, but his premises were narrow. He must have felt this, for his mythology—the tragic and valuable part of his thought—is grotesquely unscientific, like Marx's economics. His myths of the Id, the Superego, the Ego, and his whole topography of the self, along with the primal fable of slaying the father, were acknowledgments that *the* scientific method did not suffice.

To translate the situation into Ehrenzweig's terms, we may say that Freud as scientist had externality illusions. These illusions may be as deceptive as the illusions of art Freud so distrusted. Some basic Freudian concepts such as the Oedipal complex are not real as a fever is real; they have only a parascientific validity. At best they resemble Newton's laws, which reified mathematical formulas into "forces." Speaking of the Newtonian system, Wittgenstein observes that "the law of causality is not a law but the form of a law," a logical net, "not about what the net describes." Freud's skepticism about the undependable animal called man is justified; but unhappily he was deluded into thinking his science more dependable. Thus he fell into his own kind of blindness and undervalued art.

As scientist, then, Freud is subject to the very criticism he makes of the artist: he supposes that an illusion is reality, since scientific law is our formulation of the reality-principle, not reality itself. Like other scientists of his day, he postulated reality in surrogate form, a form that may alienate from reality. So far as art is actually a fantasy mistaken for reality, Freud is, like Plato or Bacon, privileged to scorn the artist; but one must add that the scientist cherished his own fantasy.

Fortunately another view of art is implicit in Freud's work, a view never fully articulated although he constantly and almost against the grain seems to have felt that the artist can do what the scientist cannot. For the artist can play, and play is a devotion to pleasure that is therapeutic, giving a sense of identification with reality that heals the alienation of the scientist from reality, his puritan renunciations. Freud concedes that the sharing of the emotional experience so enriching to every culture is promoted by the artist rather than by the scientist. Freud could never quite abide by his professed contempt for art and, however unwillingly, tended to sanction it as a means of knowing reality advantageously. Unconsciously, perhaps, Freud wished to endorse art as Lust, as knowledge, and he implies that the artist stands in a relation to reality quite different from the scientist, a relation of love and acceptance instead of a relation of precaution, practicality, or hate. Freud says the artist works, as he always did, by magic. Consumed by his desires, the artist has a talent to present us with a visionary fulfillment of these desires, and his address to our emotions creates illusions convincing enough to seem valid. Nobody resembles Plato more closely than Freud in his official depreciation of art and his temperamental sympathy for art and the artist.

This shamefaced endorsement of art is doubtless the ground for Freud's mythmaking, the poetry that cannot be purged from his scientific thought. The stern refusal of pleasure Freud demanded as puritan and scientist disappears in this other attitude, tolerant as it is of Eros, creativity, and communion. Art as union with reality, not as resistance to it or defense against it—that is a note Freud strikes in one of his most poetic passages on the "oceanic sense" of life where he deals tenderly with the tragic isolation of the self as soon as the self finds its identity by feeling its alienation from the world outside. At the opening of *Civilization and Its Discontents* Freud ponders how the ego in its earliest phase was not detached from the world but embraced it with a feeling that was cosmic. Unfortunately this cosmic expansion has shrunk until the self with its "sharply outlined" consciousness of its own identity senses that it is excluded from its first total "oneness" with the entire universe. Thomas Mann understood this oceanic unity better than Jung, whose participation-mystique has promoted some very factitious and self-conscious mythmaking. It is not the myth which is oceanic, but the artist's faculty for responding to reality as Wordsworth did, totally, involving the universe in the immediate occasion, which then becomes a "whole experience." To quote Ruskin again: the artist is one who expresses the mind of manhood by the hands of childhood.

The oceanic sense stands in contrast to another Freudian myth that has a harsher poetry—the myth of the birth of consciousness in the primal naked cellular organism whose first response is a dim awareness of the peril in the world outside the self, a recoil causing the vulnerable protoplasm to withdraw as deeply as it can inside itself. By this defensive response, the inorganic crosses the threshold into life; the world is hostile, and if the organism is to survive, it must retreat within itself. Its first encounter with reality brings only a sense of pain, danger, and rejection. Otherwise life could remain indifferent to reality outside, for whatever gives pleasure can be absorbed or "introjected" into the organism. But discovery of the external induces only antagonism, precaution, and refusal.

Thus Freud's *other* myth tells us that our primal relation to the world is hate, which is an older response than love since it springs from our instinctive rejection of the world outside. The stimuli beating in upon the narcissistic cellular self quickly teaches it a hostility that repudiates everything that could cause pain. Thus it hates and wills to reject or destroy whatever can disturb it. As instrument for self-preservation, therefore, the ego is not originally devoted to pleasure but to prudence, calculation, and all the imperatives that later manifest themselves in nineteenth-century science. It is almost as if Freud were rewriting Genesis to suggest that the human condition is better represented by Cain, who hates, than by Adam, who loves and is given to Lust in its widest and most poetic sense. If the developed ego, or consciousness at its highest pitch, is the distinctive human faculty, then consciousness according to this myth is not erotic but given to the privative task of self-maintenance by maneuver that go by the name of thrift.

This horrid myth brings us back to *Lear,* where aging is a result of hating, where man is a naked, unaccommodated animal; if pleasure appears in this world, it does so in the perverted form of conquest, a hideous correlate to Freud's opinion that education is "an incitement to the conquest of the pleasure-principle, and to its replacement by the reality-principle." And, he added, science comes closest to making this conquest. The Freudian tragedy is that the moralist who yearned for the pleasure of abandoning the self to the oceanic should have been driven back upon a hate-relation inherent in the premises of science since the renaissance. How perverse that Freud should have sought pleasure by scientific discipline. Is it any wonder that a moralist as humane as Freud should have implied, though obliquely, the need for some other relation to reality, the Eros-relation of art?

Opposed to the ego-principle of survival is the receptive Eros-principle. The origin of love is the yearning of the self to gratify its erotic instincts by means of the "organ-pleasure" that can reach out into the world and thus be transferred to objects toward which the self is extended by its strivings. This quest for pleasure by extending the ego through love is narcissistic insofar as the self introjects the loved object into itself, seeking to love itself. But there is likewise a "leaning," or anaclitic eroticism, wherein the self depends upon the body of the mother (the breast, for example) or on some other object to satisfy the craving for pleasure. The anaclitic relation is not pre-cautionary, privative, or antagonistic. By leaning on things outside, the self transforms its relation to the world from hate to love—which is, of course, naïve and unprotected.

The anaclitic, leaning relation of the child to the mother's breast is essentially the relation of the artist to the world. Freud calls it a nutritional relation. It was Ruskin's relation to the churches in Verona, which he wanted to "eat up" touch by touch; it was Degas's relation to those ugly ballet girls. This attachment to things finds its Biblical phrasing in the expression "God so loved the world." Shelley gave this anaclitic relation an ethical meaning when he defined the instrument of moral good as the imagination, "a going out of the self and an identification of the self with another and many others." This love is different from the love in "Alastor," where the poet quests for his alter-ego, someone on whom to project his idea, the imperalism of a mind making the world merely my idea of the world, an externality illusion.

Ruskin's love of the stones of Venice is a form of identification circuitously described by Freud as a masculine response. The anaclitic love of the object so typical of the male can bring about an excessive sexual esteem of the woman, an over-appreciation arising from the narcissism of the child but now projected toward the one on whom the adult male leans. The overestimation impoverishes the ego in favor of the object loved. Freud never seems to have made up his mind whether the sacrifice demanded by the anaclitic relation is profitable; yet the simple way to express this relation is to say that Adam loved Eve—a primal erotic relation that was hardly precautionary. Such love amounts to a giving rather than a taking, and it loosely resembles Keats's negative capability, a sense of identity of the self with what is outside, a commitment to a sunset or a sparrow, to an autumn stubble-field, to the pains and pleasures of others. Richard Woodhouse describes Keats's poetical character as he knew it: "The highest order of poet will . . . have [so] high an imagination that he will be able to throw his own soul into any object he sees or imagines, so as to see, feel, be sensible of, & express, . . . he will speak out of that object—so that his own self will with the exception of the mechanical part be 'annihilated.'" This empiricism is not theoretic; it is not simply accurate observing from a detached point of view. It is, instead, a mode of participating.

This is a less egocentric, a less narcissistic, conception of poetry than was held by Coleridge, who was inclined to follow the Germans in taking poetry to be a remolding of the world to transcendental vision. Keats losing himself in the life of a sparrow knows an enjoyment the child feels in its mother's body. Keats and the child find an identity outside themselves; as Keats says in a letter, we recognize ourselves by surrendering to what is without. This identification enables us to escape from our narcissism; it is a dramatic feat, a response by acceptance rather than precaution. It heals alienation, and in his essay, "Formulations Regarding Two Principles of Mental Functioning," Freud concedes that art reconciles pleasure- and reality-principles in "a peculiar way."

The anaclitic relation appropriates things by love, gains fulfillment of the self in the external world. William Barrett once wrote that the artist displaces himself far afield with a neutrality different from the neutrality of science, which is a cancellation of the self. The more widely the artist displaces himself, the greater his defense against his neuroses, one of which is anxiety about the hostility of the world. The artist may be neurotic, but his art is not. Swift was mad, but Swift the author of *Gulliver* was not. As is often said, the difference between the artist and the neurotic is that the artist loses his neurosis insofar as he is an artist. The surrogate existence available to the artist is an escape from what Keats called the egotistical sublime, for that resembles a hate-relation comparable to the scientific imperialism, which was a form of monologue. Art is a way of dialogue—the kind of dialogue Cézanne carried on with Mt. Ste. Victoire or Keats with the Urn. In the scientific monologue of the nineteenth century the voice of man was silenced: only things were there, and the observing of them was a joyless act. The scientists could not participate.

Freud seems to have recognized that art is an act of participating and therefore like play. In fact, one can distinguish between Freud's view of art as daydreaming and art as a mode of play. He admits that the fantasy of the daydream is not the same as children's play, an imaginative activity like art; in playing the child participates in a world he creates "while separating it sharply from reality." The child's play is a way of rearranging life without rejecting the world. Freud takes up the notion of play while discussing the repetition-compulsion, for play is an imitation, and when they play, children restate in action whatever has most deeply impressed them in their daily experience. By playing, they make themselves "masters of the situation." Elsewhere Freud also notes that the child has pleasure in playing with language, just as the artist enjoys playing with his medium. Adults, he remarks, cease to play; but when they are unhappy they indulge their fantasies. And he notes that children take play seriously, like the artist. Thus he makes his brilliant comment that "The opposite of play is not serious occupation but—reality." The scientist is intent upon reality.

In brief, Freud implies that there are two ways of attempting to make ourselves masters of our situation, one by science and one by play, or art. What Freud has overlooked is that science is not necessarily "serious" but in its most inventive aspects a mode of play. Here again the distinction between science and technology becomes relevant, since "pure" science is like a variant of play, positing a thesis, then finding where it leads, as when one devises a new geometry by premising that parallel lines meet. This order of geometry arises from no utilitarian motive but from impulses that ordinarily express themselves in children's games with their arbitrary rules leading to participating in a world sharply separated from reality. So, too, the artist plays with his medium. The technologist may be quite as ingenious, but he usually operates in a world where play tends to vanish.

Unlike Freud, the new scientist finds the barrier between art and science breaking down. As Koestler says, science is no longer shackled to the accurate observing of reality, but is free to speculate wastefully and playfully, at home in the world of the Red Queen, who notes that after breakfast one can believe as many as six impossible things. The world of the Red Queen is not, however, the world of Iago—who also believes six impossible things. Iago is playing a game quite different from the games played by children, artists, or scientists today. Iago for all his ingenuity devises a game that is wholly joyless. He calls it sport: he plays *with*, but he cannot *play*. As detached observer he is outside the game which he engineers but does not enter. He does not participate.

In *Beyond the Pleasure Principle* Freud makes one of his most liberal concessions to the artist, granting that it is unnecessary to assume any "particular imitation impulse as the motive of play," for play is an overflow of pleasure, and the economics of dramatic art, notably in tragedy, is distinguishable from child's play insofar as the enjoyment is evoked primarily in the spectator instead of in the actor. The economy of play and art is cathartic or homeopathic by expenditure.

According to the Freudian principle of ambivalence Eros is associated with Thanatos, love with hate. Children's play, springing from high spirits, is often cruel; and tragedy conceals its sadistic motives only imperfectly. We tease those we love, and Kierkegaard said that God torments those whom He would save. The artist loves the world but must master it by deforming it. Nietzsche took art as a form of rebellion, an effectual resistance to what is outside, for man is a creature who can refuse. Yet the artist's refusal is not a negation, as Blake noted: "Without Contraries is no progression. Attraction and Repulsion, Reason and Energy, Love and Hate are necessary to Human existence." While rejecting the world as it appears, the artist does not cease to love it, but gains command of it by a manipulation kindred to organ pleasure or play. The artist's transformation of things can be an act of narcissism, so far as they are made to conciliate the desires of the artist. Tragedy has narcissistic features, since it is one way of making man superior to the calamities that afflict him. It is a rebellion against our failures, inuring us to misfortune; it accepts and refuses. But this narcissism is a neurosis of health, an appropriation without alienation.

Rebellion and Craft

Freud looked upon love as a cure for narcissism, "a flowing-over of the ego-libido into the object." What he calls idealizing in love resembles what we call idealism in art, for both tend to cure repressions or perversions by elevating the object. This reliance on the loved person or object, even in idealized form, is an anaclitic relationship capable of fulfilling infantile love in another mode; and conversely, whatever satisfies infantile love becomes, in the adult attachment, elevated toward an idealizing eminence. The idealizing or deforming of the object occurs when the artist enters a dialogue that is also a competition with the id. Kandinsky "learned to battle with the canvas, to come to know it as a being resisting my wish (= dream), and to bend it forcibly to this wish." Gide spoke of the novelist's vocation as a "rivalry between the real world and the representation which we make of it to ourselves." In this competition there is no false objectivity, as when the observer tries to cancel himself out. In so withdrawing, the scientist rejected himself. But Cézanne entered into a searching dialogue with fruits, with dovecotes, with bare Provençal houses and fields. Van Gogh's dialogue was with starry nights and the sun itself.

One of Wallace Stevens's achievements was to bring back into poetry a rebellious and loving dialogue with nature, a chant of men who perish on summer mornings when quails spontaneously cry. Stevens does not reject Eden and is untroubled by Eliot's apprehensions about Sweeney, the uncultivated apeneck. While Eliot was devoting so much attention to his medium (which often seemed like a constraint) Stevens was recovering a lost romantic discourse with the climate and studying how the poet intelligently competes with figures floating in the contention between the thing as idea and the idea as thing. His "greatest poverty is not to live in a physical world," but he also needs fictions. And the fiction does not appear unless we have a sense of real things, which, as Keats said, "come doubly strong" to the poet's vision. Stevens saw Eden in equatorial Tehuantepec; but he also saw Eden in New Haven or "three or four hills and a cloud." He cherished earth "like the thought of heaven." His poetry is seeing Hartford in a purple light. The fiction of the poem brings among common things "the leaven of what is not." Without refusing the "essential prose" of ordinary evenings, without being seduced by his own ideas grounded in such prose, Stevens proclaimed (answering symbolists who took flight for an absolute) "the oneness of man and his world." Eliot longed for some original Eden, but one may ask whether he had any real affection for the world. Stevens found his Paradise in the Connecticut valley, where "being imperfect" has a gaiety.

> After death, the non-physical people, in paradise,
> Itself non-physical, may, by chance, observe
> The green corn gleaming, and experience
> The minor of what we feel.
>
> (*Esthétique du Mal*)

And what we feel is "merely living as and where we live." Although he was a skilled performer, flamboyantly clever, Stevens's technical finesse did not inhibit his affection for dreary cities. His verse itself, when brought into contrast with symbolist verse, to which he was deeply indebted, seems like play and focuses some primary questions about the relations of art to technology, about hedonism and alienation, about the economy of art and its necessary exuberance. Better than almost anyone for a century Stevens illustrates Norman O. Brown's remark that "language is an operational superstructure on an erotic base." Mallarmé's *Hérodiade* is a superstrutcure of language without an erotic base; so is much of the language of *Parnasse,* of decadent literature, of Pater's meticulous style. In reading Stevens one is reminded how much even writers like Joyce sacrificed to method. It is not merely a question of language but of the writer's whole relation to the world as it is revealed in the Goncourts's *Germinie* and Huysmans's almost technological exercises in fiction. The most literary accomplishments have often diminished gratification, leaving only constraint, partly because they were obligated to methodologies or, worse, to mere data. Flaubert, tormenting himself by reading books on club feet lest he blunder in describing the medical episodes in *Madame Bovary,* hated the facts he had to master and ended by despising the world his novel created. His very research was inspired by disgust. His book is not so much a competition with reality as an attack upon it.

At the opposite pole of fiction is Dickens, whose art is at once rebellious and erotic, distorting the world while loving it. His ebullience pours into evil as well as good; he cherishes and hates London slums; he is enchanted by Fagin, Squeers, Pecksniff, Sikes, Gradgrind, and Uriah Heep. He dotes on the ugly and exhibits the grotesque as one of the most inventive categories of art. He suffers from none of Flaubert's externality illusions, and his affections overflow into what he cannot morally tolerate. His novels are an extravagant and irrational surplus devoted to making, not matching; his play with life is arbitrary to the degree of caricature. He cares nothing for precaution and is one of the least theoretical of novelists. His inefficiency is scandalous.

Dickens gives meaning to Baudelaire's axiom that nature is but a dictionary. He is immersed in actuality without having any compulsion to represent actuality as it "is"; he is one of the most thoughtless of all writers, relying upon a few superficial moral attitudes that seem to be rooted in his temperament, not his mind. His cavalier logic reminds us of whatever truth there may be in Freud's comment that thought is a defensive tactic, a restraint of action, the ego's instrument for holding the world at a distance: "By interposing the process of thinking, it secures the postponement of motor discharge." Since thought arrests action, it is a cause of detachment or even alienation. Dickens's novels are a vehicle for motor discharge; his drama is a mode of gesticulating, mimetic in a physical sense like Greek drama, which was a stylized activity incorporating the dance. The same verdict of thoughtlessness can be brought against Browning, whose art resembles that of Dickens in that it too is a kind of motor discharge. Santayana was not far wrong when he spoke of the brutality of Browning's verse. Browning is as capable of identifying with the evil, the ugly character as Dickens is; he relishes sneaks, liars, criminals as well as saints, endowing them with a vitality that is the vibration of his own appetites. The same would be true of that other great caricaturist, Daumier. Caricature, in fact, is usually one of the most effective ways of resisting things as they are without being estranged from things as they are.

In his contest with reality the artist does not always win, but the poem or the painting may occur as a by-product of the agon. Wordsworth's poems are a residue of his rebellion against the nature he loved, a resistance to "the mighty world of eye and ear," an attempt to read into sense experience something that sense experience could not give, the light from his own mind and a primal sympathy with man. When Keats saw the Elgin marbles he felt that his spirit was too weak to meet the challenge of these abiding forms; yet his tragic resistance to their overwhelming presence gained him, dimly, a vision of a magnitude bringing reassurance and calm.

Much of Cézanne's career was spent in a tormenting competition with his mountain, which he obsessively kept destroying and recreating. It unceasingly defied him, though each of its profiles was hypnotizing. His struggle to realize, to paint his *petites sensations,* yielded a series of works dominated by a necessity existing within Cézanne, not the mountain, which served only as occasion for his artistic venture. He could not withdraw from the mountain, even if he was compelled to destroy its contours. De Sanctis wrote, "To create reality a poet must first have the force to kill it. But instantly the fragments draw together again, seeking one another, with the obscure presentiment of the new life to which they are destined." Cézanne's rebellion against the mountain is not like Flaubert's rebellion against his society—a rebellion the more alienating since it attempted to posit realities that Flaubert hated. Cézanne's mountain as he painted it is a countergeography answering the geography he cherished. To create this countergeography he exploited the mountain; but his exploiting was, unlike economic exploitation, fruitful of human experience, a surplus value that endowed the mountain with a new organic life.

In dealing with these stubborn contours Cézanne waived the scientific realism of his day and fell back upon the affectionate realism that continually led Degas back to the wings of sordid theatres, which enchanted him. Degas did not admire his ballet girls any more than Flaubert admired Emma Bovary; but he delighted in these dancers as Flaubert never allowed himself to delight in his figure of Emma. Degas's testimony that realism itself can be anaclitic or even erotic is repeated in George Eliot's finding "beauty in commonplace things." This loving realism is not dependent upon a technique but upon an attitude in the writer or painter. In Eliot's case it is an untheoretic and agnostic acceptance of evidence, placing the novelist *terre à terre* with her characters. Eliot is as attentive as the studio realist and protests that the novelist has no vocation to represent things as "they never have been and never will be." She insists on accepting people "as they are: you can neither straighten their noses, nor brighten their wit, nor rectify their dispositions." So she is content to tell her "simple story, without trying to make things seem better than they were; dreading nothing, indeed, but falsity, which, in spite of one's best efforts, there is reason to dread. Falsehood is so easy, truth so difficult." Her realism tolerates pity and love; it is an unrationalized compliance with life, making it different from the realism of Flaubert, Zola, and even Balzac. It is close, perhaps, to the untheoretic realism of Courbet, or to that of Browning's Lippo Lippi, who takes pleasure in mere recognition of things.

The realism that is committed to method is different from this affectionate realism, for methodologies draw realism toward literary technology. The case is conveniently clear in painting, where, for example, the Little Masters of the seventeenth century are known as realists, though there is a great difference between a realist like

Vermeer and painters of still life like Heda, Kalf, or Pieter Claesz. However clearly Vermeer distances his world, seeing it from the angle of an observer who is, nominally, excluded from what he sees, one of the most striking effects of the painting is, by implication, Vermeer's presence, his private and intimist regard. Everything is saturated with the sensibility of the excluded painter, who invites us to be aware of his mode of vision. Vermeer's absence, like Degas's absence, is a subtle mode of appearance. He observes, though his observing is not scientific in the nineteenth-century sense of the term. His approach is so finely chosen it becomes highly personal and as sympathetic as George Eliot's. Our interest focuses in a responsiveness so ostensibly and so insistently withdrawn; yet the very privacy or reticence changes reportage to art. Vermeer's distancing does not alienate; it is, instead, the affirmation of a personal regard. Vermeer does not pretend to offer the world as it "is"; instead, he presents a world as seen. The seeing is more significant than what is so carefully seen. The realism turns tender and expressive.

The case with Claesz, Heda, or Kalf is otherwise. We are alerted to things as being there, but our interest is shifted to the extraordinary accuracy with which they are presented, the way light glints on silver, the texture of a peach or lobster. The painter is truly absent: here is the world as it is, recorded with dazzling competence, what we can all see if we care to. These artists distance themselves as well as their still life. Yet again there is a difference between this literal realism and the realism of the pre-Raphaelites or Zola's naturalistic novel because these painters are not theoretic. Heda, Kalf, and Claesz worked by brush and eye only, by their miraculous handling of pigment, their craft. Their realism is not methodological, but optical and muscular; there is no theory behind the skill with which they strip the world bare; they do not rationalize their observation; the hand is not in the service of the mind. That is to say, they do not have a technological approach, although their finesse in managing their métier is a technical accomplishment. The realism of Dutch still life is a game—as it is in Harnett and *trompe l'oeil,* which competes with photography. Thus play is a motive in the Little Masters, and still life is a game of matching—but without any of the anxiety attaching to a realism that is programmatic, as it is in the pre-Raphaelites, in Seurat's painting, or in Zola's novels. The Little Masters take pleasure in things.

On the distinctions between these varieties of realism can be based a thesis that the way to resist the tyranny of a technological society is craft, the artistic faculty of techné. Heda, Kalf, and Claesz are not painters in the sense that Vermeer is a painter; yet none of them is bound by the programmatic realism of the pre-Raphaelites or the naturalistic novel. The difference between nineteenth-century realism and foregoing realisms is precisely that the former tended to become methodological—that is, ideological, since ideologies or theories always contaminated nineteenth-century methods in the arts, which fell victim to the technological: every method evolved a program. And the basic difference between art and technology (perhaps between science and technology also) is that neither art nor science can be programmed.

To redeem technology from its own methods Robert Preusser has pled that engineering education should begin with the arts because "the practice of art permits creative application of its principles *while learning about them.*" As things usually stand, the engineer works from knowledge to execution, whereas the artist evolves his knowledge from execution. The craft, or techné, of the artist is an existential activity, exploratory and emergent; the craftsman's methods, a form of *bricolage,* are concessive to experience and derived from experience instead of being imposed upon experience. As Aristotle said, art deals with the variable, and Preusser calls for an engineering education that can break through the textbook formulas and lead to "something beyond the assigned task." The engineer, like the scientist, should be allowed beginner's luck.

In lecturing to M.I.T. students Anton Ehrenzweig has warned that professional skill is often inhibiting because it can so precisely chart the way ahead.[24] When the outcome is so completely controlled, then there is no "indifference for the future" such as the painter allows himself, but only a competence that results in a sterile functionalism. When functional design was in its early phases —its experimental period—the architect could work toward an undecided future and alternative solutions. But when functionalism became theoretic or academic, structure was preconceived, and architecture was subjected to engineering, treating space in static grids and establishing a new formalism under technological auspices. Adhering to the original Bauhaus training, Ehrenzweig claims that professional designing must not be governed by conscious planning alone but must allow a measure of uncertainty or "unfocusing." There was a "Bauhaus period" in early renaissance painting when the system of mathematical perspective was in its experimental stage and the painter used foreshortening, however arbitrarily, almost as a way of improvising.

The necessary pragmatism of the writer is the theme of John Dewey's greatest book, *Art as Experience*. We are irritated, Dewey says, whenever we feel that a novelist has manipulated his materials to gain an effect determined in advance. In reading a novel "one may get a feeling early in the story that hero or heroine is doomed, doomed not by anything inherent in situations and character but by the intent of the author who makes the character a puppet to set forth his own cherished idea." The predisposition to a certain outcome is felt in Ibsen and to an extent in Hardy, and sometimes in the Parnassians and symbolists. The artist's vision is not *avec* in this case but *par dèrriere* or *au dehors*, and efficiency in reaching the end in view is a symptom of technical anaesthesia, as it is in engineering. This type of plotting is an attempt to control the future, which in human experience must remain open rather than closed; it is a denial of the reality of time in human life. One of the meanings in that inexhaustible play *Hamlet* is the perversion of the intellect that takes the form of plotting, the effort to determine the future. Everyone in the play—and chiefly Hamlet—seeks to master time by some scheme of action that insures an outcome. But unlike the others, Hamlet at last learns how improvising is more helpful than plotting, since improvising is a way of utilizing the present; and the present is the authentic tense in human experience. Thus Hamlet's plots always fail him, and the present does not work for him until he begins to improvise, as he does in grappling with the pirates and in forging the letter that sends Rosencrantz and Guildenstern to their deaths. The lesson sticks, and when he has the invitation to duel, he follows the king's pleasure in a readiness to meet the present moment: "If it be now, 'tis not to come; if it be not to come, it will be now; if it be not now, yet it will come. Let be." So he stops his plotting, his planning the future, and surrenders to the present moment, improvising his way to the solution of his problems. Earlier he had told Gertrude how sweet it is "when in one line two crafts directly meet" in a knavery that resembles Iago's bloodless expediency. This vicious craft is an engineering feat, a version of technical anaesthesia. It is not the existential craft of the artist who works in the present by the improvising that resembles *bricolage*, the craft that is adaptable to occasions, that is open to the future.

In contrast to technological or professional closure, craft has a certain pragmatism of the muscles or the pen, adapting itself to the indeterminate, the margin of uncertainty, the chance beloved of art. Dewey refers to the necessary relativity of technique, for if method is valuable in art it must be constantly open to agnosticism. "Because the artist is a lover of unalloyed experience, he shuns objects that are already saturated." The limiting use of method in Zola is not experimental after all; the method falsifies the data. His naturalism was not open to the relativity of technique that marks a difference between craft and technism. In his Journal for January, 1847, Delacroix noted, "There must always be an element of improvisation in the execution of a painter," who will "make new discoveries as his work proceeds."

The lack of this agnosticism and adaptability is evident in the most ambitious system of technology the nineteenth century produced, Auguste Comte's positivism. The positivist, that archetypal bureaucrat, hoped to engineer life and art by his methodology:

> As the chief characteristic of Positive Philosophy is the paramount importance that is given, and that on speculative grounds, to social considerations, its efficiency for the purposes of practical life is involved in the very spirit of the system. When this spirit is rightly understood, we find that it leads at once to an object far higher than that of satisfying our scientific curiosity; the object, namely, of organizing human life. (*A General View of Positivism*)

Comte hoped to penetrate every domain of human experience by controls that tightened Bentham's utilitarianism into a total methodology: "Thoughts must be systematized before Feelings, Feelings before Actions." Committed to his belief in progress, Comte wanted to insure the future by programming: "Progress then is in its essence identical with Order, and may be looked upon as Order made manifest." The positivist did not shrink from programming art, itself an instrument for human engineering. With an insolence pardonable only because it is so well meant, Comte explains, "Guarding ourselves, then, against errors . . . we may now consider the esthetic character of Positivism. In the first place it furnishes us with a satisfactory theory of Art, a subject which has never been systematically explained. . . . Art may be defined as an ideal representation of Fact. . . . Its sphere therefore is co-extensive with that of Science. Both deal in their own way with the world of Fact; the one explains it, the other beautifies it."

The system: Comte illustrates the abiding danger of culture since the renaissance, the danger of the programmatic. Politics became programmatic, science became programmatic, art itself felt the pull toward the programmatic, and as Comte suggests, ethic became subdued to the programmatic. And the program always subscribes to an ideology; in turn each ideology generates its own bureaucracy (which is a political version of academicism). Then too, a dissociation of politics from ethics appeared with Machiavelli, who is the political archetype of the modern world precisely because he made policy programmatic. In most societies before the renaissance politics was itself a form of ethic. In the tribal phase of culture, represented by the Old Testament and Homer, the ethic of the hero was political; and in the Greek city-state, as in the Roman empire, the official piety was closely associated with rituals of men living with men in a state regulated by *themis,* law, justice. But Machiavelli brought into politics a nearly technological tactic or method divorced from any satisfactory ethic. It was left for Shakespeare to attempt some reconciliation between political strategy and morality in plays like *Henry IV,* Parts 1 and 2; *Henry V; Hamlet;* and *Antony and Cleopatra.* The attempt failed, and by the time of Comte the politics of positivism waives the whole ethical issue in favor of organizing society. The ideology is total, a human engineering that aspires to absolute Order. It is left for Lenin to assert that in politics there is no morality—only expediency.

The isolation of politics from ethics (or the conversion of policy to ethic) may also account for the isolation of

politics from art; for as politics became increasingly programmatic and ideological, it resorted to propaganda.
The normally apolitical mentality of the artist is at least
partly due to his distrust of and distaste for the official
line—that is, propaganda. The artist has increasingly
been forced into a position that leaves him isolated from
policy. It is a position neither Milton nor Dryden would
understand.

And so far as science became programmatic during the
nineteenth century the artist felt instinctively at odds
with science, even though, perversely, various artistic
movements themselves tended to be programmatic. But
the artist quickly learned to distrust the academic system,
and Ruskin warned against the theories that were really
nothing more than programs imposed upon the painter at
the expense of his craft. He realized that the academic
doctrines were a sterile technism masking under the name
of art. The official doctrines of academies were based
upon methods that were repeatable. Repetition brings
boredom, and one of the relevant definitions of the artist
is that he is essentially a man who refuses to be bored.

The programming did not become total until our century, and a great deal has been written in despair about
the drift toward a one-dimensional society breeding one-
dimensional men, subject to an absolute administrative
machinery. We have been told that technological problems produce technological solutions in an ever-widening
circle that closes upon itself. To an extent it seems true
that even the opposition to techniques can be pacified by
technical controls that extend into areas hostile to technology. There is even evidence that the painter who re-
volts against the public has been absorbed into the
system thanks to the technique of public relations by
which the most avant-garde performance becomes fashionable, the most marketable of all painting because it
is antagonistic. Thus the vanguard painter becomes accessory to the establishment, which now thrives on the

nihilistic. This is one of the most damaging ways to conciliate the artist's independence or rebellion. There seems to be no exit. Yet the artist has been the most difficult of all men to corrupt by ideologies, the most resistant to programs. There are signs that art, like science, has emancipated itself from the tyranny of the technological by a return to the primal empiricism of craft.

VI

Proximity

❦

Organic Design

LONG AGO LEWIS MUMFORD remarked
that art is merely the humanizing of technics—it is "that
part of technics which bears the fullest imprint of the
human personality." The inhumanity of technology
has been due to its excluding the human personality in
the interest of an idea of Order, an abstraction that has
tyrannized over science and technology since the renaissance. In literature and painting and architecture
this idea of Order has expressed itself in canons of
Style, which to that extent were a manifestation of
technological imperatives. The rebellion against the
idea of Order has been more or less continuous in
the arts, and Naum Gabo has defined the limits of the
idea of Order in painting: "In Art more than any-
where else in the creative discipline, daring expedi-
tions are allowed. The most dizzying experiments are
permissible, but even in art the logic of life arrests the
experiments as soon as they have reached the point when
the death of the experimental objects becomes imminent."
The arrest occurs at the instant when the experiment

is worked through to a solution that can be formulated into an official method, a program, a style. Then method becomes an academism with an attached ideology and closes the experiment to further exploration. The sabotage of the idea of Style has been violent in painting, and is being supported by the rebellion against Style in the new French novel and among the new French critics like Roland Barthes, who is agent for a brand of neorealism: not *écriture* but only *langage*. All this repudiation of Style is symptomatic of what has been occurring also in science and advanced technology, which have sabotaged official methods and opened up the wider meanings of the terms observation, theory, law. As Gabo notes, science has found itself "confronted with conclusions which had before seemed impossible, in fact the word 'impossibility' disappeared from the lexicon of scientific language."

Upon reaching these limits the scientist, like the artist, has been forced to abandon the idea of Order, and advanced technology has broken away from the narrow confines of engineering with its precise and economic formulas. That is, science and technology have returned to the empiricism of craft, which is antiideological in that it does not require the idea of an Order; it tolerates chance, the variable, the contingent, the immediate, and the concrete in place of the abstract. And it allows the involvement of the technician or scientist, as craft allows the involvement of the artist in his "style." Again, to quote Naum Gabo: "The elements of a visual art, such as lines, colors, shapes, possess their own forces of expression independent of any association with the external aspects of the world; their life and their action are self-conditioned psychological phenomena rooted in human nature . . . they are not merely abstract signs, but they are immediately and organically bound up with human emotions."

Recent discussions of the relations between technology, science, and the arts have probably added little to what

John Ruskin wrote a century ago, for Ruskin was revolting against methodological solutions, whether industrial or academic. Ruskin's ideal in all the arts is essentially a craft ideal, harmonizing the technological with the aesthetic and the human. He recognized architecture as the dominant and most utilitarian of arts, the one standing in closest relation with technics, and he repudiated the pseudofunctionalism that has made so much of our building an engineering academism. In a sentence that refutes our technological scholasticism he remarks, "The architect is not *bound* to exhibit structure; nor are we to complain of him for concealing it, any more than we should regret the outer surfaces of the human frame conceal so much of its anatomy."

Ruskin urged the architect to design sculpturally, for like the Greeks he sensed that the basic mimetic impulse is plastic; it is scaled to the human organism and responsive to the haptic and tactile. Modeling, or carving, is the most organic of the arts: "We have seen that sculpture is to be a representation of true internal form. Much more is it to be a representation of true internal emotion. You must carve only what you yourself feel as you feel it." Because it is a tactile as well as a visual art sculpture is a maximal realization of sensuous experience, "imitative sculpture being defined as an art which, by the musical disposition of masses, imitates anything of which the imitation is justly pleasant to us; and does so in accordance with structural laws having due reverence to the materials employed." Sculptural figuration is "the simplest primary form" capable of expressing the mimetic instinct that is "zooplastic and life-shaping." This Hellenic sense of the primacy of sculpture is a reaction against the overvisualizing illustrative arts of his day.

Thus Ruskin applies to architecture a sculptural criterion, and in so doing makes a distinction between engineering and architecture, an art that satisfies the life-shaping impulses which gave him an appetite for drawing the stones of St. Mark's touch by touch. Ruskin's response to architecture is kinaesthetic: "There is sensation in every inch of it, and an accommodation to every architectural necessity, with a determined variation in arrangement, which is exactly like the related proportions and provisions in the structure of organic form." His distinction between architecture and building is a sculptural one, "for though architecture and sculpture are not separate arts, there is an architectural *manner* of sculpture" just as there is a sculptural manner in architecture; and when architecture ceases to be sculptural, it declines, as it did when gothic ceased to be sculptural: "Sculpture, founded on love of nature, was the talisman of its existence; wherever sculpture was practised, architecture arose—wherever that was neglected, architecture expired." How unlike all this is to the theory of Le Corbusier in his purist phase, appealing to logic as a constant instrument of human control (and *for* human control?), the instrument of "maximum economy" to be used by an art of conception addressed "to the elevated faculties of the mind." The modular method, a way of insuring order, subdues everything to form, since "the highest delectation of the human mind is the perception of order." And the sensation of order "is of a mathematical quality." So the purist concludes that "the creation of a work of art should utilize means for specified results."

Ruskin's appeal to the sculptural may sound like Berenson's tactile and life-enhancing values; but Berenson's aesthetic is essentially a visual one, requiring the translation from optical to sculptural. The extreme refinement of Berenson's aesthetic moment is closer to decadent Beauty than is Ruskin's organic sensibility, which is thoroughly anaclitic and even erotic. Ruskin's immediate, sensuous response is similar to Wordsworth's appetite, feeling, or love, bringing its own credentials and an assurance of irresistible union with material form.

Opposed as he was to the industrial order, Ruskin was tolerant enough to grant that iron and glass could be used organically: "There appears no reason why iron should not be used as well as wood; and the time is probably near when a new system of architectural laws will be developed, adapted entirely to metallic construction." He anticipates Sir Herbert Read's proposal that the machine and factory must adapt themselves to the artist, not the artist to the economy of the factory and the machine. By insisting upon the primacy of craft over theory and mechanism Ruskin accommodates technology to art: "Art may be healthily associated with manufacture, and probably in the future will always be so; but the student must be strenuously warned against supposing that they can ever be one and the same thing, that art can ever be followed on the principles of manufacture. Each must be followed separately; the one must influence the other, but each must be kept distinctly separate from the other." The separation, however, is one of principle rather than practice. William Morris was not so categorical about separating art from the machine, and urged that the craftsman could use the machine expressively if he acceded to his instrument by adapting his design to what the machine can do.

The idea of design served Morris as a means of reconciling art with technology; for the term design was associated with the decorative arts, and Morris became the great champion of ornamental and decorative crafts, the so-called minor or applied arts that did not have the kudos of the fine arts. Yet the notion of design involves some of the most revolutionary tendencies in the modern arts; it is a point of intersection between industry and art and marks the rise of an art that rejects a three-dimensional vision, the depth or distance factor that has been overvalued since the renaissance. Within renaissance painting itself there was a reaction against the three-dimensional when Giovanni da Udine, working with

Raphael, decorated the *Logge* of the Vatican with shallow grotesques inspired by Pompeiian stuccolike ornament. These grotesque designs on the surface were as organic as the stereometric, or classic, style, and they mark a phase in the disintegration of that style.

Similarly, the most decisive movement in the modern arts has been to return to the surface, the frontal plane, the two-dimensional, and to refuse all the implications that formerly attached to the notion of depth. As Robbe-Grillet says, the appearance of things is not a mask for concealed meanings; we live in a flat world where the obvious is the essential and depth is a fiction we no longer need: the significant is there on the surface—obvious but nonetheless inscrutable. And the most inscrutable mystery for modern science is the everyday matter-of-fact concreteness that so fascinated Whitehead. The reality is the immediate occasion, not the abstract law, which distances or misplaces the concreteness and makes us believe in a fiction of depth, the concealed meanings rejected by Robbe-Grillet. Accordingly the arts and sciences have become thoroughly phenomenological; they do not seek for structures concealed in the background of appearances, since the structures are inherent in the appearances. The design is on the surface as a built-in circumstance or, if the term is allowable, an intra-structure, the fact embodying the value, the meaning. The fact, so to speak, no longer has a legendary meaning but refers only to itself. The surface is the core.

The significance of this return to the surface is suggested in William Morris's insistence that the decorative arts and crafts have none of the fake cultural values of the "fine" arts, with their merely accessory prestige. Morris moves "beyond culture." Like Ruskin he was scornful of *beaux-arts* training and hoped to redeem art from the academies by pulling it back to the craft of designing that was taught in schools of "applied" arts. Morris always denied that ornamental arts are the lesser arts, for they are practiced by the hand, learned only through exercising the métier: "I wish specially to impress this upon you, that *designing* cannot be taught at all in a school: continued practice will help a man who is naturally a designer: . . . but the royal road of a set of rules deduced from a sham science of design, that is itself not a science but another set of rules, will lead nowhere." In the name of craft Morris gets beyond art; and the instinct to ornament pulls design toward the surface.

In returning to the existential practice of design Morris laid a foundation for the Bauhaus and also, without being aware of doing so, repudiated all the specious notions that had clustered about the three-dimensional theory of Alberti:

> By the word pattern design . . . I mean the ornamentation of a surface by work that is not imitative or historical, at any rate not principally or essentially so. Such work is often not literally flat, for it may be carving or moulded work in plaster or pottery; but whatever material relief it may have is given to it for the sake of beauty and richness, and not for the sake of imitation, or to tell a fact directly; so that people have called this art ornamental art, though indeed all real art is ornamental. ("Some Hints on Pattern Designing")

Morris asks of the designer an intelligible clear line that is formal and organic, and the organic pattern or contour need not be copied from nature itself: "It is impossible to imitate nature literally; the utmost realism of the most realistic painter falls a long way short of that. . . . You may be sure that any decoration is futile, and has fallen into at least the first stage of degradation, when it does not remind you of something beyond itself, of something of which it is but a visible symbol." Freely admitting that pattern designing is a convention, Morris insists that its "convention shall not be so to say a conventional convention." The decorative is, for Morris, an organic, life-enhancing, zoomorphic linear form tending toward the abstract; and it is flat. So in the name of the ornamental Morris refuses depth; the surface can be organic.

Ruskin saw no conflict between the plastic and the decorative, which could also be organic: "The greatest art yet produced has been decorative." In contradiction to his advice to render nature exactly as it is observed (the pre-Raphaelite program) Ruskin admired the Byzantine because it was ornamental and abstract; he goes so far as to say "no art is noble which in any wise depends upon direct imitation for its effect upon the mind." Thus he contrasts "men of facts" with "men of design," who are superior since they express their enjoyment by the vitality of abstract line.

This aspect of Ruskin's thought was extended by Wilhelm Worringer, whose *Abstraction and Empathy* is a metaphysical defense of the art of the surface. To represent the third dimension (the deep space of naturalistic painting) is to shackle art to "things of the outer world" and to corrupt the idea of imitation. Worringer claims that art "does not begin with naturalistic constructs, but with ornamental-abstract ones," the "vigorous urgent life" of the line, a topography of our own spirit. The Byzantine contour on the surface destroys the natural forms of things to recreate them in another world; the mosaic and interlace are rebellions against nature, obeying the urge to make, not to match. Thus Worringer finds in the barbaric design of northern art a redemption of man's spirit from its immersion in time (a coordinate of deep space) and matter. Tinged as it is with the imperialism of Hegel's thought, Worringer's aesthetic of the plane is a mode of rejecting the world.

There is a quite different return to the plane in the aesthetic of Art Nouveau, which bridges decadence with the new functionalism leading toward the Bauhaus. This fragile and decorative design revised traditional modes of imitation and did away with the third dimension, the distanced or window view of composition. Art Nouveau had within it two different modes, both functional: the spare, economic, rectilinear, though delicate, severity of Mackintosh, and the equally spare and functional, but more seductive and erotic, line released in the fancies of Beardsley, Horta, and Guimard. Radically antiacademic as it was, Art Nouveau signifies the same return to the surface that was apparent in T. E. Hulme's quest for the hard dry image, the architect's curves, and also in Gide's new design for the novel as an assemblage of motifs in a purely fictional plane. Above all, Art Nouveau, with its graphic flamboyance, was a restoration of craftsmanship.

The restoration of craft was almost an obsession with William Morris, who sought in ornamental design to liberate the play of hand that would "satisfy the aspirations of men set free from the tyranny of commercialism" and from recipes for Fine Art. Morris's crisp line was not the application of a formula:

> . . . our eyes are apt to get dulled to this eventfulness of form in those things which we are always looking at. Now it is one of the chief uses of decoration, the chief part of its alliance with nature, that it has to sharpen our dulled senses in this matter; for this end are those wonders of intricate pattern interwoven, those strange forms invented, which men have so long delighted in: forms and intricacies that do not necessarily imitate nature, but in which the hand of the craftsman is guided to work in the way that she does, till the web, the cup, or the knife, look as natural, nay as lovely, as the green field, the river bank, or the mountain flint. ("The Decorative Arts")

That is to say, Morris does not treat design as a technology but as a craft; and the functionalism of the modern arts has, by contrast, itself been a form of technology.

The Agnosticism of Craft

The return to the surface—the obvious—in recent painting and fiction has recovered some of the untheoretic craft activity, the sense, as Morris says, of the eventfulness in things we constantly see or hear. Like the recent scientist, the contemporary novelist or painter detects that the ordinary, the commonplace, the superficial, the quotidian is the very mystery most inaccessible to reason and explanation and method. The immediate occasion is sufficient unto itself, and this recognition has led to a new humility, as well as a new frustration. If the significance is on the surface, then the need for depth explanation has gone, and the contingent, the everyday happening, is more authentic than the ultimate or absolute. The acceptance of the apparent is nothing less than the breakdown of the old three-dimensional vision of renaissance painting and the Newtonian world; it does not even require the aesthetic sensibility of Art Nouveau, its clarity of design. The old systems of meaning—the Newtonian solid geometry locating things at appropriate distances or the theoretic order of Alberti's perspective, which foreshortened—are suspect. Novelist, painter, and scientist have given up foreshortening. Plot itself was a mode of foreshortening. To accept the accidental or casual is to recognize the irrationality of the obvious, to dispense with the need for a logic accounting for everything by cause and effect, action and reaction.

Science has reverted to an empiricism capable of endorsing the immediate data of experience that are not always assignable to a theoretic explanation. The data are the system; the matter-of-fact concreteness may or may not be explained by natural law. Accidents happen, and accidents are real. The existential tolerance for the data as given has led science toward an operationalism that in some ways resembles the Happening or action painting, which is a kind of *bricolage*. Existence is itself structure, and in quantum mechanics contradictions may be a sign of actuality. Consequently a great many notions about consistency, exactitude, precision, and controlled observation have been outmoded. The scientist is now less concerned with universal laws than with studying the way things are in all their contingency. The new science has been described as an account of what scientists do—what operations they go through in an activity requiring teamwork that de-emphasizes the individuality of the scientist until he has something like the status of the craftsman who worked namelessly on the fabric of a cathedral.

The recognition of the actuality of the contingent, the accidental, as well as the necessary has had effects in advanced technology and even engineering. We are told that the engineer must learn to exploit the accidental, freeing "configurations and their placement from premeditated control."[25] In the new engineering, "concepts do not necessarily precede discoveries and, in fact, often preclude them." If technology ceases to be an instrument directed as efficiently as possible toward known ends and is itself transformed into a vehicle for discovery by accommodating the accidental *as* accidental, then it is open to craftsmanship and the chance loved by art; method becomes craft, or craft method.

All this is to suggest that advanced technology has become less programmatic, that science has become less ideological. The same tendency is evident in the so-called new radicalism of the younger generation devoted to civil rights. Ever since the Port Huron Statement, student movements have been less concerned with formulating programs for a democratic society than with getting things done in the South and depressed areas. They also have been dealing with the situation as it is by a kind of operationalism that minimizes system and method in favor of commitment to the immediate occasion.

In these ventures, as in much current science and art, method is what is created, what goes on, what is discovered. The process of creating is the sum of what is created. Formerly an artistic method was a way of wresting from nature its concealed meanings, its "content," whereas now the writing itself is a way of participating in what goes on, a methexis instead of a mimesis. For example, when Fautrier or an action painter paints, there is no representation in the older sense of the term, since the act of painting is what is represented. Action painting identifies the content of the work with the process of the brush; there is no such thing as a proper or exact method, nor is method a vehicle for representing a subject. The method is the meaning, and action painting discloses nothing beyond the painter's instrumentalism in painting. Such painting destroys illustration, and a great deal of painting since the renaissance has been simply illustrative. The action painting illustrates nothing beyond its own activity. It is self-evident.

This kind of self-evidence, where existence refers only to itself, its coming into being, not something beyond, operates in Jasper Johns's painting, where ordinary objects establish their presence. Flags, targets, letters, numerals are accepted as the data of experience, and Johns states that he uses them precisely because he does not have to invent anything: "That's what I like about them, that they come that way." Thus they can be used entirely without partiality and establish themselves in the work without any reference whatever to our attitude. They do not claim any immunity of an artistic sort. So he uses ordinary letters and numerals because a more distinctive typography would smack of "art." These things standing as we ordinarily see them prescribe the dimensions and the design of the painting, which is self-evolved. They are flattened on the surface exactly because they conceal no "depth" or referential "meaning." Something of this denial of depth is also heard in the recording of everyday conversation in Raymond Queneau's *Exercices,* which repeat the spoken language as if it were registered on a gramaphone: "You ought to get an extra button on your coat."

Queneau whimsically calls his recordings exercises in style, thus satirizing the formalism that has passed for literature. His dialogue renounces all "magic" of phrase and recovers a "classic" neutrality, a residual writing that is the naked idiom, or "white writing." In the name of truth Roland Barthes has urged discarding all the academic ideals of *vraisemblance,* taste, objectivity, genre, and whatever may go by the name of style, which has given writing in the past a specious depth called literature. The very notion of style or "literature" has led to the acceptance of an academic Blue Guide that designated the "cultural" values of French authors, imposing the standard of the dictionary. The very notion of a "character" has become a convention, and ideals of the *Beau* and the *Bien* have made literature a scholasticism. There is no *idiome sacré* for the writer, and the celebrated French *clarté* is a logical absolute that requires interdictions. The vocabulary of realism was itself an artifact. There is no such thing as "literature"; there is only language in all its immediacy and ambiguity. To use a certain language is to have a certain kind of experience; the language of a writer *is* his subject; what he says is how he speaks. In wiping away the notion of style Barthes is doing for literature what curators have been doing for paintings by cleaning them. How many fraudulent notions of style and culture have gathered about paintings that were simply dirty or overpainted? By discarding canons of genre and clarity and taste Barthes is rescuing idiom from Art, which was a superfluous dimension. The zero degree of writing moves beyond culture. Grammar and idiom *are* meaning.

Barthes merely represents what has happened in painting and in science, the reaffirming that reality must be taken at its face value regardless of meanings that are "beyond" or final. In short, depth has become expendable, or at least irrelevant. The fashionable talk about the disappearance or death of "God" is a way of recognizing that we have lost interest in ultimates, in absolutes, in universal laws, in categories like Art. The provocation of the immediate and the superficial has unsettled the old per-

spective that discovered "real" meanings in a depth view.
Gone, too, with the old foreshortening is the premise that
order implies symmetry. One of the premonitory features
of Art Nouveau was its asymmetrical design. And Art
Nouveau arose among the minor arts—the graphic arts,
furniture design, glassware, tapestry, typography. It was
an activity accessory to the so-called fine or major arts; it
did not aspire to the grand musuem values of culture but
offered what we need and use day by day. It was based
upon craft rather than art, and craft is the existential
experience in art, making aesthetic theories unnecessary.
The craftsman works according to the existential principle that the meaning of our life is in what we do hour
by hour; the value inheres in the episodes.

The recovery of meaning in the obvious is doubtless
what explains the vogue of *chosiste* art in all its current
forms. The *chosiste* accepts the surface, the apparent, the
superficial as the real—without any compulsion to explain it. Obsessed by the ordinary, the *chosiste* novelist or
pop artist refuses symbolism and all derived significance.
As Robbe-Grillet says, the writer must believe that the
surface of things is not a mask to veil hidden implications.
Things are things, nothing else or more. There is no heart
of reality behind objects. "We no longer believe in
depth." The sense of the presence of things, referring to
themselves alone, is baffling; but it also recovers some of
the mythical consciousness of the primitive mind, which
has an impression of the object there in all its intensity
without trying to measure it by something else. The presence of the thing is a kind of revelation that suffices. The
overwhelming sense that things are there is not, says
Robbe-Grillet, the old objective observing: "Objectivity
in the general sense of the term—total impersonality of
observation—is all too evidently an illusion. But *freedom*
of observation *should* be possible." If to write is to
choose, to see is to choose also.

The difficulty with the old realism was that the presence of things was not mythical; the interpretation of things ordered in a scheme disguised their real strangeness, "making them more comprehensible, more reassuring." In other words, things appeared in perspective, a foreshortening that dispelled their potency. Whitehead had this sense of the potency and mystery of things, the facts that are so stubbornly real; he identified God as the principle of concretion undiscoverable by reason; He must be sought in particular experiences. So also Robbe-Grillet finds that everyday objects by their simple existence touch the inexplicable. The object must not be exploited as a sign for accessory meanings to be read into it, since it is hermetic in its own right. If God has disappeared, He has done so partly because the world seems stranger than ever.

Heidegger's definition of art as a disclosure of the thingly character of the thing accords with this *chosiste* temper. It is difficult, he says, to let a thing be simply the entity that it is: "The thingness of the thing is particularly strange and difficult to express." Thought meets maximum resistance when it tries to penetrate this thingness, and "the unpretentious thing evades thought most stubbornly." The old depth perspective was a way of mastering the thing by assigning to it adventitious meanings, supplemental structures. In *chosiste* art "the work lets the earth be an earth."

Stripping rationality from the object is an act of humility as well as a form of agnosticism. Doubtless the *chosiste* has a method, but it is one that induces the kind of humility with which Nathalie Sarraute quests for possible meanings in the ordinary, the commonplace, the chatter of negligible persons whose existence can be known only through subconversation, the clichés that give their lives a kind of infrastructure far more ambiguous than the firmly delineated character in the traditional novel. Her fiction arises from Heidegger's axiom that "the ordinary is basically not ordinary; it is extra-ordinary."

She detects the duplicity of the everyday, its suspiciousness, its uncertain features. For her the platitude is the contingent and the real; it is the immediate and accordingly needs attention more than does the transcendent. Her agnosticism, so tentative in its methods, so sensitive to the casual, is more tolerant than the realism of older novelists. George Eliot had something of this agnosticism, but Nathalie Sarraute is more aware of implications in the banal. In her fiction the trivial becomes numinous.

In the same vein Francis Ponge, a *chosiste* prose-poet, distrusts the ideas that have been imposed upon things. When he looks at a glass of water, he feels that ideas are only epiphenomenal—*commandées* or bespoke. Ideas require agreement or disagreement; but a glass of water enables him to live in silence before it. Ideas deceive him, but things never do because they are present. Face to face with a stove, he is able to forget himself, and his prose-poems are a surrender to things that do not solicit explanations but explain themselves, justify themselves, by their existence, which is their presence. (One recalls Keats's response to the sparrow pecking before his window.) Thus Ponge feels a *parti pris des choses*, the perplexing stimulus of objects in their multiple modes of existence. The dictionary does not help him identify or comprehend things: the glass of water in its purity, liquidity, transparence is mute testimony to its own iridescent reality which cannot be thought. Ponge asks modesty before things, a tribute to the frail contour of the shrimp, that "little monster of precaution."

Or again, Gaston Bachelard, one of the most sympathetic of agnostics before things, shows the irrelevance of ideas when we encounter space as a lived experience. At a time when the science of outer space thrives, Bachelard studies space as a personal discovery or recognition, a poetry of earth that is never dead. In his *Poetics of Space* he contrasts space as it is known to the physicist with space as we live it in daily experience. He is afflicted, he

says, with topophilia, an acute sensitivity to the contours in which we exist, the sensation of space as it is felt
within the house, within the cellar or attic; the space
inside a drawer is not the space inside a seashell or the
convolution of the snail's life, the space of the miniature,
the satisfaction of roundness. This inherent poetry of
space was already discovered by Wordsworth in the Wye
valley, a geography that was lived mutely in the blood
and felt along the heart. No geometer makes this personal
conquest of space; these poetic areas of experience cannot
be measured by physicist or surveyor. Our lived spaces
are the topology of our existence: our hands still feel the
latch of doors we first opened. Proust lived in this kind of
space, known only as uneven paving stones and his turns
on the way to Meséglises. Thoreau and Pater were others
who sensed that lakes and houses remain inscribed in
consciousness. Such spaces the architect never blue-
printed, the mason never built. Bachelard notes how hard
it is to live poetically in an apartment; elevators have
done away with the heroism of climbing near the sky. We
no longer fear the madness that is buried in the dark
walls of the cellar with its terrifying space. Robert Frost
dredged into this space in "The Witch of Coos." But then
Frost also found terror in the attic.

These spatial experiences are poetic, not scientific,
simply because the scientist uses another kind of attention. The scientist must repeat his experience if it is to be
verified, for in science "the first time doesn't count." By
the time the observation is again confirmed, it is no longer
new: "In scientific work we have first to digest our surprise." The poet, not the scientist, is the one who can trust
his first vision, before the recognition is endorsed by
duplicating it, before it is codified into ideas, theories,
laws. So Bachelard describes science as a way of reducing discovery. Knowledge in scientific form is coherent
disillusion, organized disappointment, a loss of epiphany.
The poet, who "has no past," is always living "on the

threshold of being." His images are unpredictable and unrepeatable; they validate the instant. The poet, then, has a privilege which the scientist, *as* scientist, must forgo; his world is forever new, and his surprise keeps his consciousness from becoming "somnolent" or routine. His recognitions may be disturbing, for they are not yet crystallized into explanations. The poetic or lived experience in science occurs only when the new planet swims into ken for the first time. Bachelard speaks of poetry as the appearance of an image in wholly unexpected form, an image that touches the depths before it breaks the surface to arise in a zone that supports language. The lived quality of a poetic image gives it presence, for a poem liquidates the past the moment it is written. Thus art sanctions the reality of the single intense perception, and the poet's technique is a way of experimenting that is open to the indecisive.

That is to say, the poem cannot be programmed. The poem transcends its own techniques because it is a recognition we could not predict; and the authenticity of a work of art can usually be judged by the unexpectedness of its direction or discovery. Malraux has said that art is a defense against fatality. The special modern form of fatality is the total programming attempted in our technological society. The computer appears to be the most sinister agent in this programming, a more administrative force than the internal combustion engine, about which T. S. Eliot was anxious. The computer reaches decisions, and its decisions are made under the direction of a technological imperative. Is there any reason to hope that its decisions can be other than technological? Possibly not, unless there is a revolution within technology itself. The most promising opportunity for any such revolution would seem to lie in Robert Preusser's plea that the engineer must learn to play and thus free technology from predetermined control, capitalizing on accidents that can be turned to creative discoveries. This would mean an unofficial use of the computer. Something like this unofficial use of technology occurred in the primitive phase of impressionism when spectrum analysis and photography led to a new optical sensitivity, a creative interaction between art and techniques. Monet used spectrum analysis unofficially; Degas used photography for purposes that were not technological.

Wallace Stevens has remarked that poetry is "an unofficial view of being." The artist is a person who has always had a talent for using science and techniques unofficially. Most great renaissance painters used mathematics unofficially. Andy Warhol is using set theory unofficially, as Fautrier did. He is using acrylic and silk-screen techniques unofficially. Wordsworth used the associationist psychology of his day unofficially, just as a good many novelists have used Freud unofficially. This is one reason for believing that there may be no ultimate incompatibility between science or technology and poetry or painting. Wordsworth seems justified in saying that whenever the scientist affects our daily impressions, the poet will be at his side to carry sensation into the heart of scientific discovery.

There is evidence that the computer itself can be used unofficially. The lettrist group of poets has enlisted the computer in an aesthetic adventure that has its origins in Mallarmé's enlisting typography for the open, figured pages of *Un Coup de Dês*. While it is too soon to claim that we can compute poetry, the artistic resources of the computer appear in graphic form in the shaped verses of concrete poems that are not only visual but auditory. This, too, is an art of the surface, and suggests that electronic devices like the computer can serve as an extension of our nervous system. The unofficial use of the computer makes programming as accessible to craft as the painter's air brush. John Dewey wrote an appropriate comment on these lettrist verses: "There is a tendency among lay critics to confine experimentation to scientists in the laboratory. Yet one of the essential traits of the artist is that he is born an experimenter." Even in a society regulated by computers there need not necessarily be two cultures.

The danger is not technology but the official program. The official has been as damaging in the arts as it is in technology; the history of the modern arts has been one of resistance to academic programs. In our technological culture the artist's vocation is resistance to human engineering, which is a perversion of technology. Sometimes his only mode of resistance is insolence. It is an insolence that can be justified only by considering that officials are even more colossally insolent in attempting to engineer human beings. In resisting, of course, the artist should distinguish between the official and the traditional. The official is the programmatic; the traditional is not. And everywhere mere programs are being substituted for traditions. In fact, a program might be called a devalued and unscrupulous form of tradition.

It may be that art remains our only refuge from a technological order where all can be calculated, formulated, regulated. Yeats speaks for the artist when he writes in his Diary, "Every note must come as a casual thought, then it will be my life." We can make conquests by programs—yet they are false conquests. The conquest by the artist is different. Bernard Berenson was right, after all, when he wrote that art is a conquest gained only by a moment of personal discovery. The artist is forever helping us defend this precious and unofficial moment of our being.

Notes

1. On the question of academic *vs.* applied art in England I summarize Quentin Bell: *The Schools of Design*, 1963.

2. This empiricism is fully discussed in Robert Langbaum: *The Poetry of Experience*, 1957. Langbaum explains how romantics threw themselves into the world.

3. The phrase is Gaston Bachelard's in *The Poetics of Space*, to which I have often referred.

4. As discussed by Pierre Francastel in *La Réalité Figurative* ("Espace Génétique et Espace Plastique") and also in Ernst Cassirer: *Mythical Thought*.

5. My discussion of poetic techniques in France is based upon Robert Gibson: *Modern French Poets on Poetry*.

6. On French stylizations see A. E. Carter: *The Idea of Decadence in French Literature*, from which I cite these instances.

7. Such archaizing vocabulary is illustrated in Austin Warren: "Instress of Inscape," *Kenyon Review*, Summer, 1944.

8. Regarding exactitude in the older science I have relied generally upon Whitehead and, here, Jacob Bronowski: "The Discovery of Form," *Vision and Value*, ed. Gyorgy Kepes.

9. "The Destruction of a Plastic Space," *Art History*, Vintage ed., 1963.

10. The query is put by James J. Gibson in "Constancy and Invariance in Perception," *Vision and Value*, ed. Gyorgy Kepes.

11. Gerald Holton: "Conveying Science by Visual Presentation," *Vision and Value*, ed. Gyorgy Kepes.

12. My comment on Berenson refers to his *Aesthetics and History* and *Italian Painters of the Renaissance*.

13. Metatheatre is the theme of Lionel Abel's book by that title. It is a theme also treated in another book I find basic—Ann Righter: *Shakespeare and the Idea of the Play*.

14. Such distinctions are made in Jean Pouillon: *Temps et Roman* and also in Wayne C. Booth: *The Rhetoric of Fiction*.

15. The distinction is James J. Gibson's (in *The Perception of the Visual World*).

16. In speaking of realism I have freely used Lukacs's *The Historical Novel* and his *Studies in European Realism*.

17. Here and in what follows I recapitulate Wolfgang Schoene: *Ueber das Licht in der Malerei*.

18. Degas's new view is analyzed in "The Destruction of a Plastic Space" by Pierre Francastel (*Art History*, Vintage, 1963).

19. In what follows I repeat Anton Ehrenzweig: *The Psycho-Analysis of Artistic Vision and Hearing*, which deals with the whole phenomenon of the non-Gestalt breakthrough in the arts.

20. Regarding Marx and his relation to Hegel I accept the views of Robert Tucker: *Philosophy and Myth in Karl Marx*.

21. Again Tucker: *Philosophy and Myth in Karl Marx*.

22. Pier Luigi Nervi: "Is Architecture Moving Toward Unchangeable Forms?" in *Vision and Value*, ed. Gyorgy Kepes.

23. Whitehead: *Modes of Thoughts*, chap. I.

24. "Conscious Planning and Unconscious Scanning," *Vision and Value*, ed. Gyorgy Kepes.

25. Robert Preusser: "Visual Education for Science and Engineering Students," *Vision and Value*, ed. Gyorgy Kepes.

Bibliography

I have quoted, referred to, or otherwise drawn upon the following critical sources.

Abel, Lionel: *Metatheatre,* 1963

Abrams, M. H.: *The Mirror and the Lamp,* 1953, 1958

Ashby, Eric: *Technology and the Academics,* 1958

Bachelard, Gaston: *Poetics of Space,* trans. Maria Jolas, 1964

Barrett, William: "Writers and Madness," *Partisan Review,* January-February, 1947

Barthes, Roland: *Critique et Vérité,* 1966
            Le Degré Zéro de l'Écriture, 1953, 1964

Bate, Walter Jackson: *John Keats,* 1963

Becker, George J.: *Documents of Modern Literary Realism,* 1963

Bell, Daniel: "The Eclipse of Distance," *Encounter,* May, 1963
            The End of Ideology, 1960, 1962

Bell, Quentin: *The Schools of Design,* 1963

Booth, Wayne C.: *The Rhetoric of Fiction,* 1961

Brecht, Bertolt: *Brecht on Theatre,* ed. John Willett, 1964

Bridgman, Percy: *The Way Things Are,* 1959

Bronowski, Jacob: "The Discovery of Form," Vision and Value Series, ed. Gyorgy Kepes, 1965
            "The Machinery of Nature," *Encounter,* November, 1965
            Science and Human Values, 1961

Brown, Norman O.: *Life against Death,* 1959
            Love's Body, 1966

BIBLIOGRAPHY

Bullough, Edward: " 'Psychical Distance' as a Factor in Art and an Aesthetic Principle," *British Journal of Psychology,* 1912

Butterfield, Herbert: *The Origins of Modern Science,* 1962

Camus, Albert: *The Rebel,* 1951, 1956

Carter, A. E.: *The Idea of Decadence in French Literature,* 1958

Cassirer, Ernst: *Mythical Thought,* 1955

Cassou, Jean: "The Nostalgia for a Métier," 1951 (in *Art History,* 1963)

Clayborough, Arthur: *The Grotesque in English Literature,* 1966

Cornford, F. M.: *From Religion to Philosophy,* 1912, 1957

Davie, Donald: *Ezra Pound—Poet as Sculptor,* 1965

Ehrenzweig, Anton: *The Psycho-Analysis of Artistic Vision and Hearing,* 1953

Ellul, Jacques: *Propaganda,* 1965
    The Technological Society, 1964

Francastel, Pierre: *Art et Technique aux XIXe et XXe Siècles,* 1956
    La Réalité Figurative, 1965
    Peinture et Société, 1952

Fredeman, William E.: *Pre-Raphaelitism,* 1965

Friedmann, Georges: *Industrial Society,* 1945, 1955

Gauss, Charles Edward: *Aesthetic Theories of French Artists,* 1949

Gibson, James J.: *The Perception of the Visual World,* 1950

Gibson, Robert: *Modern French Poets on Poetry,* 1961

Goldmann, Lucien: *Pour un Sociologie du Roman,* 1964

Gombrich, E. H.: *Art and Illusion,* 1959
    "Freud's Aesthetics," *Encounter,* January, 1966
    Meditations on a Hobby Horse, 1963

Green, Martin: *Science and the Shabby Curate of Poetry,* 1964

Havelock, Eric A.: *Preface to Plato,* 1963

Herbert, Robert L., ed.: *Modern Artists on Art,* 1964

Homer, William Innes: *Seurat and the Science of Painting,* 1966

Huxley, Aldous: *Literature and Science,* 1963

Itten, Johannes: *Design and Form—The Basic Course at the Bauhaus,* 1964

James, Henry: *French Poets and Novelists,* ed. Leon Edel, 1964

Kayser, Wolfgang: *The Grotesque in Art and Literature,* 1957, 1963

Kepes, Gyorgy, ed.: Vision and Value Series, 1965–1966

Kirk, G. S.: *The Songs of Homer,* 1962

Koestler, Arthur: *The Act of Creation,* 1964
The Sleepwalkers, 1959

Langbaum, Robert: *The Poetry of Experience,* 1957

Laporte, Paul M.: "Painting, Dialectics, and Existentialism," *Texas Quarterly,* Winter, 1962

Levin, Harry: *The Gates of Horn,* 1963

Lévi-Strauss, Claude: *La Pensée Sauvage,* 1962 (translated as *The Savage Mind,* 1966)

Lord, Albert B.: *The Singer of Tales,* 1960

Lukacs, Georg: *The Historical Novel,* 1955, 1963
Studies in European Realism, 1964
La Théorie du Roman, 1920, 1963

Marcuse, Herbert: *Eros and Civilization,* 1955
One-Dimensional Man, 1964

McLuhan, Marshall: *The Gutenberg Galaxy,* 1962

Medawar, P. B.: "Anglo-Saxon Attitudes," *Encounter,* August, 1965

Miller, J. Hillis: *Poets of Reality,* 1965

Mumford, Lewis: *Art and Technics,* 1952, 1960

Oertel, Robert: "Perspective and Imagination," Acts of the 20th International Congress of the History of Art, II, 1963

Olson, Elmer: "An Outline of Poetic Theory," in *Critiques and Essays in Criticism,* ed. R. W. Stallman, 1949

BIBLIOGRAPHY

Panofsky, Erwin: *Gothic Architecture and Scholasticism*, 1951

Pelles, Geraldine: *Art, Artists, and Society*, 1963

Polanyi, Michael: *Personal Knowledge*, 1958

Popper, Karl: *The Logic of Scientific Discovery*, 1959

Pouillon, Jean: *Temps et Roman*, 1946

Preusser, Robert: "Visual Education for Science and Engineering Students," in Vision and Value Series, ed. Gyorgy Kepes, 1965

Read, Herbert: *The Origins of Form in Art*, 1965
          Selected Writings, 1964

Reitlinger, Gerald: *The Economics of Taste*, 1961

Richards, I. A.: *Speculative Instruments*, 1955

Rieff, Philip: *Freud—The Mind of the Moralist*, 1959, 1961

Righter, Ann: *Shakespeare and the Idea of the Play*, 1962

Righter, William: *Logic and Criticism*, 1963

Robbe-Grillet, Alain: *For a New Novel*, 1965

Russell, Bertrand: *Mysticism and Logic*, 1917, 1957

Schoene, Wolfgang: *Ueber das Licht in der Malerei*, 1954

Steinberg, Leo: *Jasper Johns*, 1963

Symons, Arthur: *The Symbolist Movement in Literature*, 1919

Tawney, R. H.: *The Acquisitive Society*, 1920, 1948
          Religion and the Rise of Capitalism, 1926

Taylor, Frederick Winslow: *Principles of Scientific Management*, 1911

Trilling, Lionel: "On the Two Cultures," *Commentary*, June, 1962
               "The Fate of Pleasure," *Partisan Review*, Summer, 1963

Tucker, Robert: *Philosophy and Myth in Karl Marx*, 1961

Turnell, Martin: "The Criticism of Roland Barthes," *Encounter*, February, 1966

Warren, Austin: "Instress of Inscape," *Kenyon Review*, Summer, 1944

Warren, Robert Penn: "Pure and Impure Poetry," *Kenyon Review*, Spring, 1943

Bibliography

Weber, Max: *The Protestant Ethic,* 1904–1905, 1958
Weightman, J. G.: "The Obsessive Object," *Encounter,* July, 1962
Whitehead, A. N.: *Modes of Thought,* 1938
     Science and the Modern World, 1925
Wind, Edgar: *Art and Anarchy,* 1963
Wittgenstein, Ludwig: *Tractatus Logico-Philosophicus,* translated by D. F. Pears and B. F. McGuinness, 1961

ABOUT THE AUTHOR

WYLIE SYPHER is Alumnae Professor and Chairman of the Department of English at Simmons College in Boston. Born in Mount Kisco, New York, Mr. Sypher was graduated from Amherst College, received master's degrees from Tufts College and from Harvard, and a doctorate from Harvard. He has taught summers at the University of Wisconsin, the University of Minnesota, and for the 1968 summer session he will be the first Robert Frost Professor of Literature at the Bread Loaf Graduate School of English at Middlebury College, where he has taught since 1957. Professor Sypher has twice been awarded a Guggenheim fellowship for research in the theory of fine arts and literature. His book *Four Stages of Renaissance Style*, published in 1955, has become an influential work on its subject. His *Rococo to Cubism in Art and Literature* and *Loss of the Self in Modern Literature and Art*, published by Random House, are also available in Vintage editions. An anthology, *Art History: An Anthology of Modern Criticism*, edited by Professor Sypher, is a Vintage original.

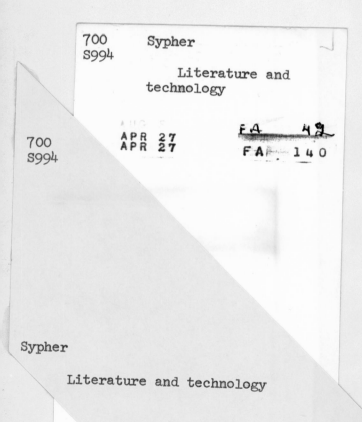

Sypher

Literature and technology